# WISDOM FROM HEAVEN

## The Message of the Letter of James for Today

### Derek Tidball



CHRISTIAN FOCUS

Copyright © Derek J. Tidball 2003

ISBN 185792 865 2

Published in 2003 by
Christian Focus Publications, Geanies House,
Fearn, Ross-shire, IV20 1TW, Scotland

www.christianfocus.com

Cover design by Alister Macinnes

Printed and bound by
Mackays of Chatham

# Contents


Introducing James ...................................................... 5

1. Trouble and how to meet it  (1:1-4, 12-18; 5:7-11) ............ 17

2. Wisdom and how to obtain it (1:5-8; 3:13-18) .................... 35

3. Wealth and how to treat it (1:9-11; 2:1-7; 5:1-6) ................ 55

4. Religion and how to practise it (1:19-27) ............................ 75

5. Words and how to control them  (1:19-21; 3:1-12;
       4:11-12; 5:12) ................................................................ 95

6. Law and how to keep it (2:8-13) ........................................ 115

7. Faith and how to prove it (2:14-26) .................................... 131

8. Relationships and how to handle them (4:1-10) .................. 149

9. Tomorrow and how to face it (4:13-16) ............................. 167

10. Prayer and how to use it (5:13-20) ................................... 183

Endnotes .............................................................................. 205

Text of the Letter of James ................................................. 219

# Contents

# Introducing
# James

The letter of James is among the most suspect books of the New Testament. It was by no means clear that it would be included in the list of authoritative books of the Christian church which we call the canon of the Bible, until very late in the day. Although guided by the Holy Spirit the process by which books were included was an informal one with several lists being drawn up at various times and in various places until a consensus picture began to emerge. The books that were eventually included in the definitive list were believed to be apostolic in origin, orthodox in content, universal in value and to have the ability to guide, nurture and sustain the church.[1]

James was often absent from the earliest lists. It is not difficult to understand why. Reading it quickly you would not find too much specifically 'Christian' content in it. If you take out the two references to Jesus Christ (1:1, 2:1) it could be purely a Jewish letter, typical of the group of writings known as 'wisdom literature'. That leads to a number of questions. How essential, people asked, were those references to Jesus? Were they not just cosmetic, perhaps added later to make the letter look more Christian? Is it primarily addressed to Jewish Christians or does it have a value for Gentile Christians as well? By comparison with some of the other New Testament writings it appears to have little theology in it. Superficially it appears to be good advice about the general problems of living. So, does it really add anything or say anything which we couldn't already find, say, in the Book of Proverbs? What makes it fit for inclusion in the New Testament? Many especially feel that it does not come off well in comparison with the letters Paul wrote. They are three-dimensional presentations of Christian truth. James is one-dimensional. They contain meat. James is little but milk. A particular issue between Paul and James is the discussion of the meaning of faith and the place of works in the Christian life. In that contest Paul is often declared the winner.

The cloud which hovered over James' inclusion in the canon has continued to hang over the letter down the centuries, sometimes more menacingly than at other times. Most famously Martin Luther, with his bias to Paul, declared James 'an epistle of straw'. He wrote somewhat dismissively of it, 'I will not have him in my Bible to be numbered among the true chief books, though I would not thereby prevent anyone from including or extolling him as he pleases, for there are otherwise many good sayings in him.'[2]

Closer examination of the letter, however, shows that none of these charges stand up. Though soaked in the mindset of Jewish wisdom literature it is a thoroughly Christian work. Time and time again we find that James is only putting into his own words the teaching of the 'glorious Lord Jesus Christ'. The echoes of the Master's words reverberate throughout the book. Its value extends far beyond the Jewish Christian community. Gentiles, as well as Jews, need to learn to live wisely in this complex and fallen world we inhabit, as well as in a less than perfect church to which we belong. James and Paul, far from being in conflict, walk in agreement with each other on so many issues. The particular debate about faith and works is not nearly the problem people have made it out to be.

James did make it into the canon. And rightly so. As part, therefore, of inspired scripture it is worth studying and is profitable, as Paul would say, 'for teaching, rebuking, correcting and training in righteousness'.[3] Two reasons make it particularly apt for the church today. We have access to more knowledge than any previous generation in history. Clever, intelligent people abound. Yet the world is dying for lack of wisdom. Knowledge and intelligence have not led to a better world. It is not more peaceful, more secure, more at ease with itself than it was. Rather, the reverse seems to be true. The greater the knowledge we possess, the less we seem to know what to do with it. The greater the intelligence we boast, the greater the folly we demonstrate. Wisdom is needed as never before. And, what is true of the world is true of the church. Resources have never been greater. Techniques and strategies abound. Theological knowledge is available in shovelfuls. Activism has reached new heights. Yet the church is frequently dying for a lack of wisdom. It seems so often to be failing because it ignores the basics. The issues in which James wished to instruct the early church – issues such as suffering, money, the tongue, ambition, an uncertain future and what sort of religion is acceptable to God – are still with us today.

## Who was James?

Just who was James and what authority did he have to write? He describes himself as 'a servant of God and of the Lord Jesus Christ' (1:1). Since we can identify five different people called James in the New Testament, any one of whom could have introduced themselves with words like these, his introduction doesn't give much away. Or, does it? There was James the son of Zebedee, the brother of John, and James the son of Alphaeus who are both listed as among the apostles. There was James the younger, whose mother Mary attended the crucifixion. Some believe 'the Younger' is just another label for James, the son of Alphaeus, rather than pointing to a different person. There is also a mention of James the father of Judas (not Iscariot), another of the disciples, but we know nothing else about him at all. We cannot even be sure whether he was a believer himself, so perhaps he is the exception to the claim that any of them could have identified themselves as servants of Christ.

The fifth James was James, the brother of Jesus.[4] He is the first of Jesus' four brothers to be named, almost certainly because he was the next oldest child in the family. The Gospels tell us that he was not in sympathy with Jesus during his lifetime[5] but at some time he was converted. How and when is a matter of speculation. We know that Jesus appeared to him after his resurrection.[6] That, however, was not likely to have been the decisive event in his conversion since he rose to prominence in the leadership of the Jerusalem church very quickly after that. Paul met with James three years after his conversion.[7] Peter sent word to him when he escaped from prison.[8] He presided over the council at Jerusalem and was evidently much respected for his wisdom.[9] And when Paul last visited Jerusalem it was James who received him.[10] His leadership in Jerusalem would have undoubtedly given him influence well beyond the confines of that local church.

Tradition tells us that James lived a life of extraordinary piety and holiness. He remained a keen practitioner of the Jewish law as well as a devoted follower of Jesus. He was nicknamed 'the Just'. In every way he was a model disciple. Josephus, a major Jewish historian, tells us that James was stoned to death on the orders of Ananus, the High Priest, about 62 AD during an interregnum between Roman governors.[11]   Ananus was a member of the aristocratic Sadducean party of Israel. Josephus also tells us that his execution provoked such an outcry, even among non-Christian Jews because of the respect in which James was held, that Ananus was deprived of his office. Although Josephus does not specifically say he was martyred for his Christian faith later information confirms that it was his testimony to Jesus that caused his death.

It is almost certainly this James who wrote the letter we have in our New Testament. Not only does the letter have all the hallmarks one would expect of a letter written by James the Just but, as many scholars agree, 'only one James was so uniquely prominent in the early Christian movement that he could be identified purely by the phrase, "James, a servant..." '[12] Any other James would have needed to describe himself further. For this James, the name alone would have been sufficient.

His self-description is astonishing. The phrase 'a servant ... of the Lord Jesus Christ' witnesses to an extraordinary transformation which had taken place in James' life. From opposing his brother he had come to serve his brother. He had not come merely to an uneasy peace with his brother; nor to accept that Jesus might have been right; nor to follow him at a distance. He had come to bow the knee and voluntarily submit to his brother's mastery over his life. He had set his life at the disposal of Jesus, his brother and his Lord. Writing this letter was part of the service he rendered to his Lord.

**Who was he writing to?**
The letter is addressed to 'the twelve tribes scattered among the nations'. While some take that to mean he is writing for Jews who had been dispersed and were living outside of Palestine, it makes more sense to understand the phrase as a symbolic reference to Christian believers, albeit perhaps Jewish Christian believers, who were scattered around the Roman world.[13] Galatians 6:16 speaks of the church as the 'Israel of God'. So we know that labels which had once applied to Israel as an ethnic group were later applied to Christians. Revelation 7:5-8 and 21:12 certainly use the phrase 'the twelve tribes of Israel' of the believers who form the new people of God, living in the last days. They were the true Israel who had come to believe Jesus was the Messiah. Many of them had to flee Jerusalem

following the martyrdom of Stephen and persecution mentioned in Acts 8:1-2. Others would have travelled and settled elsewhere because they were involved in trade or for other reasons. It would be natural for the senior pastor of the church in Jerusalem to seek to continue his care of them and his teaching ministry among them through the medium of a letter.

## Why was he writing?

Scholars have attempted to identify a specific reason for the letter. It is obvious that most of Paul's letters were written in response to a particular situation in the churches he addresses or in response to particular needs in the lives of the individuals to whom he writes. What, if anything, can we make of the occasion of James' letter?

Various suggestions have been offered as people have pieced together the clues which he trails through the book in an attempt to make a coherent picture out of them. Let me give some examples. Whilst tentative in his conclusions, Peter Davids says the letter appears to be addressed to people living in Palestine before AD 70 because the details fit what we know of the social, economic and political context there at that time.[14] The preoccupation of the letter with the abuse experienced by the poorer members of the community at the hands of the rich landowners and merchants certainly lends support to this view. Similarly, and with equal diffidence, Robert Wall says it fits Palestine before the Roman War of AD 70 where the great majority of the population was 'confined to working-class ghettos, living a hand-to-mouth existence without any hope of an improved life'. In such a situation people would either react with anger and the fires of political rebellion would be stoked, or they would compensate for their poverty by investing in religious piety and future hope.[15] But it is not the only possible conclusion that can be reached.

Ralph Martin, noting the emphasis on rejecting violence, anger and killing and the advice to leave one's future in the hands of God, suggests the letter was a call to Jews who had been influenced by the fanatical Zealot movement, who advocated violent opposition to the rule of Rome and engaged in acts of terrorism, to reject their approach to life in favour of a more Christian one.[16] Martin actually advocates a two-stage approach to the composition of the letter whereby James' earlier work – his original sermons and material – were skilfully edited into letter form and made to address a later situation. This, he claims, makes more sense of the linguistic features and polished style of the letter, which would most probably have been beyond James' abilities, than if he himself had written it in the form we have it.[17]

Yet others, like Sophie Laws, argue that it was written at a much later date in Rome. The chief reason for doing so lies in the similarity between the writing of James and the writing of other documents, like the *Shepherd of Hermas* and *1 Clement,* which we know to be from a period after James' death and which were set in Rome.[18]

No certainty is possible in answering this question. Nor is it necessary for, as Douglas Moo has recently written, 'while the social and historical situation of the readers may help us understand the problems they are dealing with, those problems are ultimately both more general and more basic than the immediate situation.'[19]

In recent days, Richard Bauckham has helpfully developed that position further. He argues, I think convincingly, that the letter is 'an official letter or encyclical which James as head of the Jerusalem church addresses to all his compatriots and fellow-believers in the Jewish Diaspora'.[20] If this is so then it is unnecessary to seek to discover the particular situation which lay behind the letter. Indeed, detailed particulars which relate only to specific situations would be set aside in favour of dealing with what were typical situations. James didn't need to know precisely what was going on in individual churches. As a wise pastor he knew enough to write intelligently and perceptively with spiritual advice which would prove of value wherever it was read. The text, he says, has 'the necessary character of an encyclical'.[21] The situations he describes are the sort of situations which could be found in many places in the Diaspora. The people he refers to and the argumentative questioners he engages with in his discussions are hypothetical. Nonetheless, James is hitting the mark. The letter is a real letter, full of encouragement and challenge. It could be read and applied in a whole variety of particular church contexts and its message would retain its relevance for many, right down, in fact, to our own day. So here is 'a resource for the churches to draw on regularly and whenever necessary. It is wisdom for them to appropriate and live by'.[22]

## What sort of letter did James write?

Again, Richard Bauckham's recent work has proved most helpful.[23] He shows how James, adopting the style and approach of other wisdom writers, would have set about writing his letter. Wisdom differs in content and style from other forms of literature, such as the law and the prophets. It was about practical insight and instruction for living. Here is theology in working men's clothes. It is composed on the basis of the teacher's own observations of life. It is their reflections and insights which form its foundation. Its authority lies both in the authority of the experience of the writers and in the sense they make of life. The authority these writings carry is implicit and depends on whether people recognise their insights as a true reflection on life or not. They don't seek to justify their insights by complex argument so much as by allusion and analogy from everyday life.

James stands very much in that tradition but he does so distinctly as a 'teacher in the style of Jesus'.[24] The closeness of thought between the teaching of Jesus and James is astonishing. Yet, equally astonishing, nowhere does James quote Jesus. Isn't that a serious weakness? Should he not quote him and then expound him? Or, should we not expect him to do so? Here we need an understanding of how wisdom writers would operate. Their approach would not be to quote their teachers. Rather they would immerse themselves in the wisdom of their teachers and then creatively and freely develop it rather than slavishly repeat it. That is exactly what James does.

To achieve his objective he calls a whole arsenal of literary weapons into play. He regularly resorts to one sort of aphorism or another, that is, a short pithy saying or general maxim. Bauckham identifies beatitudes (1:12); 'whoever' sayings (2:10, 4:4); conditional sayings (1:5, 26); couplets (4:8); paradoxical statements (1:9-10) and a multitude of strong contrasts; admonitions (1:19-20; 4:8; 5:9, 12, 16); general declarative statements (1:3-4; 2:5, 26; 3:16); reciprocal sayings (2:13, 3:6); and debating points (1:13). More fully developed are the parables and sayings which draw attention to the likeness between things, such as, 1:6, 10-11, 23; 2:26; 3:3-6, 11-12; 4:14; 5:7-8. James resorts to holding up Old Testament examples on five occasions – Abraham, Rahab, the prophets, Job and Elijah (2:21-25; 5:10-11, 17-18). He can also resort to judgement oracles which would be worthy of any Old

Testament prophet (5:1-6) and exhort people through using sharp dialogue, as he does, for example, in 2:18-23.

The variety of his literary technique, densely packed as it is into such a short letter, explains something of the apparently disorganised, fast-moving nature of the letter. The truth is that it is much more organised than, say, the Book of Proverbs, where sayings on totally diverse topics seem thrown together almost at random. After roughly setting out his agenda to begin with, James does, in fact, largely work through the agenda developing each item on it more fully, though on occasions he returns to an item more than once. Hopefully, what follows in the book will provide ample demonstration of this.

James, then, might chiefly be said to be a teacher of the wisdom of Jesus, functioning in a manner typical of the wisdom tradition of Israel. Even his discussion of law, especially his exposition of the love commandment of Leviticus 19, which we have not so far mentioned, should not be separated from his teaching as a sage. He expounds the law not as a typical rabbi, concerned to reduce it to specific rules and fragment it into a multitude of regulations, but as a typical teacher of wisdom. Wisdom and law had a close association in the Jewish tradition.[25]

Yet to describe James as a typical exponent of Jewish wisdom would be to make a fundamental mistake. All his wise insights are filtered through the teaching of Jesus. He is a Christian wisdom teacher *par excellence,* a sage of the risen Christ. In a very real sense it is not the wisdom of James which one encounters in this letter, but the wisdom of Jesus.

**Is there doctrine in James?**

As mentioned earlier, the letter of James is often considered to be of secondary importance in the New Testament because it is thought to lack theological depth. It is true that the uppermost concern of the letter is practical and ethical, as it seeks to address the moral behaviour of the churches. But what is often not noticed is that this concern is built on a strong foundation of doctrine.

In a robust defence of James' theological acumen, Luke Johnson has outlined the essential features of his doctrine.[26]  To paraphrase him: the book's focus is theocentric, and shows little concern for identifying the separate persons or work of members of the Trinity. Its picture of God is incredibly rich. He is: one (2:19); demons tremble before him (2:19); the Lord of hosts (5:4); in whom there is no change (1:17). He is not tempted by evil (1:13), nor does he participate in human anger (1:20). He is 'the father of lights' (1:17), who characteristically gives birth (1:18), and creates people in his own image (3:9). He reveals himself and his will (2:8-11), and will one day encounter men and women as their judge (2:12; 4:12). Even so, he is compassionate and full of mercy (5:11), and promises to reward those who love him (1:12; 2:5). His compassion leads him to hear the cry of the oppressed (5:4), to heal the sick (5:15), to hear prayers offered in faith (1:5-6; 5:15), and to forgive sin (5:15). This is the God who longs to enter into friendship with human beings (4:4-10).

This God is also the hope of the future for, in spite of all that is wrong with the present world in its state of enmity with him, there is a new age to come which will see misery inflicted on those who currently perpetrate evil (5:1) but will save those who are merciful (2:13; 4:12). This God demands righteous living now. His coming is near (5:8). 'The Judge is standing at the door' (5:9).

James is obviously no lightweight when it comes to theology. Perhaps our penchant for right doctrine is sometimes a cover-up for our desire not to confront the issues of right living. James will not permit such escapism.

## A personal afterword

It has been my privilege to expound James in several congregational settings over the years and, most recently, to the Belgrave Heights Convention in Melbourne at the turn of the millennium. They wanted some wise words for the new millennium. There are none wiser than those of James. I am grateful to the people there for the warmth of their hospitality, if not for the warmth of their weather. In what was supposed to be the middle of their Australian summer I had to borrow an overcoat to keep warm. As always, a number of people have contributed to the writing of this book but I would particularly like to thank Simon Johnston for reading the manuscript and correcting a number of errors. I have tried to indicate the source of quotes and ideas in the endnotes. If I failed to do so I apologise.  I have also included a number of biblical references in the endnotes so as not to interrupt the text itself too much. Placing them there does not indicate they are unimportant and the reader is encouraged to consult them. The NIV Inclusive Language Version has been used throughout. In order for you to read the relevant biblical passage from the Letter of James, the text of his letter is found on pages 219 to 224.

May the wisdom of James help us to live wisely in the midst of some very foolish times so that we can further enhance the splendour of 'our glorious Lord Jesus Christ'.

# 1

# Trouble and How
# to Meet It

# (1:1-4, 12-18; 5:7-11)

**1. Accept its reality,  1:2**

**2. Consider your reaction,  1:2**

- ◆ Foolish responses
- ◆ Wise responses

**3. Understand its value, 1:3-4**

- ◆ Trouble produces stable disciples
- ◆ Trouble produces finished products

**4. Envisage its reward, 1:12**

**5. Discern its nature, 1:13-18**

- ◆ An error to be rejected
- ◆ A truth to be accepted

**6. Contemplate its Lord, 5:7-11**

- ◆ The creation of the Lord
- ◆ The coming of the Lord
- ◆ The compassion of the Lord

American football has always been a mystery to me in spite of the attempts of numerous transatlantic friends to explain it and unravel the delights of Superbowl over the years. The players never seem to get anywhere. Some years back when the Chicago Bears were playing the New York Giants one commentator claimed that during the game Walter Payton, the Chicago's running-back, had clocked up over nine miles rushing too and fro. 'Yeah,' said his companion, 'and that's with someone knocking him down every four and a half yards.'[1]

If that seems to capture your experience of the Christian life, then James is for you. We may be unsure, as the introduction explained, whether James wrote his letter because of a particular situation of suffering that his readers were facing or whether he was writing in a more general vein. But whichever, it is clear that learning how to face trouble was something they urgently needed to do. In his opening chapter James sets out the agenda which he will address in the rest of his letter. Top of that agenda is the theme of suffering. Immediately we are confronted by his direct, honest, punchy and uncomfortable wisdom.

## 1. Accept its reality, 1:2

James is a realist. He's no doorstep evangelist seeking to sell his readers a cheap gospel while keeping the small print from their view. He will have none of the health and wealth gospel which promises that once they have made Christ their Lord believers will live in some specially protected cocoon which will exempt them from trials and suffering. Not for him the glib teaching which says that the moment we face difficulties or illness we should pray in faith and they will miraculously disappear. He might even have difficulty singing that wonderfully old-fashioned hymn 'Trust and obey' which speaks unguardedly in one verse like this:

> Not a shadow can rise,
> Not a cloud in the skies,
> But his smile quickly drives it away;
> Not a doubt nor a fear,
> Not a sigh nor a tear,
> Can abide while we trust and obey![2]

He knows that the shadows can rise, the clouds can gather, the fears can mount and the tears well up in our eyes as we face some of the cruelties, injustices and sicknesses of our world. That is why he does not say 'if you face trials' but '*whenever* you face trials of many kinds' (1:2). They will come. They are bound to do so. They are a reflection of the fact that we are still living 'between times'. The Kingdom of God has been inaugurated but has not yet reached its consummation. Creation has not yet been fully restored; believers have not yet been fully perfected; and though Satan has been thoroughly defeated by Christ's death, he has not yet been finally overthrown. The world, the flesh and the devil, therefore, still conspire to cause us trouble and submit us to trials, just as they did Jesus. It is cold comfort to tell those who are really up against it that suffering is a myth, or it's all in their mind, or that it's due to their lack of faith. That's just not true. Nor is it true that all trouble or sickness is a direct punishment from God. Jesus taught his disciples that there was not necessarily a direct connection between a particular sin and a particular experience of suffering. Much suffering was due to the general state of our fallen world and was an opportunity for God to display his grace in people's lives.[3] Occasionally God may exercise discipline in the lives of believers through sickness, as 1 Corinthians 11:28-30 suggests, but most of it stems from our living in a still-yet-to-be-fully-redeemed world.

Realising this will help us to handle suffering constructively and at the same time release us from becoming introspective. The danger with thinking that we should be exempt from suffering because we are Christians is that when it comes we spend all the time asking, 'Why me?' Then we look inwardly either for a sin of commission or omission. That is, we either spend time looking for what sin we did commit to cause the suffering or what good (like exercising faith or praying) we omitted to do which would have prevented it. James is more realistic and too familiar with his brother's words to pretend that any of us can get through life without trouble. Jesus frequently told his disciples that suffering would be part of their lot in life so that they should hardly have been surprised when it came.[4]

Reading ahead, we can see the sort of trials James' readers were undergoing. They came in all shapes and sizes, much as they do for us. There was the scourge of poverty (1:9-11), the anguish of injustice

(5:4), the nightmare of persecution (5:6), and the misery of ill-health, possibly stress-related (5:14). Then there was the disappointment which arose from their continuing to struggle with the strong forces of temptation that were still in them (1:13-15), and the discouragement of belonging to a less-than-perfect fellowship (4:1-3). None of these trials disappeared quickly, as they might have hoped. So, in the absence of the problem being removed, other ways of coping with it, more mature ways, had to be discovered. What wisdom does James offer? He begins with our reactions.

## 2. Consider your reaction, 1:2

Given that suffering, trials, troubles – call them what you will – are bound to come, how do we react to them? People react in different ways. A lot of factors, like our personalities, upbringing and stress thresholds, will condition how we respond. Some people are naturally more laid-back than others; some more naturally anxious than others. Even so, basically we will react in one of two ways: either foolishly or wisely. Truth to tell, James doesn't mention the former, choosing instead to concentrate on the latter, but it might be helpful to mention some typically foolish reactions.

### *Foolish responses*

However understandable it may be to respond foolishly to trouble it does not help the situation. If anything, it exacerbates it. Foolish responses are expressions of our 'old natures' and reveal that deep down we don't really believe God is in control of our lives and can be trusted with them. They show that we remain the centre of our own universes. They prevent us from benefiting spiritually from the pressure points and keep us spiritually immature. Furthermore, they give an opportunity for the devil to triumph once again in our lives.

Among the foolish reactions we might name are: unrestrained anger and resentment, either at God or others; self-pity; impatience; anxiety; and vengeance or some desire to find a way of getting our own back. Then there is the slow drip of discouragement where, because we have not responded to the trials in a spiritually healthy way, we allow ourselves to be dragged down by our tribulations until we are altogether spiritually disabled.

A different, but equally foolish, reaction is that of denial or escapism. People under pressure can resist the well-meaning advice of their friends to slow down and deny there is a problem until it is too late and they crack up. A lot of men refuse to visit the doctor when they discover some worrying abnormality on their bodies in case they find out they are seriously ill. Like these people, Christians can pretend that all is well when patently it is not and refuse to admit and face up to trials and troubles. Let's just pretend everything's fine and hope the clouds go away, we think. When asked by others how we are, we cover up; refusing to mention our real needs either because we fear rejection or do not want to express weakness. So we summon up a false bravado. Some people's version of the Christian life is much like Liberace's version of Tchaikovsky. 'My whole trick,' he once confessed, 'is to keep the tune well out in front. If I play Tchaikovsky, I play his melodies and skip his spiritual struggles. Naturally, I condense. I have to know just how many notes my audience will stand for. If there's time left over, I fill it up with lots of runs up and down the keyboard.'[5] But that, of course, was not Tchaikovsky.

James has a much more constructive approach to our struggles than that. He doesn't want us to spend time just doing runs up and down our spiritual keyboard. He wants us to enter into the struggles and respond to them in a way which will lead to our growth in God.

*Wise responses*

According to James, the wise response to trouble, surprising as it may seem, is to 'consider it pure joy'. Or, as J. B. Phillips paraphrased him, 'When all kinds of trials and temptations crowd into your lives, my brothers and sisters, don't resent them as intruders but welcome them as friends.'[6]

In using the word 'consider', James is inviting us to pursue a deliberate and decisive act. We are to stop and consciously think about how we are to react rather than just drifting into the usual, foolish responses which is what normally happens when our spiritual gearbox is in neutral. And the spiritual gear we are to engage is that of joy – 'pure joy', or, 'nothing but joy'. He calls us to an unnatural reaction of deep, steady and unadulterated thankful trust in God. Thanks, James! Most of us were hoping for something more sympathetic than that! It is only as we read further and James begins to teach us the value of suffering that we shall see that his advice is not the invitation of someone who has lost his mind but the wisdom of one who makes great spiritual sense. 'Joy is one of the big words of our Christian faith.'[7] Jesus told his disciples that he longed for them to experience complete joy, even when the path of life was to take them through suffering, and he still does.[8]

Robert Wall helps us to understand what James means when he explains that 'joy is not a human emotion but a theological perception'.[9] Joy is not about emotional pleasure. We do not respond to trials with joy because our feelings are telling us we like what we are going through. James is not encouraging masochism, nor that we should be glib about suffering, nor indifferent to the cause of justice. We respond with joy because we know some of the deeper issues involved which helps us to interpret suffering not as the miserably negative force which others perceive it to be, but as an instrument in the hands of a sovereign, wise and gracious God using it for our good. It is a call to put God into the whole picture of life; the bad times as well as the good. There really is any number of reasons why we can be joyful. We can be joyful because God is still sovereignly in control, no matter what. We can be joyful because facing trials drives us nearer to Christ who himself suffered and faced trials. We can be joyful because trials are one of God's ways of reshaping us until we are fully like Christ. We can be joyful because trials are a sign that God has not given up on us and it points forward to the day when we shall no longer suffer. So, although we will not be thankful *for* all circumstances, we will be thankful *in* all circumstances. It is some of those deeper reasons which James now explains.

### 3. Understand its value, 1:3-4

In the pain of his bereavement, C. S. Lewis mused as to whether God would be seen by some as a 'cosmic sadist' mindlessly inflicting grief on his creatures.[10] But James assures us, in teaching that closely parallels Romans 5:1-5, that suffering serves a twofold purpose and is, therefore, the wise strategy of a loving God. Suffering serves a shorter-term and a longer-term goal.

### *Trouble produces stable disciples*

'... the testing of your faith develops perseverance.'

The idea that testing produces perseverance and proves reliability is evident in a multitude of ways in our ordinary lives. We have no problem with it there. Metals are tested before being used to build an aircraft or a bridge so that we can have confidence that they will not fail us at the crucial moment. Precious metals are tested to prove whether they are genuine and will hold or increase their value, or whether they will quickly reveal themselves to be fake and worthless. Athletes undergo strenuous training to prepare for the crucial race and the winning tape. Students are tested, in exams or assessments, so that the learning process may go deeper and the knowledge they have acquired in the classroom stay a little longer in their minds. Alec Motyer, in romantic and optimistic mood, uses the illustration of a young couple in love. Their love, he writes, is a tentative opinion until they face successfully the various tests which prepare them for marriage. 'Thus what began as a tentative belief ends as a fixed, steady, unchangeable character of life.'[11]

What is true in our ordinary lives is true as well in our spiritual lives. Peter wrote of suffering as a means of proving the genuineness of the believers' faith.[12] James' concern is that testing increases the believers' stamina. It produces staying power, endurance, steadfastness. And as Jesus said, it is 'by standing firm you will gain life'.[13]

In our contemporary culture such virtues are not highly prized. Short-termism is in. Postmodern culture exalts a Lego-style approach to building our lives. We take the blocks and build one thing today and then dismantle it to build something entirely different tomorrow. We float in and out of jobs, and in and out of relationships. We live only for the moment, for today. It breeds a superficial type of person; one who is frequently ill-equipped to face the realities of life. Whether we can build anything worthwhile this way or, at least, anything worthwhile which will last for the future is doubtful. Most great achievements require perseverance. When we transfer that instant mentality to our faith it is fatal. God is not looking to us for an occasional flirtation with him but for an ongoing, steady, developing and faithful relationship which persists no matter what. If he is the eternal God, he deserves nothing less.

### Trouble produces finished products

Trials are a means of helping us to grow strong so that we endure till the end. So, James shifts his focus from the process of enduring what we are undergoing now to the end result we can anticipate in the future. He envisages that if we endure through the trials and testings we will eventually be 'mature and complete, not lacking in anything'.

The word which the NIV translates as 'mature' is the word *teleios,* which means 'perfect'. It is the word Jesus himself had used in the Sermon on the Mount when he said to his disciples, 'Be perfect, therefore, as your heavenly Father is perfect.'[14] It is the word Paul used to capture the vision of what we shall be like when God has finished his work of reconstruction in our lives.[15] It speaks of wholeheartedness, 'a fully-rounded uprightness'[16] and of our being like Christ.

It is a tall order. Most of us are far from there yet. It is a future goal, but one for which we aim now. Without the trials, troubles and suffering we would never get there. They help to wean us off our reliance on ourselves and on things, off asserting ourselves, off centring on ourselves and help us to centre on Christ. They rub off the rough edges, dethrone the false ambitions, and deflate our pompous pride. They teach us to look beyond passing feelings to long-term certainties. They are God's messengers for our good.

James then uses a very similar word to underline his meaning. Through suffering we will not only become 'mature' but 'complete' (*holokleros*). According to Peter Davids this word adds little except that it simply 'stresses the incremental character of the process'.[17] This maturity does not come in an instance. No dramatic experience of the Holy Spirit will produce it in a flash. It is the product of a lifetime. It is the culmination of the work of a skilled master craftsman, carefully refashioning our characters.

The use of these two words – 'mature and complete' – alerts us to the importance James places on the issue. Why use two words when one would do? When we look more closely we discover that we are being introduced here to something of extreme importance to

James; to a theme which will constantly recur. Richard Bauckham goes so far as to say that it is this idea of completion, of being fully integrated, of being wholehearted, of total consistency, which is 'the overarching theme of the whole letter, encompassing all the other major concerns James raises'.[18]

His goal is to see his readers whole. That means to be totally focused on God; to be integrated as individuals and integrated into the Christian community; to be completely surrendered to pursuing God's will and God's ways, to reject all compromises, to shun all that would fragment our lives and pull us in different directions and to exclude all that is incompatible with our goal. Paul had told the Corinthians to 'aim for perfection'.[19] James is saying a hearty 'Amen' to that!

Our temptation is to try to soften James' words. Surely he doesn't mean to be quite so fanatical? Have we not so many other demands on us in our busy lives; so many other exciting opportunities to pursue? Must we really conduct our spiritual lives with quite so much single-mindedness? James' response to such questions would be robust. If at the end of the day you want to stand before God as mature and complete people in Christ without any deficiency, 'lacking in nothing', then you must pursue the goal with all your strength and understand the cost of suffering which is involved. If you want to risk standing before your creating and redeeming God, ashamed because of your halfheartedness and shortcomings, so be it.

Alec Motyer sums it up:

'Doctor,' we might say, 'does the medicine have to be so nasty? Does the treatment have to be so severe?' And he replies, 'Don't you want to be better?' So then, do you want to be like Jesus? Do you want to come to the full enjoyment of your salvation? Do you want, when you reach heaven, to have your perceptions and faculties so sharpened and sensitized that you will be able to see the glory? There is no other way.[20]

## 4. Envisage its reward, 1:12

After putting further items on his agenda James picks up the theme of suffering again in verse 12. The verse forms a short bridge between what he has already said about suffering and what he is going to say about it. Verses 3 and 4 had looked forward to the time when perseverance would have served its purpose and believers were at long last perfect. In that day, he now adds, 'they will receive a crown of life.' Eventually all the suffering and irritating troubles of this life will prove to have been worthwhile.

Although perfectly straightforward, even this brief verse contains a number of riches we should not miss. The New Testament does not always seem as embarrassed as we are to talk about the future rewards of those who have remained faithful and served Christ sacrificially. Here the reward is of a 'crown of life' which far exceeds the transitory crown which victors in the ancient games would receive or the crown of gold that any king could put upon his head. The life referred to is life eternal, life lived in the company of the ever-living God. When John Chrysostom (347-407), the golden-tongued preacher of the ancient church, preached on this he remarked, 'We see no garments or cloaks, but we see crowns more valuable than any gold, than any other contest, prizes or rewards, and ten thousand blessings stored up for those who live upright and virtuous lives on earth.'[21] To be precise the reward is for those who have persevered in the faith and who have graduated through suffering.

But it is just there that James presents us with a paradox. Although the crown is unattainable except to those who have passed the test of suffering, it is a crown which is given to us not because of our own achievements but because of God's promise – a promise made 'to those who love him'. Paradoxically, then, what guarantees the reward is not our works but his grace. This paradox is no different from others which run through scripture. The children of Israel who left Egypt possessed a new land because God had promised it to them. It was theirs, unequivocally and irrevocably, because God had given his word and marked it down as theirs. Even so, they would not have possessed it unless they had believed the promise, crossed the Jordan, fought the battles and occupied it. So it is with us. God, in his grace, promises those of us who love him, however imperfectly, a crown. Without his promise there would be no reward to look forward to. But we will only receive it by passing through much trial and tribulation. 'There is none that goeth to heaven without their trial. As the way to Canaan lay through a howling wilderness and desert, so the path of heaven lieth through much affliction.'[22]

## 5. Discern its nature, 1:13-18

Having returned to the subject of suffering, James proceeds to take his analysis of it deeper. His tone becomes more urgent as he seems either to address a common misunderstanding that was already in circulation among his readers or to anticipate a misunderstanding that someone might fall into in the future. The fault lay in mixing up temptation and testing, and blaming both on God. But there is a world of difference between them. A temptation is put in front of us by someone who hopes we will fail and give in to it. A test is put in front of us by someone who hopes we will pass and grow through it. Trials, testing and suffering have a positive role to play in the Christian life; temptation, a negative one. His readers dare not confuse the two. To help them understand this James sets out an error which is to be rejected, followed by a truth which is to be accepted.

*An error to be rejected, verses 13-15*

The error is to blame temptation on God. He tests his people but he does not tempt them. He tested his friend Abraham by commanding him to sacrifice his only son, Isaac, in order that Abraham could prove the genuineness of his faith.[23] After the death of Joshua, God left other nations in Canaan rather than mopping them up, 'to test Israel and see whether they will keep the way of the Lord and walk in it as their ancestors did.'[24] He sent ambassadors from Babylon to King Hezekiah, whose reign had till then been one of unalloyed success, 'to test him and to know everything what was in his heart.'[25] Job is the most outstanding example of testing in the Old Testament.[26] On each occasion God was seeking to confirm that his servants had a robust faith which was not dependent merely on what he gave them but would hold true even when he gave them nothing or took away from them what they had. But in no instance did he seek to destroy their faith or cause them to sin.

Indeed, the mistake, as James points out, is 'very elementary'. God could not tempt people because it is totally incompatible with his nature to do so. Three aspects of God's character make it impossible for him to tempt people. First, he is holy (v. 13). Secondly, he is a life-giver (v. 17). Thirdly, he is trustworthy (v. 17). His holiness means that God cannot himself be tempted by evil and, given that, it is illogical to believe that he could possibly tempt others, since that in itself is evil. Leslie Mitton puts the point succinctly: 'There is nothing in God to which evil can make its appeal.'[27] How, then, can he be accused of being the source of temptation?

Add to this his generous and life-giving nature. The gifts God gives are 'good and perfect', not sullied and tainted. He gives like this because he is 'the Father of heavenly lights' – a description of God unique in the Bible – which is almost certainly an allusion to God as the creator of the stars at the beginning of time.[28] How can a morally incorruptible being whose nature is to give life and spread light tempt people into sin, rob them of goodness and disseminate darkness?

The thought of light gives rise in James' imagination to the idea of shadows, for where there is light, there shadows fall. And that leads him to affirm a third aspect of the character of God which makes it absolutely impossible for us to believe that he can be the source of temptation. Shadows move around. They lie first in that direction and then, as the day progresses and the sun goes on its course from east to west, they move and lie in the opposite direction. They cannot always be relied upon to be in the same place. But God can always be relied upon. His character does not change. Mitton, again, sums the point up superbly: 'His goodness is not occasional or fitful, but unceasing and unfading, steady and persistent.'[29] So, says James, in effect, don't argue that because God hasn't tempted people in the past it means he won't do so in the future. God demonstrates the very consistency which James longs to see in his readers' own lives. We can depend on him not to tempt us to sin.

### *A truth to be accepted*

So where does temptation come from? If we can't blame it on God, who can we blame it on? James says we have no one to blame but ourselves. A fuller biblical answer would mention the world and the devil as well as the flesh.[30] But James' narrow-angle lens causes him to focus on the evil desires within each of us and, in view of what he is to reveal about the state of the church to which he is writing, it is wise that he should do so. To have mentioned the other sources of temptation and produced a wide-angle picture of them at this point would no doubt have caused them to shift the blame elsewhere rather than take responsibility for themselves. It is a feature of the day in which we live that we are always looking for someone else to blame.

Pastorally, I have had a number of people come to me who wanted demons exorcised from their lives because they were causing them to live in sin, or so they said. Now, I am quite sure that demons exist and are capable of doing just that. But in most cases their problem was nothing to do with a demon. It was to do with their own immorality and disobedience. The answer lay not in a demon that needed exorcising but a sin that needed confessing. The answer lay not in deliverance but in repentance.

As a wise pastor, James correctly diagnoses their situation, and ours, and explains what they, and we, need to know about temptation. The source of temptation is our 'own evil desire'. It comes from within. Two or three years ago a family in Canada were plagued by spooky events in their house as lights flashed on and off and phones rang inexplicably. Having failed to identify the source of the problem themselves, they eventually called in the police who commenced an eighteen-month investigation during which they monitored the disturbing happenings. Only after that length of time did they identify the source of the problem. It was traced to the teenage son of the family who masterminded all the incidents from their own basement. Their problem came from within, from one of their own family members. So it is with us.

The problem has its seat in 'desire'. Strictly speaking 'desire' is a neutral word since desires can be good or bad, although we have to admit that desire by its very nature tends to push the boundaries and so is more than likely to lead us into sin.[31] But it is clear, because of verse 13, that the desire James has in mind is 'evil desire' and it must be dealt with immediately. To confront the desire once is not sin. To give it house room is. It is foolish to entertain evil desires, for we all know that they will quickly take over and lead to our downfall. The lethal potential of uncontrolled desire is dramatically expressed. It's as if it's a hook neatly concealed by bait. It seems so attractive but once it enters its prey it quickly drags its victim away to destruction.[32] James' fishing analogy (if that's what it was) is immediately followed up by an analogy from the maternity hospital. If desire is conceived then an inevitable pattern follows: conception is followed by birth, the birth of sin. Sin grows up and in turn gives birth but this time what it delivers is death. How different, as Chrysostom pointed out, from a normal pregnancy. There conception gives rise to pain but after the pain of childbirth there is much joy and relief. Here the sequence goes into reverse. The desire is normally conceived in the pleasure of sin but once the birth has taken place it gives rise to pain, misery and ultimately to death.[33] The only answer is not to give in to the initial temptation and then it will come to nothing.

How different, too, is the way God works in our lives. In verse 18 James brings this section to a conclusion by taking up the image of birth again. Only this time, in strong contrast to what he has said so far, it is to demonstrate the new birth God gives. This birth is conceived in his own loving will, rather than our own fallen minds, as the verse stresses through its emphatic opening words, 'he chose us'. The delivery takes place 'through the word of truth' rather than through the deceptive words we hear when desire entices and coaxes us to do wrong. Evil desires promise much sweetness but deliver only bitterness and pain. And this birth leads to something significant not just for us who receive it but for the whole of creation. Born again believers are the first instalments of a new, fully redeemed creation which comes into being when Christ returns to reign over all. We are the promise of better things to come on the day when our cosmos is renewed. James only mentions the larger picture in passing, in half a sentence, leaving it to Paul to expound it more fully in Romans 8:19-23. What a thought! Our personal spiritual experience is connected to the destiny of all creation. Here, if ever, is a 'good and perfect gift of God' which we can live by now. We do not have to give in to the deceptive seduction of evil desires. God, through his creative power and sovereign grace, is recreating us.

## 6. Contemplate its Lord, 5:7-11

James circles a third time over the subject of trials and testings, although his writing is more spiral in form than circular because each time he revisits the subject he lifts us to a higher plane. His initial approach led us to learn the value of trials for our own spiritual growth. His second discussion helped us to distinguish between trials, testings and suffering on the one hand and temptation on the other. Now, thirdly, as he addresses the question of injustice from which his readers suffer, he invites them to respond to it with patience. In doing so he is not encouraging them to bear their grievance with stoicism, nor with a typically British stiff-upper-lip-grin-and-bear-it type attitude. He is not calling for a 'passive waiting but an active focus' on the Lord.[34] It is because there is a sovereign Lord who reigns supreme and who is not indifferent to our plight that the call makes any sense. So, although at one level these verses seem to be about us and the need for patience, at another they are even more about the Lord and his sovereignty. Three things are said of God.

*First, James speaks of him as the Creator Lord, verses 7-11*
How has God the Creator made the world to function? Farmers can tell us. He has made it to produce the resources we need for food – slowly. The seasons are part of his plan. Farmers know that they cannot rush the process of the harvest. 'The early autumn rains are needed to prepare the soil for the seed and the seed for germination. The late, or spring rains, are needed to cause the seed to swell and develop in the ear. The buffeting storms are needed to mature the harvest and produce a rich crop.'[35] The process cannot be hurried. How foolish we are if we try to reach the harvest too soon. All we will do is spoil the crop. The Creator Lord says, 'Be patient.'

*Secondly, James speaks of him as the Coming Lord, verses 8-9*
The Creator Lord is also the Coming Lord. When the Lord does come he will sort the issue out on our behalf and vindicate those who have been treated unjustly. Some may live as if the Lord has left his creation for good and as if there is no day of reckoning to come. But, far from it. 'The Lord's coming is near.' 'The Judge is standing at the door!' The Lord is waiting in the wings. So we need not act precipitously by taking the law into our own hands. We can leave it to the Lord, who will do a better job of it and may well do it soon. And in the waiting we will have gained, for we will have been transformed into his likeness.

*Thirdly, James speaks of him as the Compassionate Lord, verses 10-11*
The prophets and Job are called to the witness stand to give evidence of the final important aspect of God's character, that he is full of compassion. In life they suffered horribly and suffered unjustly,

but with the benefit of hindsight we look back on their experiences and see them very differently. We regard them as blessed because of the perseverance they showed. Their lives testify to 'what the Lord finally brought about' when in the end they were vindicated. Through it all they testify to the unchanging nature of God as one who is 'full of compassion and mercy'. From the earliest days of Israel onwards that was who they had understood God to be like.[36] Just because they experienced momentary difficult and adverse circumstances, there was no reason to believe that God was anything different. His compassion and mercy remained constant. His compassion held on to them, brought good out of their suffering and triumphed through them. As Thomas Manton, the Puritan Bible commentator, wrote, somewhat quaintly to our ears, 'But God doth not change; there is no wrinkle on the brow of eternity; the arm of mercy is not dried up, nor do his bowels of love waste and spend themselves.'[37] Just so. What he allows us to suffer in our lives he allows out of love. One day, when righteousness finally triumphs, we shall see the reality of that love more fully than we do now. But though in the meantime the clouds may sometimes hide the sun we dare not doubt its existence, nor the unfaltering nature of his compassion for us.

John Bunyan suffered many trials during his life, including twelve years of imprisonment for his preaching of the gospel. The cost to his family, as well as to himself, was horrendous. Yet he testified that the key to his life was 'to live upon God that is invisible'. In 1684 he wrote a rich exposition of suffering based on 1 Peter 4:19, entitled *Spiritual Counsel*. In it he affirmed his belief that no suffering comes except by God's appointment and that God does nothing without good cause. Therefore we should receive thankfully what comes from his hand. He also affirmed that there was more of God to be discovered in suffering than when all was well. He explained:

> We are apt to overshoot, in days that are calm, and to think of ourselves far higher, and more strong than we find we be when the trying day is upon us ... We could not live without such turnings of the hand of God upon us. We should be overgrown with flesh, if we had not our seasonable winters. It is said that in some countries trees will grow, but will bear no fruit, because there is no winter there.[38]

Bunyan understood James' wise counsel. Troubles can be welcomed with joy because they are the means by which God chooses to fashion us to perfection; because we can be sure he is the God who is full of light and who only ever showers us with good and perfect gifts; and, because we can rest in his sovereign power which will ensure that justice and righteousness will prevail at the end. The Lord, 'full of compassion and mercy,' will triumph.

# 2

# Wisdom and
# How to Obtain It
# (1:5-8; 3:13-18)

**James, the teacher of wisdom**

**1. James expresses a fundamental need, 1:5-8**

- The need for wisdom
- The supplier of wisdom
- The recipients of wisdom

**2. James explores a startling contrast, 3:13-18**

- Two wisdoms: different in origins
- Two wisdoms: different in character
- Two wisdoms: different in results

**3. James explains an elementary solution**

- We need to admit our need
- We need to develop our focus
- We need to remember our fallibility

Why do clever people do such silly things? President Clinton, the most powerful politician on earth, risked impeachment for a brief fling with Monica Lewinsky. He kept the presidency but lost the moral respect of the American people, all for one fleeting moment of pleasure. Peter Mandelson, the spin doctor who orchestrated Tony Blair's election as British Prime Minister, had a reputation for manipulating the press with consummate skill. Yet he fell foul of them when they discovered he had told them a lie about his personal life. Failure to deal truthfully with the press cost him his role in the British Cabinet, not once but twice. Jonathan Aitken, in less happy times than now, was sent to prison for lying under oath in a court of law whilst waging a high profile campaign to wield the sword of truth and cut out the cancer of lies in the British press. The roll call of stupidity among public figures could continue. In recent years, the news has been full of stories of intelligent and powerful people (usually men) who have demonstrated anything but intelligence in their private lives and public dealings.

Judging from the television, it's not just powerful people who do stupid things. Ordinary people, who for the most part appear quite sane, demonstrate a capacity for behaving in absurd ways. One only has to watch the series of programmes which were briefly fashionable under the title of *Neighbours from Hell; Holidays from Hell; Garages from Hell* and so on to discover that it is people just like you and me who behave foolishly. In fact, we only have to look at our own lives to realise we are all capable of living unwisely.

In his marvellous book *Celebration of Discipline,* Richard Foster wrote, 'The desperate need today is not for a greater number of intelligent people, or gifted people, but for deep people.'[1] He was right. The world does not need cleverer people to solve its problems, nor an increase in the volume of intelligence that already exists. It needs greater wisdom. Intelligence and wisdom should never be confused. In days when knowledge and information have become so accessible through the Internet it is even more vital than before that we learn the difference between the two. The former has to do with information, acquiring knowledge and the quickness of understanding. The latter has to do with the ability to apply knowledge and information in a way which is beneficial and constructive both for oneself and for the wider community. We may have gargantuan quantities of knowledge and intelligence and still live silly, unhappy lives. We may have just a little wisdom and lead lives of rich peace and contentment. The measure of wisdom is not what one knows, but how one lives.

The poet William Cowper perceptively expressed the differences between them.

> Knowledge and wisdom, far from being one,
> Have at times no connection, Knowledge dwells
> In heads replete with thoughts of other men;
> Wisdom, in minds attentive to their own.
> Knowledge, a rude unprofitable mass,
> The mere materials with which wisdom builds,
> Till smoothed and squared and fitted to its place,
> Does but encumber whom it seems to enrich.
> Knowledge is proud that he has learned so much
> Wisdom is humble that he knows no more.[2]

**James, the teacher of wisdom**

Nothing is more characteristic of James than the idea of wisdom. If the characteristic word in Paul's writings is faith, the characteristic word in Peter's is hope, the characteristic word in John's is love, then the characteristic word for James is wisdom.

His letter, as we saw in the Introduction, is the New Testament counterpart of the Old Testament Book of Proverbs. Here, we briefly recapitulate what was said in the Introduction about James as wisdom literature (since any author knows that readers often foolishly pass over such matters and rush on to the later chapters) and introduce some new aspects of it. In content, style and perspective James stands in the wisdom tradition of Israel. That tradition reflected spiritually on everyday life and how people could manage their lives well, avoiding discomfort in relation to God, others and even themselves. The tone of the wisdom writings was gentle. You would look in them in vain for the confident thunderings of the prophets. Yet they were just as persuasive as any saying introduced by the words 'thus saith the Lord'.

Richard Bauckham defines the wisdom teacher, James included, like this: he is a sage who instructs with the authority of his own experience, observation, insight and reflection. Typically the sage gives reasons why the behaviour he commends should be adopted. Typically he uses analogies and examples from common experience, which help his hearers in a certain way. He shares with them a perspective on life and the way to live it.[3]

For all its likeness to earlier wisdom writings and despite its lack of many obvious Christian reference points (there are only two explicit references at 1:1 and 2:1) the letter of James is emphatically not locked into the era of the old covenant. James writes as a follower of Jesus and is 'a creative exponent of the wisdom of Jesus'.[4] But this does not mean he is quoting Jesus all the time. In harmony with the way wisdom teachers functioned, James was not required to repeat the words of Jesus – although allusions to them abound – and then expound them. Rather, it is clear that he is shaped and inspired by Jesus' teaching but re-expresses it in his own creative way, crafting his own words and images to convey its meaning. He owes a debt to Jesus that goes well beyond the mere parroting of his words.[5] He owes a total perspective and worldview to Jesus.[6] He writes with the same commitment to living a life that is ethically radical as we find in Jesus. He has the same vision of the community of disciples living under the rule of God and shunning hierarchical structures as Jesus. He places the same emphasis on the imminent coming of God's judgement as Jesus. He has the same view of God as generous, compassionate and merciful as Jesus. Like Jesus he speaks in black and white terms with no room for compromise. Like Jesus he is concerned about our speech and the inner source of our words and actions. Like Jesus he is passionate about the poor and has no room for the prideful status-conscious attitudes which are found in conventional society.

We find all that, and more, in the wisdom James sets before us. But before we explore some of those themes in their own right, we need to look at what James thinks about wisdom itself, wisdom, that is, as a topic in its own right. Wisdom is the second item on James' agenda. He speaks of it immediately after the topic of suffering, introducing it in 1:5-8 and developing it more fully in 3:13-18.

## 1. James expresses a fundamental need, 1:5-8

*The need for wisdom*
The vision James has set before his readers is of their lives being fashioned by trials and suffering until they reach completion and are 'not lacking anything'. We can imagine his readers responding to that by saying that that is all very well but it seems so far off and idealistic. What they could do with was some help with their shortcomings now. One of their deficiencies was a lack of wisdom as to how to live through the difficult times they were facing. If that single lack were supplied it would make such a difference to so many other things. James had just taught them to see their sufferings in a positive light. Doing so would help them to bear the load more easily, stop them from reacting foolishly (so making the situation worse) and help them to see life from God's perspective. Why couldn't they have seen that for themselves? What they needed was a good dose of wisdom. They needed an insight into living which would enable them to live wholesome, contented and ordered lives whatever their circumstances. God had made the world to run on certain lines but it now seemed so out of sorts with itself, so distorted and disjointed, because of sin. They needed to know how to function in such a world and how they could live quality lives rather than lives that were undernourished, depleted and stretched to the limit. Wisdom would give them the answers.

It seems a trifle unnecessary for James to say, 'If anyone lacks wisdom...' Who among us would claim we had all the wisdom we need to negotiate our way through this complex and crazy world? Who has got enough wisdom to know how to bring up our kids; live unsullied lives in a sex-soaked culture; to make good moral choices in a world made increasingly complex by the advance of medical science; or, to cope with the acceleration of the communications revolution and the availability of indiscriminate knowledge? Or, who knows how to live simply and contentedly in an affluent culture when globally 1.3 billion live on less than 70 pence a day and more than 800 million people do not have enough to eat?[7] Certainly our society does not seem to know the answers. The psychiatrist Oliver James has documented the way in which we seem to be handling the unprecedented prosperity and opportunities we enjoy with total ineptitude. The more we have, he says, the less we are satisfied. Never has there been such affluence on the one hand and never has there been such a high incidence of clinical depression on the other. Wealth and choice seem to breed discontent. Rather than being satisfied:

> We compare ourselves obsessively, enviously, and self-destructively, thus corrupting the quality of our inner lives. No sooner do we achieve a goal than the goal posts move to create a new more difficult one, leaving ourselves permanently dissatisfied and depleted, always yearning for what we have not got, a nation of Wannabees.[8]

Does James – the writer of the letter, not the psychiatrist – really need to be so tentative in his question? Of course, we lack wisdom. All of us lack wisdom. And we could do with it.

## The supplier of wisdom

Fortunately, there is an abundant source of supply available if only we are prepared to reach beyond ourselves for it and not look within and assume we can depend on our own resources to provide it. It is plentiful because it is God who supplies it and he 'gives generously to all without finding fault'. Such is his nature. Gerard Hughes highlighted the way in which God is portrayed as generous in the ministry of Jesus. Hughes pointed to the parables and talked of the 'foolish prodigality' of a God who leaves ninety-nine sheep to go in search of one lost one. He wrote of the financial imprudence involved in forgiving a debtor who owed ten thousand talents, and, in paying a full day's pay to those who were last minute workers. The miracles of Jesus demonstrate the same generosity. The 180 gallons of excellent quality wine produced at the wedding in Cana seems 'an unnecessarily large quantity', especially at the tail end of the feast. And to feed five thousand and have twelve baskets full of food left over seemed extravagant. 'The Father,' Hughes concludes, 'is presented as a God of overflowing goodness, whose one desire is to share what he has with as many as possible.'[9] That is certainly how James sees God.

In describing God like this James uses a unique word in the New Testament. *haplōs* sometimes means 'generously' and sometimes means 'simply', or 'straightforwardly'. It can be translated either way. But the meaning here is crystal clear: when one comes to God to ask for wisdom the simple request is going to be met with a ready response. When we ask for support from human agencies we are accustomed to having to argue our case, to fill out multitudes of off-putting forms, and often to cajole officials who seem stubbornly unwilling to part with the money we need. Indeed, they often seem to protect it as if it was their own. When we make an insurance claim we almost expect to be refused because somehow we managed to miss some clause or another in the small print. But we dare not project these common human experiences on to God. We have no reason to believe that he will respond to us as the arch or eternal bureaucrat. Quite the reverse. James amplifies the point. To God's generosity James adds his liberality. He is generous 'to all'. To God's liberality James adds his magnanimity. Unlike the official who seems to delight in catching us out and in preventing us from receiving the help we had hoped for, God gives 'without finding fault'. This God, as Jesus showed us, is waiting to answer our request with enthusiasm.

### The recipients of wisdom

There is, however, just one stipulation. 'Having described the willing father,' as Peter Davids puts it, 'James turns to the other side of the transaction, the waiting child.'[10] Whilst there can be no doubt that God is willing to give, the question remains as to whether we are in a position to receive. If we want to receive we must ask with wholeheartedness and integrity. Single-mindedness is the requirement. There can be no room for divided loyalties and vacillating commitments. If we really think we can supply the lack of wisdom ourselves, we will not receive it from God. If we think that we can find a supplier elsewhere, perhaps among the rich and powerful on earth, we will not receive it from God.

Here James is in typically uncompromising mood; a mentality which we shall encounter time and again in this short writing. It is found, for example, very clearly in 4:4. The manner in which we ask for wisdom demands an either/or approach not a both/and one. We can't have it both ways. Using graphic terminology he presents the person who wants to cover all his options like a wave buffeted around on a stormy sea. It is at the mercy of the winds. The wave has no power of its own. It has no will to go in any particular direction. It cannot determine its own direction. It is at the mercy of other forces. The point was vividly brought home to me one time when I was expounding this passage in Australia at the time of the Sydney-Hobart yacht race. That year the storms beat furiously and several yachts were wrecked. Being on an open storm-tossed sea was a perilous position to be in. That describes exactly, James says, the two-minded person who believes a little of this and a little of that but will not stake his or her life completely on God. In reality such a person is a practical polytheist, believing in the God and Father of Jesus Christ and other gods at the same time. They want to hedge their bets by believing as much in other solutions to life's problems as in the living God. The people who approach God like that will never receive wisdom.

God will give, but we must ask with a singular determination.

## 2. James explores a startling contrast, 3:13-18

When James next returns to the subject of wisdom it is to set out more fully what he understands by wisdom. In doing so he is simply giving fresh expression to the ancient teaching of the Book of Proverbs, which stated that 'The fear of the LORD is the beginning of wisdom'.[11] He is also putting in summary form much of the wise teaching of Jesus. James explores his meaning by contrasting what he means by wisdom with what conventional society usually considers it to be. The two kinds of wisdom differ in their origin, their character and their results.

*Their different origins, verse 15*

(i) The origin of earthly wisdom
Underneath it all, wisdom is a spiritual issue, not a matter of education, experience, money, or technique. It is a matter of one's relationship with God. In a devastating put-down, James declares that conventional wisdom, much prized by the world, is in reality 'earthly, unspiritual (and) of the devil' (verse 15). Its focus is purely this world. It does not concern itself with anything beyond what one can see and enter into now. The world is a closed system; one, as the sociologist Peter

Berger aptly described it, as 'a world without windows'.[12] People who live in such a world do not look beyond their own immediate experience nor believe in any reality superior to themselves. They deny the very possibility that the unseen and eternal might be real and they certainly do not let them govern the way they live. They do not bow before the transcendent. There is nothing more important for them than 'earthly things'[13] and nothing larger in their universe than themselves.

To pronounce such a world view as 'unspiritual', as James does, is to state that there is an absence of soul about it. Conventional wisdom gives freedom to the body, so that its appetites might be immediately fed; and to the mind, that its logic might be crucially followed. But it has no room for the soul. Feeling and reason dominate. The spiritual dimension of our personhood and our need to enjoy a relationship with God are simply airbrushed out of the human picture.

Ironically, there is a grand unseen manipulator pulling the strings of such wisdom. Truth to tell, while people may deny that the realm of the demonic exists, or at least that it is to be taken seriously, it is that very realm which influences the way people think and act. James' critique of conventional wisdom reaches its climax as he dismisses it as having its ultimate origin in the devil himself. The devil, of course, has great skill in the art of deception. He is, as Jesus claimed in an argument with the Pharisees, 'the father of lies' and lying is his 'native language'.[14] What he sets before people looks so reasonable and so attractive. But it proves to be a fatal attraction for, as we shall see, such wisdom destroys community and ruins lives. Yet, generation after generation goes on being fooled by it. The world, the flesh and the devil, then, conspire to make a pseudo-wisdom look attractive.


(ii) The origin of heavenly wisdom

By contrast, there is a genuine wisdom which has its origins in heaven. It is given to us by the One who made us, and who, therefore, has some claim to be taken seriously by us. Logically, our Creator should know, if anyone does, how we can best live our lives and how we can conduct them so that we dwell in harmony with others and with the world in which he has placed us. It would seem sensible to listen to him. This means that we will not find such a wisdom within us, as

New Age philosophies teach us. We are not self-sufficient in wisdom, but need to look outside of ourselves to our Father in heaven to supply it. The fundamental difference between the two wisdoms is that the earthly makes self and the heavenly makes God the ultimate reference point of life.

Bill Hybels reported on an interesting experiment which illustrates what happens when we refuse to use external reference points. Twenty pilots who were all very capable of flying their aircraft when visibility was clear but had never done any instrument training were put in a flight simulator and made to fly through thick fog and storms. Each of them crashed their plane in 178 seconds. 'It took,' he commented, 'seasoned pilots with skilled intuition less than three minutes to destroy themselves once they'd lost their visual reference points.'[15] Life often requires us to fly blind, and it is already apparent that James' readers are having to fly through fog and storms. To do so without crashing requires us to use the external reference of the wisdom that comes 'down from heaven', that is, the wisdom which is revealed to us through Christ.

*Their different characters, verses 14 and 17*
Telling the difference between earthly and heavenly wisdom is not difficult. They are so different in character they can be spotted a mile off.

(i) The character of earthly wisdom
Earthly wisdom is characterised by an extreme and destructive individualism. Its chief components are 'envy and selfish ambition'. It can never truly rejoice in someone else's success because it is eaten up by jealousy. It always makes a priority of Number One and looks out for its own interests before being concerned with the interests of others. It is seen in lives which appear to be 'driven', always striving forward for more, for greater, for better and never satisfied with what has been achieved or acquired so far. The Greek moral philosophers considered this quality of jealousy to lie at the root of many of our ills. If left to fester, they said, it would inevitably lead on to other ills such as slander and even murder. There is plenty of evidence, ranging from Shakespeare's plays to tomorrow's newspapers, that they were right.

The word James couples with 'envy' and which is translated in the NIV as 'selfish ambition' (*eritheia*) is quite an unusual one. We pick up its meaning outside of the New Testament when we learn that Aristotle used it of factional power-hungry politicians. Obviously some things don't change![16] We're familiar still with the type of politician who isn't really interested in serving the community, whatever the election publicity might say, but who is prepared to sacrifice any principle or do as many U-turns as necessary if only it will mean they can get into power or maintain the power they already have. There you see a typical example of earthly wisdom.

It is significant that James says such vices should not be given room in our hearts. These ugly characteristics are what come naturally to us, given our fallen human natures. Jesus had argued with the Pharisees that what made us unclean was not whether we'd gone in for the sort of ritual washing of hands and plates they advocated but what lay deep within us. As he explained, 'What comes out of a man is what makes him "unclean". For from within, out of men's hearts, come evil thoughts, sexual immorality, theft, murder, adultery, greed, malice, deceit, lewdness, envy, slander, arrogance and folly. All these evils come from inside and make a man "unclean".'[17] Given that, James says we should eject such thoughts, just as he had earlier said we should eject temptations, as soon as we become aware of them. To give them house room is foolish.

As Christians we dare not exempt ourselves from the searching challenge of these words and make the mistake of thinking this is a problem only for those outside of the church. It's perfectly obvious that it was a major problem among the believers to whom James is writing, as the verses which immediately follow demonstrate (4:1-3). And contemporary experience of church life compels us to admit that that it still remains a problem. Even the most saintly among us struggle with 'envy and selfish ambition'. F. W. Robertson of Brighton, the celebrated preacher of a former age, was supposed once to have prayed, 'Lord, I would sooner your work was not done at all, than done by someone better than I can do it.'[18] His prayer might have the merit of being a good deal more honest than some of our prayers but it is no more right because of that. Thomas Manton pointed out that envy and selfish ambition often disguise themselves 'under the mask of zeal'.[19] Many a church meeting has been wrecked by people pretending to be concerned about the cause of Christ who were actually playing politics and bolstering their own power position in the church. Many friendships have been destroyed because people have related in the way people do in the world rather than as they should in Christ.

James follows his reference to 'envy and selfish ambition' with two curiously difficult phrases which instruct us not to 'boast about it or deny the truth'. What he seems to be saying is that if we live enviously and ambitiously, out for Number One, it is stupid to brag about it because it is obvious to everyone else that we are being foolish. No one is fooled by us however much we dress it up. People may say nice things to our faces but our folly is plain for all to see and they laugh at us behind our backs. What 'truth' does he have in mind which he encourages us not to deny? It makes sense, in view of the previous phrase, if it is a reference to denying the truth about ourselves. We do not fool others so it is all the more pathetic if the only person we end up deceiving is ourself. Some people are painfully lacking in self-awareness and it leads them into all kinds of folly. They are so difficult to handle. They put themselves forward for the most inappropriate jobs. They consider themselves to have gifts which they are plainly lacking. And they consider themselves to be God's answer to a number of situations where the plain truth is that they are part of the problem. Better, says James, not to pretend and come clean about ourselves or else eventually we might well be unmasked for the fools we really are.

(ii) The character of heavenly wisdom
Wisdom from heaven could not be more opposite. It, too, is evident in one's behaviour where it becomes manifest in the living of 'a good life' and by the doing of good works 'done in humility'. If it is evident in one's behaviour it is even more evident in one's character. It is not just the specific acts that one does which reveal whether we are wise or not but also the kind of person one is reveals it. In verse 17, James begins his description of this wisdom by first using the catch-all word 'pure'. This is followed by a string of seven adjectives which itemise different aspects of the meaning of purity. Several of these are

alliterated in the Greek and would have been easy to remember. They are reminiscent of the fruit of the Spirit described by Paul in Galatians 5: 22-23. Paul would say the Holy Spirit produces the fruit of righteousness within our lives because we are incapable of producing it naturally. James is saying the same thing in a different way. Living like this comes 'down from heaven'. To be full of the Spirit is for James not about having supernatural or ecstatic experiences but about living wisely in all the flesh-and-blood reality of our routine and mundane lives; and about relating harmoniously with others in the day-to-day ordinariness of our lives.

So, top of the list comes purity. That's the word that sums it all up. According to Proverbs 15:26, the thoughts of the pure are pleasing to God. To be pure is to live innocently, with moral integrity and blamelessness. 'The unsullied chastity of a virgin bride'[20] illustrates its meaning best as Paul appreciated when he stated that his ambition was to present the Church to Christ 'as a pure virgin'.[21] It speaks volumes that today 'being innocent' is usually used in a disparaging way. It denotes someone who is precious, naive and can't cope with the world and is likely, therefore, to run into trouble. What was once prized as a positive virtue is now ridiculed as a negative weakness. How counter-cultural wisdom from above is!

The seven adjectives which then follow 'purity' lend colour to its meaning. 'Peace-loving' means what it says. Rather than being awkward, arrogant and antagonistic in nature, the wise person will value peace and adjust their own behaviour, attitudes and ambitions to guard it and, where it has been lost, to restore it.

The next word, which the NIV translates as 'considerate', is the word 'gentle'. It means we will be generous in our reactions with other people, forgiving their faults, exercising patience over their failings and seeing their mistakes in the best light. We will not be demanding and exacting of others. This requires that we take time to understand them and try to put ourselves in their shoes. We will seek the missing piece of the jigsaw puzzle which explains their behaviour, without which we would fail to understand why they are as tiresome as they are.

To be 'submissive' is not a call to give in to anyone regardless of whether they are right or not. It is to be 'open to reason'. It is the opposite of being stubborn, strong-minded and unyielding. It requires that we listen to others before making up our minds and that, because we are open to reason, we will climb down graciously when we have got things wrong.

The quality of 'mercy' which follows next is best illustrated by what James had already written in 2:12-13. Mercy is the exercise of compassion to others. It is the opposite of insisting on one's rights. Once more, this aspect of wisdom stands in sharp contrast to the spirit of the age in which we live which has placed an unparalleled stress on our 'rights'. The first reaction these days when someone lets us down or something goes wrong is to find someone we can sue. Usually the only people to profit are the lawyers. But the litigious streak now runs deep within us all. James calls us to let go our rights and use mercy in large doses – to be 'full of mercy' – rather than to be tight-fisted in dispensing it.

Similarly, we are to be 'full of good fruit'. Mercy is not meant to be a nice warm feeling we have towards others but a disposition which actually issues in practical and constructive action.

The sixth quality is more difficult. The word 'impartial' (*adiakritos*) is used only here in the New Testament. Since *diakritos* refers to doubt and wavering, its opposite must mean something like to be settled and straightforward. That would certainly be consistent with James' wider concern, as we have already seen, for example, in 1:6. He wants us to be wholehearted people, people of integrity, rather than unstable or double-minded people. We should not blow hot and cold in our relationships with others but prove ourselves to be persons of steady reliability. If trustworthiness is hard to find anywhere else our neighbours should always know they will find it in us.

The final aspect of wisdom is 'sincerity'. Mark Twain knew that the secret of success is sincerity. Therefore, he advised, 'If you can fake it (sincerity) you've got it made.' Did you hear of the Freudian slip which an unfortunate printing firm suffered one year? It failed to proof-read its own Christmas card adequately and sent it out with the greeting, 'We fake an interest in all our customers.' James calls believers to total integrity in their relationships. We need to produce the genuine article; not a sincerity which some spin-doctor has manufactured just to preserve some nicely-managed image.

As I write there are yet again lamentable pictures from north Belfast on our news. The situation, at least as presented by the media, looks like this. Catholic children who wish to take a direct route to their school are compelled to pass through a few hundred yards of Protestant territory. For more than a week they have been barracked and threatened by their Protestant neighbours and, on one occasion, the target of a blast bomb thrown in their direction. Their faces show the fear they feel. It is but one of the many events which demonstrate the wisdom of the world in action. Both sides are the hostages of worldly wisdom. Catholics insist on walking down that street because it is their right to do so, even though there is a perfectly acceptable route which they could follow that would remove the cause of their provocation at a stroke. Protestants are equally to blame. Arrogantly seeking to protect their territory, they behave in a way which the rest of the world finds both deplorable and unbelievable. How different Northern Ireland would be if both sides of the political dispute rejected the foolish wisdom of the world and lived instead according to the wisdom from heaven. Peace would break out overnight. If we needed convincing of the truth of James' words, there it is. The wisdom of the world has nothing to boast about. It simply shows itself up for the absurdity it is.

Even more poignantly, as I typed the above words, unknown to me the tragedy of the terrorist attacks on New York and Washington, on 11th September 2001, was unfolding. They, and the hawkish response made by some American politicians, stand as a monumental sign of earthly wisdom. The magnitude of the destruction is hard to grasp. Lives have been lost in their thousands, businesses and wealth massively destroyed. The world stands on the brink of an uncertain future. Worldly wisdom costs lives. If only the world would receive the wisdom that comes down from heaven!

*Their different results, verses 13, 16 and 18.*
Throughout these verses on wisdom James has been weaving a thread which highlights the effect of living according to the one pattern or the other. The wisdom of the earth and the wisdom from heaven lead to diametrically opposite results not just for the individuals who live by them but for the neighbourhoods, communities and nations of which they are members.

## (i) The result of earthly wisdom

Earthly wisdom inevitably leads to 'disorder and every evil practice' (verse 16). The unavoidable consequences of people living simply for themselves is anarchy. No community or society can function healthily if that is the foundation on which its members wish to build. The logic simply doesn't add up. If 'envy and selfish ambition' rule I will succeed at the expense of someone else who will fail. We cannot both fulfil our unrestrained ambitions. If, for example, I wish to satisfy my sexual desires by having intercourse with a female who is unwilling then, living by the logic of earthly wisdom, I will impose myself on her regardless of her feelings or of any respect she might deserve as a person who also has a right to decide how she will live her life. If I want to occupy a certain territory which is already 'owned' by someone else, then, according to earthly logic, I am likely to fight for it and my opponent is likely to defend it. War will follow. The clash of unrestrained wills inevitably means one becomes powerful and the other destroyed. 'Envy and selfish ambition' lead at the very least to our distancing ourselves from one another and, at worst, to destroying the very possibility of any sense of community or civilisation. Earthly wisdom is anything but conducive of a peaceful way of life. The flattened towers of the World Trade Center in New York tragically say it all.

## (ii) The result of heavenly wisdom

'Wisdom from above' yields entirely different results. It leads to a life of moral goodness. It gives rise to relationships that are strong and healthy because the partners in them respect each other, restrain their natural desires and show respect for each other. 'Humility' is key to such behaviour. In a former day the Greek word *prautēs* would probably have been translated as 'meekness' rather than 'humility'. But meekness has been so confused with weakness that it is probably no longer wise to do so. The confusion began long ago with the Greeks regarding meekness as a vice rather than a virtue. Meekness, however, is a word which originally spoke of strength; albeit a strength which had been disciplined and channelled to constructive ends, rather than one which rides roughshod over others. Jesus pronounced those who were meek, 'blessed.'[22] And he spoke of himself as meek.[23] We are therefore simply being called to imitate him. In him, surely, we see wisdom and strength perfectly blended together.

Exercising humility will lead us to 'raise a harvest of righteousness'. It is evident that in using that phrase James has something very active in mind because he connects it with peacemaking. To Paul, righteousness essentially meant being in a right standing with God. But he would have been the first to claim that those who were in a right standing with God would actively pursue 'rightness' in all the other areas of their lives. You cannot be in a right relationship with God and not live righteously in your dealings with others. Speaking the truth, behaving with integrity, acting ethically, living morally, proving trustworthy are inevitable. But it is more than that. Being righteous before God will also mean we long to create right relationships in his world. We will seek to live at peace with others in our own personal networks of relationship. But we will not stop there. We are called to pursue peace beyond our own circles, for we are called to be peace-*makers* (not just peace*keepers*) in the wider circles of our communities and society. The harvest of righteousness will call us to take the sort of initiatives that the members of ECONI[24] have done in Northern Ireland. In response to the call of Christ,[25] echoed here by James, they have bravely crossed the party lines, withstood the opprobrium of Protestant zealots who have accused them of naivety and betrayal, and risked the misunderstanding of Catholic republicans in order to make peace and bring harmony to that divided province. They understand what Jesus and James meant and they are seeking to live obediently to the vision. No one pretends it is easy. But all know it is both right and worth it.

Earthly wisdom destroys community and ruins lives. Heavenly wisdom produces wholesome individuals, builds community and constructs healthy societies.

## 3. James explains an elementary solution

How can we get such wisdom? As he has been explaining the nature of true wisdom, James has given us some scattered clues. We do not learn it from a textbook or in a classroom. We learn it in a life lived before God.

*First, we need to admit our need*
The first lesson to learn if we want to be truly wise is that we are
needy people. If we persist in believing either that we are already
wise or that we have adequate resources within us which will make
us wise we are condemned to continue living in ignorant folly. We
need to reach out in humility to God so that he might supply what we
lack. Only as we set aside our pride and express our deficiencies will
we acquire wisdom. Worldly wisdom salutes self-sufficiency. It says
that one of the worst weaknesses possible is to become dependent on
others. To have to rely on someone else and lose one's freedom is
considered by many a great disgrace. Yet, spiritually speaking, it is
the beginning of wisdom.

*Secondly, we need to develop our focus*
Our culture celebrates diversity. When we buy sweets, we pick-and-
mix. When we buy clothes we mix-and-match, or mix-and-clash, as
the case may be. In terms of thinking our modern minds have been
described as being homeless. We're like intellectual vagrants who
cannot settle to one set of convictions but are always on the move to
somewhere else. In terms of relationships we're into constructing
our marriages and families first this way and then reconstructing them
that way. In terms of our identity we're constantly recreating ourselves.
No one really knows who we are.

   But if we want to be wise, we need to develop focus. Asking God
to supply us with wisdom is a start. But the way we ask is all-important.
If we ask only half-seriously we will end up disappointed. If we would
quite like God to give us wisdom but we also want to look for it
elsewhere at the same time we shall never acquire it. The life that
wants to be wise needs to learn to focus on the voice of God to the
exclusion of other voices. Unless we are truly hungry for it our needs
will go unsatisfied.

*Thirdly, we need to remember our fallibility*
The moment we think we have become wise, we cease to be wise.
We never grow beyond the role of the learner. Jesus said, 'Take my
yoke upon you and learn from me, for I am gentle and humble in heart
and you will find rest for your souls.'[26]  The yoke needs to remain in
place for the rest of our lives. The learning needs to go on continuously.

Until the day of Christ, when God's work in us will be complete, we are always liable to slip back to our old ways. Self will rear its head in unguarded moments. Envy will spring up when least expected. Ambition will lie dormant for years and then revive. We'll be happy to sacrifice our rights for so long and then discover that deep down we weren't really so happy to do so after all. Living wisely calls for a daily crucifying of self; a daily determination to consider the interests of others above our own; a daily resolve to walk the way of Christ. Only then will wisdom eventually blossom in our lives.

The volcanic explosion of information technology which has taken place within very recent years means that we have far more knowledge and information at our fingertips through a computer keyboard than we can handle. We can download quantities of material to which our grandparents would never have had access even after a life of research. When we use a search engine to find out about a topic the number of sites we discover boggles the imagination. We could never work through them all and, even if we could, how could we discern what was valuable from what was nonsense among them? As the world gets cleverer so the need for it to get wiser is more and more evident. Unfortunately as knowledge increases wisdom seems to be on the wane. Knowledge can be acquired anywhere. But wisdom seems in short supply.

Here is one area where the people of God are called to stand out as different. We are called to live not according to the wisdom which is earthly, unspiritual and devilish but according to the wisdom which comes 'down from heaven' which was personified in Jesus Christ. We are called to imitate him. That's really all that James is saying. Be Christlike. If we do so we will provoke, as he did, a reaction. The reaction may be one of envy, of hostility, or of conversion. But it will not be the response of indifference from which the church has suffered for so long. We should be praying hard, 'Lord, make us wise.'

# 3

# Wealth and
# How to Treat It
# (1:9-11; 2:1-7; 5:1-6)

## 1. The perspective of the Kingdom,  1:9-11, 2:5-7

- ◆ The principle of status reversal
  The high status of the poor
  The low status of the rich

## 2. The problem of the church,  2:1-7

- ◆ The practice of conventional values

## 3. The principles of the Scripture

- ◆ Is God biased to the poor?
- ◆ Is God opposed to wealth creation?

## 4. The perils of the wealthy,  5:1-6

- ◆ The sin of hoarding
- ◆ The sin of injustice
- ◆ The sin of indulgence
- ◆ The sin of corruption

## 5. The practice of the believers

None of us ever believes we are rich. No matter how much we possess we can always compare ourselves upwards. There is always someone who has more than we do, so we convince ourselves that we are not to be counted among the wealthy. Recent studies of lottery winners show that even those who have won millions are not content. For all they have, they feel they could do with more. It seems we are never satisfied; condemned ever to be 'a nation of Wannabees'.[1]

Yet, without fear of contradiction, we in the western world are rich by any measure; especially when compared with the people who lived in James' day or those who live in much of the developing world of our own day. The people of James' time, no matter what their wealth, had:

> never ridden in a car,
> never flown on an aeroplane,
> never turned on an electric light,
> never used a phone,
> never watched a TV or listened to a radio,
> never slept on an interior-sprung mattress,
> never washed dishes in hot tap water, let alone used a dishwasher,
> never mowed a lawn,
> never had surgery,
> never used penicillin,
> and never switched on a computer.[2]

If that isn't rich, what is? Like it or not, when the Bible addresses the rich it is addressing those of us who live in the modern western world. So those of us who have ears need to hear what it says.

Money, or the lack of it, is one of the most potent forces that shape our lives. The currency may have changed over the years but the significance of riches has not. Many of the problems James' readers faced were caused by the behaviour of rich people of whom some, but not necessarily all, were members of the church. So, it is not surprising that the third item on James' agenda, after suffering and wisdom, is how to deal with wealth, or perhaps, more strictly, the wealthy. The theme crops up at a number of points in his writing. He addresses both the poorer ordinary members of the congregation and financiers, merchants and large landowning farmers (see, for example, 4:13–5:6). Two particular problems become evident. First, the presence of wealthy people was causing havoc in the church because it brought conventional social divisions to the surface. Secondly, the practice of wealthy people was causing havoc in the marketplace because it resulted in heartache and financial ruin to many. How should Christians deal with such issues? What should their response be?

## 1. The perspective of the Kingdom, 1:9-11, 2:5-7

*The principle of status reversal*
James begins his teaching by setting out the radical perspective of the kingdom of God – a perspective which would cause them, and us, to re-evaluate totally the way we see things. Part of the problem which James exposes is that members of the church, rich and poor alike, were still thinking in conventional terms and judging people by the customary measurements of the world. They had not sufficiently reconstructed the way they saw the world according to the teaching of Jesus. They had not been nearly radical enough in their thinking.

The ancient world revolved around the axis of honour and dishonour. Honour was a key value in ancient cultures and the motive which determined how people lived and reacted to one another. It was the foundation on which nations and societies were built. From early days onwards children were taught to take pride in their race, tribe or family and to uphold their honour. If someone brought dishonour on their people, say by committing a crime or losing a contest, they would expect to be shamed and know that they were risking severe punishment, even expulsion from their group. To insult a group's honour would be to provoke them to a vigorous, often vengeful, response. Honour had to be defended. Honour and wealth were connected. Within most societies the esteem in which one was held depended on the wealth one possessed. The rich were honoured above the poor. They had the duty to dispense patronage and the poor had the duty to know their place and be grateful for it. That was the way it was. It was the way people were taught to think from their cradle onwards.[3]

Then came Jesus. He turned things upside down. He gave honour to those whom conventional logic would have denied it because of their ritual impurity, racial background, social position or financial poverty. He healed a woman who was 'unclean' because of a long-standing haemorrhage[4] and he touched lepers who were among the untouchables of his time.[5] His compassion extended to those of other races[6] and he embraced those with dubious reputations.[7] He taught that God rejected those whom most would assume were worthy of God's favour and accepted those who were assumed to be subject to God's disfavour.[8] On one occasion he retorted to the Pharisees that, 'What is highly valued by people is detestable in God's sight'.[9] Here was a Messiah who, as Mary had foreseen, 'has brought down rulers from their thrones but has lifted up the humble. He has filled the hungry with good things but has sent the rich away empty'.[10] Throughout the Gospels, Luke's in particular, we see that the rule of God entails a reversal of all that is conventionally accepted with regard to social, economic, and so religious status. Salvation is about the reversal of one's status before God.[11] God's kingdom is an upside-down one and his economy works in the reverse way to normal.

Those who claimed to follow Jesus should have been well aware of this before James wrote about it in his letter. Yet, the way his readers were behaving suggested these believers, at least, had not grasped Christ's teaching in this area. Their behaviour could, in fairness, be interpreted in one of four ways: either that they were ignorant of this basic teaching and had never been taught it; or, they knew it but had forgotten it; or, it was so hard to get their heads around and they found it difficult to live contrary to their surrounding culture; or, that they were deliberately flouting the teaching of the one they called 'Lord'. So, with perhaps uncharacteristic patience, James once more goes over the mandatory principle of the Kingdom of Jesus, that of status reversal. Then, to drive the point home, he applies it to the way they ran their church.

### The high status of the poor, 1:9; 2:5

James first mentions 'believers in humble circumstances' which, in the context, must mean that they were financially impoverished. Yet, whatever their bank balances might suggest from the standpoint of spiritual reality these poor people actually occupied 'a high position', the sort of position one would normally associate with the rich (1:9).

On what basis could James makes such a claim? 2:5 gives us the answer. Three factors meant they merited high status in God's Kingdom. First there is the *choice God made*. God had chosen the poor to be his own. They may be marginalised and rejected as of no significance by others, but God has deliberately elected them and promoted them to positions of intimate friendship and significant influence in his Kingdom.

Secondly, there is the *currency they used*. They were 'rich in faith'. When travelling overseas it is important to have the right currency with you. I was once briefly a millionaire. The only trouble was that I was a millionaire in Polish Zlotys which, at the time, were worthless anywhere else but in Poland. From memory it amounted to about £36 sterling. The rich of the world may be wealthy in monetary terms but money is not the currency of eternity. In the Kingdom of God, the currency is faith. It costs nothing, financially. The economic poor can have as much access to it as the financially rich. No one is excluded. But the rich, used to dealing in more tangible currencies, tend to exclude themselves by dismissing the currency of faith as unimportant.

Thirdly, there is the *future they faced*. While the poor may have had little in this world the day would come when they would inherit the riches of God's kingdom, an inheritance which comes purely as a result of God's gracious promise towards 'those who love him'. The rich may want to buy their way in – they are used to doing that – but they will not be able to do so. Entrance to his Kingdom and all the abundance it possesses is on the basis of a relationship with God which requires nothing but devoted love and, consequently, the steady offering of a life of obedience.

### *The low status of the rich, 1:10-11; 2:6-7*

From the high status of the poor James turns to the low status of the rich. It is a matter of dispute as to whether the rich people James mentions in 1:10-11 are Christians or unbelievers. Some commentators believe James had rich unbelievers in mind because he does not refer to them as brothers.[12] The stress on the folly of their boasting about wealth, which is a useless currency in the next age, suggests they haven't yet come to terms with the next age at all. And, nowhere else in his letter does he clearly state that the wealthy people he is writing about are Christians. But, even so, it is more natural to regard them as rich believers; the flip side of the poor believers whom he has already addressed. What is said about them fits just as well if they are Christians as if they are not.

They are strongly advised to 'take pride in their low position'. The low position means they must adopt a position where they are consciously dependent on God, a position in which they can live in 'poverty of spirit' even if they are rich in monetary terms. James tells them three things which should encourage them to cultivate humility before God. First, *they should be aware of their transience*. Recalling Isaiah 40:6-7 James uses a graphic image of life. In the Mediterranean area the spring season was brilliant but brief. No sooner had plants sprung up and displayed their glory than the biting, scorching heat would burn them up forthwith. What the heat did not finish, the south-east wind soon would. Nothing lasted. Flowers were here today and gone tomorrow. And so are all of us, however rich we may be.

Secondly, *they should be aware of their impotence.* They may be well respected in 'the city', powerful people who take decisions that affect the future of thousands of others, but one decision is totally outside of their control: namely, the timing of their 'fading away'. That lies in the hands of God. They cannot bank on tomorrow, let alone their retirement. Their lives might unexpectedly be cut short, 'even while they go about their business'; an issue to which James will return in chapter 4. Since the awful events of 11th September 2001, no one should need convincing of the tragic truth of his words. We are powerless to prolong a life which God has determined should end.

Thirdly, *they should be aware of their liabilities.* In 2:5-6 and 12, James gives a further reason for them to exercise poverty of spirit. He paints the unpleasant, but all too familiar, picture of the rich throwing their weight around and riding roughshod over the poor. They are the ones with money and that gives them power, or so they think. If they meet opposition to their plans they can put up the money to mount a lawsuit against anyone who gets in their way; confident that those they despise will be too impoverished to defend themselves adequately in court and so their plans would triumph. There is only one problem with that. Wise businessmen take all the potential liabilities of a decision into account before taking a decision. These foolish businessmen stopped calculating their liabilities too soon. They had only considered the immediate profit margin, not the longer-term accounts that would be submitted to the divine tribunal in eternity. They are accountable to God for the way they have treated others.

James' language is strong, perhaps even intemperate by our standards. The NIV somewhat tamely translates the oppressive action of the rich, in verse 7, as 'slandering the noble name of him to whom you belong'. The word translated 'to slander' is the word 'to blaspheme' (*blasphēmeō*). Why does James consider the mistreatment of poor people in the marketplace as not simply unjust but actually blasphemous? What makes it blasphemous? Proverbs 17:5 provides us with the answer. It is blasphemous because the people they abuse are people made in the image of God and to insult them is, therefore, to insult the one who made them. One cannot engage in oppressive relations with fellow human beings without invoking the wrath of the God who created them. 'So when the practice is open and clearly sinful,' Manton says in support of James' forthright approach, 'it is not good to come with a contemplative lecture and lame homily, but to fall to the case directly.'[13] Perhaps some diffident pastors should learn from James.

## 2. The problem of the church, 2:1-7

*The practice of conventional values*
The clear teaching of the Kingdom of Jesus is one thing. What the church does with it is another. The problem with the church is that it has been relatively good over the years at preaching one thing and practising another. So James sets his readers, and us, a test. 'What would actually happen,' he asks, 'if a rich man and a poor man came to visit? How would they really be treated? Would the church show favouritism or a bias towards the wealthy?' In James' original the word for 'favouritism' (*prosōpolēmpsia*) could be translated literally 'receive the face'. In other words, would they respond merely to what they see externally, on the surface? The test is, would the welcome the rich man and the poor man received be different because

of their wealth and social standing or would they be greeted evenhandedly?

The case study James presents sounds as if it might actually have happened. In an episode which Guy King once called the tale of 'the short-sighted usher',[14] James envisages two strangers, one rich and the other poor, arriving at the church. You can tell their income bracket from their clothing. The rich man is dressed in a way which suggests he was a member of the Roman Equestrian class. Not many others would have had gold rings and even if the visitor was wearing them purely as jewellery, rather than as a badge of office, it would send out signals that here was a man of considerable social significance. The ushers, no doubt, stand to attention, are profuse in their greetings, ingratiating in their attitudes, and then conduct the man with ceremony to a good seat. By contrast, when the poor person who is shabbily dressed enters, their welcome is grudging and perfunctory. He is left standing or told, 'If you must sit, sit on the floor'[15] on a level with the rich man's footstool.

In their behaviour the ushers are demonstrating the basic problem of the church. Its teaching and its practice clash. The values of the Kingdom have not been worked through to their behaviour. They haven't understood that the way they treat people is a spiritual not a social issue. The Bible will not allow us to defend this class-ridden action in the name of politeness or convention. Social inequality has no place in the church. James explains the spiritual implications of such behaviour and points out that two vital issues are at stake. The first is our understanding of the Lord Jesus himself. Do we not believe in a 'glorious Lord Jesus Christ' (verse 1)? If so, what do we see in him? Did not he who was the Lord of glory lay aside his majesty and the trappings of his regal status to become a human being who wore the dress of the peasant class?[16] Did he not provide us with a model in status reversal and did his teaching not make clear that the values of his kingdom were the converse of those of conventional society? How, then, can we say we believe in him if we so flatly contradict both his example and his teaching? To claim to be following him is clearly disproved by actions like those of the ushers James describes. In the light of who Jesus is and what Jesus did we must agree that, 'if we sidestep our responsibility to the poor, the helpless, the outcaste, we are not making a marginal error but failing in the life of faith itself.'[17] How we treat others is as basic as our faith in him. It is that fundamental.

The second spiritual issue involved is our understanding of ourselves. In adopting this class-conscious behaviour we have given ourselves a status to which we have no right. We have put ourselves in the position of judge (verse 4) and have proceeded to evaluate people's worth by entirely false standards. We have 'got above ourselves' and assumed, quite wrongly, our right to assign people to different classifications and discriminate between them. But that responsibility belongs to God alone. We are among those to be judged, rather than to do the judging. Therefore we should restrain ourselves from judging others and adopt instead a position of humility.

The incident James describes is all too real. It can neither be dismissed as purely hypothetical, nor trivialised as a mistake the church would have made then, but would not, of course, make today. I remember a friend starting a sermon on this passage by giving a special welcome to the city's Mayor who was (supposedly) in the congregation that evening. He also gave an effusive welcome to a very wealthy businessman whose yacht was to be found in the local Marina, when it was not sailing in the Mediterranean. Many heads turned when my friend pointed in the direction where the fictitious visitors were supposed to be sitting, and we were caught in the well-laid trap! A female colleague has described how on many occasions people make the assumption that when she says she works at London Bible College she must be on the domestic or administrative staff and the conversation quickly dries up. Once it is known that she is on the faculty suddenly the attitude and conversation change. Suddenly people treat her with a respect which was absent before.

One Saturday morning I was dressed in casual clothes (actually, probably my gardening clothes) and popped into the main college building. I made the mistake of asking the leaders of the Christian conference who were using our premises if all was well and was immediately told of one or two things which were not. They particularly had trouble with some PA equipment they couldn't get to work (mainly because they had not followed the instructions they were given!) and I tried to oblige by seeing if I could get it going. I failed. (In defence of my incompetence it should be pointed out that I had not been given the instructions!) Throughout the conversation I had been called, 'Boy', which from one perspective was very flattering. Eventually I revealed that my job in the college had nothing to do with video and audio equipment but that as Principal I would see if I could rouse another member of staff who might know what to do. How embarrassed they were. How drastically the attitude changed. I was 'Boy' no longer, but 'Sir'. I was angry that they would speak to any of my colleagues, or students, in such a condescending fashion. It was a deeply revealing moment.

If James had simply reminded us of the principle we would have argued that we lived by it. But in giving us the illustration he unmasks the truth and exposes the inconsistency of our practice. Social discrimination remains a perennial problem because there is something inherent in our human nature which makes us favour those from whom we have most to gain.[18] But such a 'worldly' tendency must be resisted because of the spiritual issues involved. James Adamson sums the lesson up in a nutshell. 'Do not try to combine faith in Christ with the worship of social status.'[19]

## 3. The principles of Scripture

Behind such teaching lie some hard questions about wealth. While we cannot engage here in a full exposition of the Biblical principles concerning wealth and poverty two basic questions may be introduced. Those who seek a fuller understanding of the Bible's teaching in this area can find it in Craig Blomberg's excellent study *Neither Poverty Nor Riches*.[20]

### Is God biased to the poor?

'God's bias to the poor' is a slogan which some have loudly proclaimed in recent times. It has its origins in James' words, 'Has not God chosen those who are poor in the eyes of this world to be rich in faith and to inherit the kingdom he has promised to those who love him?' (2:5). Those who advocate it have been largely, but not wholly, associated with a movement known as 'liberation theology' which grew out of the pastoral experience of handling poverty in Latin America.

It seems to tap into a rich seam of biblical teaching. The Old

Testament law was particularly sensitive to the needs of widows, orphans and strangers, that is, those who had lost the usual means by which financial support would be obtained. Psalm 68:5 states, 'A father to the fatherless, a defender of widows is God in his holy dwelling'. Psalm 82:3 commands God's people to 'defend the cause of the weak and fatherless; maintain the rights of the poor and oppressed.' Proverbs 14:31, like Proverbs 17:5 which we have already mentioned, closely associates the honouring of the poor with the honouring of God himself. It does seem possible, on the basis of these and other texts, to paint a picture in which the economically poor are more spiritually privileged and the rich are more spiritually vulnerable.

However, caution must be exercised about such a position. There is no automatic spiritual blessing in poverty. The blessing does not derive directly from the poverty so much as from the sense of dependence on God which poverty induces. If that dependence is absent, poverty might prove to be as much of a spiritual liability as wealth is when it results in arrogance. In its realism, the Bible not only recognises that poverty may *result in* spiritual blessing but that poverty might equally be the *result of* sinful behaviour. Proverbs 10:4, for example, asserts that 'lazy hands make a man poor'. It does not mean by this that being lazy is a virtue. Far from it. The Bible teaches that we have to look at why the person is poor, not just the fact of their poverty. In the case of James' readers they are poor because they have been treated unjustly. It is not due to their own indolence or carelessness. So, if they respond to their situation by trusting their lives into the hands of God and leaving him to provide for them, then, indeed, they would be blessed. Poverty which increases dependence on God is a vehicle of blessing.

The command in James 2:1, and the application of it in verse 4, not to show favouritism is based on Leviticus 19:15. There, the Old Testament law called for the exercise of a totally impartial administration of justice. 'Do not show partiality to the poor or favouritism to the great.' Only a justice which refused to be open to manipulation from either side of the wealth divide would be adequate to reflect a righteous God. There was to be no bias, either way. It is wrong, therefore, to say that God is biased to the poor. Even so, Ronald Sider has pointed out the need not to reject the position out-of-hand.

He affirms that 'God is not partial. He has the same loving concern for each person he has created.' But then he adds this further explanation, to my mind, persuasively:

> Precisely for that reason he cares as much for the weak and disadvantaged as he does for the strong and fortunate. By contrast with the way you and I, as well as the comfortable and powerful of every age and society, always act toward the poor, God seems to have an overwhelming bias in favour of the poor. But he is biased only in contrast with our sinful unconcern. It is only when we take our perverse preference for the successful and wealthy as natural and normative that God appears biased.[21]

And he adds that God is never neutral in the battle for justice. Consequently, he is on the side of the poor.

Whilst the phrase 'bias to the poor', then, may be unfortunate and, like any slogan, it is not adequate to deal with all the questions about wealth and poverty which we wish to ask, from where we stand in the complacent and rich western world it contains a real element of truth.

### Is God opposed to wealth creation?

Let's now ask the opposite question. If there really are genuine spiritual advantages in possessing little, does it mean we should seek to remain poor and discourage the making of money? Is God opposed to the creation of wealth?

Once more it is not possible to give a simple soundbite answer to that question and the Bible certainly does not do so. God is presented as a God of unimaginable wealth. He owns every animal in the forests and the cattle on a thousand hills are his.[22] The riches of the earth are his to dispose of in sovereign freedom. Frequently the Old Testament refers to material blessing as a sign of God's blessing – a picture which is transposed under the new covenant as blessings are to be found 'in Christ' rather than in material possessions.[23] Furthermore, God is said to be honoured as 'the wealth of the seas' are brought to a restored Jerusalem and the riches of the nations are made available for his pleasure.[24] Add to this the mandate given to humanity at creation to 'fill the earth and subdue it.'[25] Men and women have a calling from God to develop the rich resources of the earth, not for selfish ends, but as responsible stewards of creation for the well-being of all. We are encouraged to enjoy good things, providing we do so with thanksgiving to the God who gave them to us and consecrate them to him.[26] Wealth creation, then, would seem not only to be a legitimate aspect of our life on earth but a necessity if we are to fulfil our calling on earth.

Nonetheless, the road to wealth creation is littered with signposts, warning us of the inherent dangers in our fulfilling that calling as *fallen* men and women. Wealth too easily becomes an end in itself. It all too easily becomes our idol and we end up serving it.[27] It can become a way of satisfying our private indulgences and reinforcing our self-centredness, rather than enhancing the lives of others. And, all too often, wealth induces anxiety in us rather than bringing us satisfaction and contentment.[28] Our eagerness for it can lead us into temptation and all kinds of evils are committed in pursuit of it.[29] We need to be aware that money is not a neutral commodity. 'According to Jesus,' Richard Foster argued, '... behind money are very real spiritual forces that energise it and give it a life of its own. Hence, money is an active agent, it is a law to itself and is capable of inspiring devotion.'[30] Hence we should handle wealth with care.

In the light of that, Richard Foster's practical advice is to adopt 'Ten Rules for Simple Living' so that we may avoid the pitfalls of wealth and release ourselves and our money to be available to serve God's purposes. In summary they are:

1. Buy things for their usefulness not their status.
2. Reject anything which produces an addiction in you.
3. Develop the habit of giving things away.
4. Refuse to believe the advertisers and pedlars of gadgets.
5. Learn to enjoy things without owning them.
6. Develop a deep appreciation of creation.
7. Look with healthy scepticism on the buy now, pay later philosophy.
8. Obey Jesus' instructions about honest speech.
9. Reject anything which breeds oppression in others.
10. Shun whatever will distract you from your main goal.[31]

## 4. The perils of the wealthy, 5:1-6

When James returns to the subject of wealth later in his letter, he narrows his focus to the rich and addresses them with some robust and uncomfortable words. There is general agreement that these are not wealthy Christians that he is addressing at this point but landowners outside the church who were gobbling up small farms and concentrating wealth in the hands of a few. These canny businessmen would have exploited the opportunity presented by poor harvests and droughts to force smallholders off the land. Many who had suffered in this way would have been thrown into the labour market to compete for the scarce opportunity of being employed as a day-wage earner. And even there the rich landowners would be able to dictate the terms of their employment. Exploitation abounded.[32]

The forthright language James uses might seem offensive to the ears of nice Christian congregations in middle-class areas of the affluent West. But it is by no means unique to him. All James is doing is taking up the language of the prophets about the day of the Lord – the day when God will settle his accounts – and applying them to the situation his readers face. He echoes the words of Isaiah 13:6; 22:12; and Amos 8:3-8 and 5:11. If rich people are concerned about 'the bottom line' then they ought to understand, he tells them, what the ultimate bottom line is. It is the day of the Lord. God will one day settle all his accounts. But he will choose the time when he does so.

I love the story John Blanchard tells about this. A man wrote to his local newspaper during a period of debate about observing the Sabbath. He boasted:

> 'I have been conducting an experiment with one of my fields. I have ploughed it on a Sunday, I sowed the seed on a Sunday, I irrigated and tended it on a Sunday. I reaped it on a Sunday – and I want to tell you that this October I have had the biggest crop in the whole neighbourhood.' The editor published the letter but he added this footnote – God does not settle his accounts in October.[33]

When the day of settlement does come the wealthy might find that their accounts contain a number of outstanding liabilities that need settling or bad debts which they have accumulated because of the way they have lived. Four such liabilities are now mentioned as James enumerates sins which are particular perils to the rich.

### The sin of hoarding, 5:2-3

The Jews traditionally measured wealth in terms of food, clothes and precious metals. The truly wealthy person was likely, then, to have stockpiled them. They would all make good investments. But James, taking up the words of Jesus in Matthew 6:20, points out how foolish such a stance is. Food rots, clothes get eaten by moths and precious metals corrode. There is nothing secure about such investments. On the other hand, there is something dangerous about them. Rather than being an asset they are really a liability. As James writes with a fierce passion in condemnation of hoarding, the images tumble into his mind and out through his pen and crash into one another on his parchment. Metals corrode ... corroding metals can eat into your flesh ... flesh gets eaten away too by fire ... and fire is associated with judgement on the last days. Hoarding is not just futile, it's destructive. It invites the fire of judgement.

Why is hoarding viewed so negatively? Three reasons suggest themselves. First, because it shows the wrong priorities of the heart. Secondly, because it demonstrates an indifference to the poor. Thirdly, because it shows a wrong reading of the times. 'You have hoarded wealth,' James reminds them, 'in the last days.' But they'd obviously not appreciated the significance of the fact that they were living in the 'last days'. Only one more act was to follow the 'last days' – the act of God's judgement. If they'd really believed that they were in the last days they would have been more concerned about what God would think of them than they were about how their shares were performing on the stock market.

### The sin of injustice, 5:4

The economy of the time was a subsistence economy where wages were necessarily paid on a daily basis. That is why the rights of the workers were safeguarded in the law. Leviticus 19:13 forbade anyone to hold back the wages of a hired worker overnight. So did Deuteronomy 24:14-15. Malachi 3:5 put those who defrauded labourers of their wages on a par with sorcerers, adulterers, and perjurers. Economic justice and financial integrity mattered to God.

Those who have money already are always tempted to make more money. And James knows that one way they did so was not to pay their bills on time. So they got rich at the expense of their workers, who were left, without the wages they deserved, to get poorer. But just as centuries before Abel's voice was heard by 'the Lord Almighty'[34] after his brother had killed him, so the voice of those deprived of their living (even if only temporarily deprived) would reach the Lord of all transcendent majesty and call forth his judgement.

### The sin of indulgence, 5:5

What did these wealthy people do with the money they should have been passing on to others? They used it to live in luxury. With callous indifference to those who would have been pushed to scrape together a basic meal, they spent their money on indulging themselves. Two words are used to describe their selfish opulence. First, he uses the word *etruphēsate,* which speaks of living in prosperous ease. A related word is used by Peter, who was equally unhappy about the situation, to talk of people who passed the night away in revelling.[35] Without a care in the world they can party. The food and the drink will flow in abundance. And the band will play, covering up the cries of the hungry. Their cries are, however, still picked up by God whose ears are acutely attuned to the poor. Secondly, James uses the word *spatalas*. The Greek translation of the Old Testament, known as the Septuagint, had used that word when describing the lifestyle of the inhabitants of Sodom in Ezekiel 16:49. The indictment against Sodom read, 'She and her daughters were arrogant, overfed and unconcerned, they did not help the poor and needy.' Their lives, in other words, were totally self-centred. And that is the essence of sin.

Another graphic picture comes into James' mind. These overfed partygoers remind him of a herd of pigs who are being fattened for the slaughter. They may not realise it but their self-indulgent lifestyles are simply preparing them for their next appointment in the slaughterhouse of God's judgement.

### The sin of corruption, 5:6

The final accusation is that the wealthy corrupt the process of law. They use the very law which was designed to protect the innocent to obstruct justice and crush those who get in their way. The story is as old as the story of Naboth's vineyard[36] and as recent as today's newspaper. The pattern is seen again and again from before Ahab to after Robert Maxwell. Wealth means power, and the wealthy wield power, often through the courts, to get their own way, trampling on those who oppose them. The reason why the poor did not oppose the rich was either because they were powerless to do so, lacking both the money to mount a challenge and the contacts to make it effective, or because they had chosen a strategy of non-resistance. The result was that some people had lost their lives whilst the rich went on their unfeeling way, amassing greater and greater fortunes. But their behaviour unmasks them for what they are. They are not bold and fearless champions but 'brutal bullies, picking as the victim of their outrages' those who are too weak to stand up to them.[37]

Professor Tasker believed that this verse seemed to be something of an anticlimax and 'brings the section to an end on a note of majestic pathos.'[38] Why does he call the pathos 'majestic'? Where is the majesty here? It seems anything but majestic. But, as he argued, James' point is that the poor may not respond to injustice here and now and defend themselves either through the courts or by using violence against their oppressors. But their non-resistance, in line with the teaching of Paul in Romans 12:19, leaves the door wide open for God to step in eventually on their behalf. It is a 'majestic pathos' because he, the Lord of Lords, will come to their defence in a manner which is far more satisfactory and final than their paltry attempts at securing justice for themselves could ever be.

## 5. The practice of the believers

So, how are we who are contemporary believers to live in the light of this teaching?

* We must contemplate Jesus, the 'glorious Lord' who 'became poor so that we through his poverty might become rich'.[39]
* We must re-engineer our thinking so that we estimate wealth and status according to the values of the Kingdom of God, not conventional wisdom.
* We must shun favouritism and renounce discrimination.
* We must behave obediently and keep the law of the Lord.
* We must cultivate contentment with what we have.

* We must practise generosity.
* We must meet our obligations with integrity.
* We must live in the light of the future.

Living in the light of the future drastically changes one's attitude to wealth and poverty. Those who despise the poor, evaluate people according to their wealth, try to protect their futures by hoarding money, or behave extortionately towards others, and who live in self-indulgent luxury, believe that the world is a closed system where only what you can see, touch and count here and now matter. But such people are friends of the world, and consequently enemies of God.[40] Indeed, it is impossible for them to be friends with God for they have left him completely out of their reckoning. Friends of God bring him into the picture. They know he evaluates people by a different set of measures. They trust him and know he will provide when they have need. And they know that whatever injustice they face here will one day be put right as he comes to judge the earth. They have, then, no need to tread on others, to curry favour with those of high status, or manipulate their financial transactions to their own selfish ends. They can take money or leave it. They will always treat people as valuable. They will always live in integrity and walk in obedience to God's will. They know that friendship with God is not only about how you pray and what you do in church but also about how you handle money and what you do in the marketplace.

# 4

# Religion and How to Practise It (1:19-27)

# 4. Religion and how to practise it

**Pure religion is:**

**1. The pursuit of personal holiness, verses 19-21**

- The principles stated
- The reason given
- The implications described
- The means provided

**2. The discovery of liberating law, verses 22-25**

- The problem he identifies
- The illustration he uses
- The solution he proposes

**3. The practice of social righteousness, verses 26-27**

- The Old Testament background
- The contemporary application

When we say 'religion' most people think of church buildings, otherworldly priests and inhibiting rules and regulations. Religion belongs to a past world which has little place in the present, except as a purely individual affair of the heart. It's based on myths which can't stand up to examination. It is the cause of conflict and war. The world, they think, would be better off without it.

A typical tirade against religion occurred recently in *The Times*, written by Libby Purves under the title 'For God's sake, keep Church and State apart.'[1]  She argues that the terrorists who wish to destabilize the Western world are motivated by religion, albeit 'an extreme perversion of Islam'. What makes them so frightening is that 'they do not want anything that the pragmatic modern mind can understand'. Since they believe that their suicide mission will lead them to Paradise there is nothing anyone can do to dissuade them from their murderous intent. From that base, she launches into a wide-ranging condemnation of the role of all religion in the public domain. European religion burnt witches, sponsored the Inquisition and the Crusades, and dictatorially enforced puritanical morals on an unwilling people. 'Maybe – only maybe,' she continues, 'there have been times when the conjunction of religion and power was useful.' While she is prepared to admit that faith nourishes the human spirit and without it human life is impoverished, 'for God's sake,' she pleads, keep it out of the corridors of power. Whether it be Christianity or Islam, in the field of education, science or politics, religion needs to be kept out. Her article concludes, 'Religion belongs in the heart, not the statute book or the chemistry lab. We should know that by now.'

Her evidence is, of course, selective and her understanding of the role of religion is limited. It would be possible by careful editing to write an altogether different article on the positive contribution that the Christian religion, at least, has made to humanity in the pursuit of justice, liberty and a better world. She names Cromwell as a 'narrow, emotionally deficient fanatic', forgetting that he liberated Britain from a much greater oppression than he himself imposed. Even so, she has a point. We must confess with penitence a long shameful history where liberty has been suppressed, crimes committed and wars started in the name of the God and Father of Jesus Christ. We should take serious note of her warning that imposing morality, whether Christian or that of another religion, on people leads to an oppressive state rather than a wholesome way of life. But then some Christian commentators have said that for a long time. It was the missionary statesman Lesslie Newbigin, for example, who once wrote that, 'The project of bringing heaven down to earth always results in bringing hell up from below.'[2]

The key problem with Libby Purves' approach, however, is that she has no vision of what authentic, pure religion is like. Nor do scores of people who only ever experience the distorted perversions of it which are all too common. Given this difficulty, quite a number of evangelical Christians want to distance themselves from 'religion' and say that what they are about is not 'religion' but a 'relationship with Jesus Christ.' The distinction, however, is not so easily made either in theory or practice. James does not shy away from the word 'religion' even though he would have experienced as much debased religion as we do. Instead he boldly advocates it, but religion of a pure, not a tainted, kind.

The corruption of religion has a long history. The preaching of the Old Testament prophets was directed against precisely such distortions. The children of Israel persistently erred in believing that the covenant promises would protect and bless them if only they kept up the ritual observance of their faith. They had no comparable commitment to the ethical dimensions of the covenant. Isaiah 58 points out that keeping days of fasting was useless unless accompanied by loosening of the chains of injustice, feeding the hungry, clothing the naked, sheltering the strangers, not exploiting the workers and abstaining from violence. Jeremiah, too, in his great Temple Sermon in chapter 7, denounced Judah for trusting in Temple rituals while happily continuing to commit theft, murder, adultery, perjury and idolatry. They failed to realize that being the people of God made demands on them in every dimension of their lives and they had reduced their covenant relationship, quite wrongly, to pious, empty ritual. Such religion, Amos thundered, far from pleasing God, provokes his anger and he refuses to acknowledge it.[3]

This perennial danger of debasing religion was evident when James wrote his letters to Christian believers. Using somewhat unusual words he describes his readers as religious (*thrēskos*) and their faith as religion (*thrēskeia*) and he confronts the issue head on. The words he chooses have to do with the worship of God through the observance of religious rites. 'If you want to be religious,' he says, 'this is how to do it. This is the religion God requires you to practise.' And it's not the religion you are practising at the moment. Verse 26 packs a punch. In a few phrases it critiques typical religion and dismisses it as false. John Blanchard has brilliantly summed it up like this: false religion lacks restraint ('yet you do not keep a tight rein on your tongues'), lacks reality ('deceive themselves'), and lacks results ('their religion is worthless').[4]

It doesn't take much thought to see how different it is both from what they were practising and from what many average churches, especially evangelical ones who are sucked into their busy round of self-serving programmes, practise today.

Although the focal point of his argument is reached in verses 26-27, we need to back up a bit and take in the previous verses which round out the picture of a religion which is acceptable to God. The whole section tells us that religion which pleases God is about the pursuit of personal holiness (verses 19-21); the discovery of his liberating law (verses 22-25) and the practice of social righteousness (verses 26-27).

## 1. The pursuit of personal holiness, verses 19-21.

*The principles stated, verse 19.*

Three brisk precepts head up the discussion. 'Everyone should be quick to listen, slow to speak and slow to become angry.' Robert Wall believes that these commands are so significant that the rest of James' letter is essentially composed as a commentary on them; with the first being explored in 1:22-2:26, the second in 3:1-18, and, the third in 4:1-5:6.[5] That may be a bit over-neat but there is clearly some merit in his view. Nonetheless, we must examine the statement in its immediate context as well as in its broader context.

At one level, the teaching is transparent. Why do conflicts arise? Where does division come from? What causes breakdown in any community, the church no less than the world outside the church?

Surely it is our self-centredness, self-assertiveness and self-protectiveness. Self is at the root of everything which is wrong with us and our world. We are full of ourselves and therefore we delight in dumping on others our ideas and wisdom, expecting them to listen to us while we happily ignore what they have got to say to us. The failure to listen causes misunderstanding, and misunderstanding breeds resentment and issues in angry reactions.

One of the courses at London Bible College on church leadership used to begin with a group of students simulating a PCC, Elders' or Deacons' meeting. The unusual feature was that though the business was real, each group had a non-participant observer in it whose task it was to report back at the end of the day on what they had experienced. Unprimed, but without fail, the observers reported that no one in the discussion had listened to anyone else. They were all so full of the contribution they wanted to make that they cut across each other, jumped in before others had finished, ignored what had previously been said and went off at tangents which had more to do with their own agendas than the one they were supposed to be working at together. That, in microcosm, is how many of us behave perpetually. Fortunately, within the groups of Bible College students referred to, it never led to violence. But elsewhere, anger erupts, either out of the frustration of not being heard or the mishearing of what was said, and violence ensues.

It is all too familiar a picture of the national and international stage. But James' concern is not the political scene. It is the body of Christ. There, both at local church and the inter-church level, our inability to listen carefully to one another is injurious to the name of Christ. That is why some Christian leaders have devoted a great deal of their time talking with and listening to those with whom they differ about church government, modes of baptism, charismatic experience or the role of women. Cynics may dismiss such conversations as a waste of time. But James might suggest that they are a natural outflow of the righteous pattern of living that God desires.

A prime example of how such injunctions are to be obeyed is found in the leadership John Stott has exercised in the evangelical world during the last decades of the twentieth century. He has initiated as well as participated in many discussions where Christians differ from each other, including some with Roman Catholics. As his biographer mentions in reporting on one set of these discussions, 'He made it very clear that dialogue, courtesy, a willingness to learn, even a search for unity, implied no doctrinal compromise: "Reunion with Rome is inconceivable without the reformation of Rome." '[6] Agreement was rarely reached, at least in any deep and enduring way, but clarification of each other's position, the removal of barriers and reduction in animosity certainly occurred.

Many of us will feel far removed from such highbrow discussions (and perhaps that is why we are threatened by them) but few of us fail to recognize the importance of James' words for our relationships within our local fellowships. How the quality of our relationships would improve if we accepted his simple advice.

Robert Wall suggests that rather than being a general plea for listening, James is in fact pleading for us to listen to the words of the law of God, and being 'quick to listen' is to be understood as being prompt in our obedience to it. Since James mentions the law in verse 25 he may have a point. But surely the words are not meant to be restricted to the law alone and are of more general application. That is certainly how James develops them when he comes to write about the tongue in chapter 3.

*The reason given, verse 20*
We might be expected to obey a command of Scripture for no other reason than that it is God who has decreed it. Yet, in his goodness God often supports his commands by giving us the reasons for their existence. So it is here. We should avoid anger, which we will best do by listening instead of sounding off, because 'human anger does not bring about the righteous life God desires.' In translating it like this, the NIV has chosen a particular slant which may be legitimate but is not necessarily required by the original Greek which is a little more crisp. Literally it reads, 'for the anger of men does not work the righteousness of God.' The idea of righteousness crops up several times in the letter (2:21, 23-25; 3:18) and may mean being in right standing with God or living in right relationships with others. So here, the meaning may be either that human anger is unacceptable to God to whom we must give account of our lives as a righteous judge, or,

that it is not a proper way of achieving the right relationships God longs to see among his people.[7] Either way, uncontrolled anger is clearly wrong and both violates our good standing before God and destroys right relationships with others.

*The implications described, verse 21*
Those who are silent, patient and peace-loving among us may well feel they are on safe ground here. By disposition, they are happy to listen, too shy to speak and, being slow burners, it takes a lot to get them to reach seething point and boil over. But the meek should not be too quick to congratulate themselves simply because they are not wired up to be excitable individuals by disposition. An ancient pastor of the church, Gregory the Great, advised the clergy of his day to admonish and instruct not only the passionate but the meek as well. The meek, he reasoned, might in reality use their meekness to justify spiritual lethargy and they may be too tolerant of spiritual indiscipline.[8] James strongly advocates the virtue of meekness but even so those who exhibit it are as much in his sights as others are. His reason for including them is different from that of Gregory's but no less demanding. The obligation laid on us all, the meek no less than the volatile, is to rid ourselves of 'all moral filth and the evil that is so prevalent' within us.

If we really are quick to listen, especially to God's word, then it will not be long before we discover something either in our external behaviour or internal attitudes which is inconsistent with walking in a right relationship with God. And all such wrongdoing and wrong-thinking needs jettisoning from our lives, just as we regularly throw out the rubbish from our homes for the refuse collectors to remove. In fact, the word he uses for moral 'filth' would be the natural word for soiled garments or medical waste.[9] Why would we want to keep hold of them? We dare not tolerate even the slightest sin. The high ideal James sets before us is that *'all'*, not just some or even most, of the impurities be removed from our lives. It is typically uncompromising of James to put such a demanding goal in front of us. It is exactly what we might have expected from his emphasis on perfection, completion and integrity to which the letter constantly returns. He knows it's a tough standard because he admits that evil is 'prevalent'. It's all around us, and within us. We are being seduced in every direction and encouraged to commit sin. It's a battle situation. It isn't easy. But our ambition must be clear and unwavering. All wrong of whatever kind should be ejected from our lives.

*The means provided, verse 21*

How is such a goal to be reached? Fortunately, God has provided us with the resources we need. We are not expected to attain it without help. The resource God has given is 'the word planted in you.' Two aspects of that phrase deserve attention. First, using an agricultural metaphor, the word is said to be 'implanted' within us. The word is not an external reference point but an inner source of life and growth, just as the roots of a tree, implanted in the soil, enable the tree to grow. This is what the prophet Jeremiah promised would happen in the era of new covenant. 'I will put my law in their minds and write it on their hearts.'[10] In the age of the Spirit, the word of God would not need to be externally imposed by law (even though it may still be usefully taught) since we will be motivated to obey it from within as we gratefully seek to please God in response to his grace in our lives. But the image should not mislead us. The roots of a tree need to be implanted in good soil and, if it is to grow, even then it will need tending and feeding carefully. So we, if we are to profit from the implanted word, need to tend it carefully. It is wrong to think of the implanted word as if it is some computer chip with which God automatically reprogrammes our thoughts and behaviour and which he has given us as a replacement for a defective one. It is an organic not a mechanical image which is in use. Therefore, we are required to nurture the implanted word by our reading and studying of it so that it might grow up to maturity and bear its fruit through us. Without that it will never produce the harvest of which it is capable.

But just what is this 'word' which is implanted within us? Some have a desire to define it precisely. They suggest variously that when read in the context of the whole letter it is the word of the law of God, or the writings of the Old Testament Wisdom tradition or the teaching of the teachers mentioned in 3:1.[11] But most are rightly content to believe that the word is the word of the gospel, of the apostolic good news of God's salvation in Christ. It is this word which must not only be received initially at conversion but continuously and consciously reviewed so that it becomes the guiding principle of every dimension of our lives. Only then will we be able to make progress towards the goal of perfection which is set before us. Personal holiness develops as we ruminate on 'the word'. No wonder, then, that so many struggle in the area of personal holiness. The word of the gospel, the teaching of Jesus, the apostolic truth, found authoritatively recorded for us in the Bible, has a very low priority in the lives of many believers. Other voices have crowded it out. In doing so they have cut off the very source of spiritual nourishment God has provided as a means of growth and they remain impeded in their discipleship as a result.

True religion is about our growth in personal holiness.

## 2. The discovery of liberating law, verses 22-25

A common misconception about Christianity is that it is a religion of rules and regulations. We have only ourselves to blame for such a misunderstanding for, in all honesty, we have often preached negatively and legalistically. We have been concerned to improve the moral tone of our nation with the result that we have been active in opposing the liberalisation of law and have advocated tighter moral controls. We have come over as moralists rather than evangelists. Inside the church, too, we have often been concerned, again rightly so, to raise the standard of Christian behaviour and that has driven us to emphasise the 'Thou shalt nots ...' of the Christian life. Our concerns have been right but our strategies have frequently been unbalanced and people have gone away with a distorted image of the Christian message. We are not known as much as we should be as preachers of forgiving grace. Sadly, we are more known as preachers of legalistic morality.

Given James' advocacy of impossibly high standards in the Christian life we might think that he would fall into the trap of dragging Christian believers away from the glorious liberty of the new covenant back into living under the law of the old covenant. But not so. True religion is about discovering 'the perfect law that gives freedom.' Let's see why he introduces that thought.

*The problem he identifies, verse 22*
Every parent has experienced the disease of 'selective deafness' in their children. Somehow or other they have an acute sense of hearing when it comes to things which are to their advantage, or to conversation

which parents don't want them to hear, but when it comes to doing homework, tidying their bedrooms or even going to bed, they develop an acute sense of deafness! 'I didn't hear you' is the cry that gets repeated across the nation by a thousand children's voices. James' concern is with another form of hearing problem. The word is heard all right, but somehow it never leads to any practical action. It is as if by merely hearing the word his readers think they have done sufficient. But to think like that is to fall victim to a gigantic deception. To think that we can be Christians by listening without acting is a delusion of the worst kind. Listening, if it is true listening, must follow through to obedience. Here, says Douglas Moo, 'we are taken right to the heart of James' pastoral concern. However important may be the mental assent to the word, it has not been truly received until it is put into practice.'[12]

For those of us who belong to the evangelical wing of the church these words come as a special challenge. An aspect of our heritage, in which we can justly take pride, is the tradition of Bible teaching and preaching that goes on both Sunday by Sunday in regular worship and through special Bible conferences and weeks of one sort or another. Thousands of us, for example, gather at Keswick, Spring Harvest, Soul Survivor, or (until recently) at Stoneleigh, or other such venues to hear the word of God taught. Some of us go back year after year and sit through hour after hour of good teaching. We become expert 'sermon tasters' and can detect slipshod preparation or questionable theology a mile away. Next year, next day, we'll be found back in the same seat, eager to hear the word of the Lord again. But what difference does it make? Does it alter our lives? Does it lead to action? If only we were to put into practice a tiny fraction of the teaching we heard we might have a much greater impact for the gospel in our communities than we do.

I do not decry the importance of these conferences and Bible weeks. Given the dearth of good teaching many have to endure in local churches week by week they have a significant part to play. But in themselves, they are insufficient. The word of the Lord must not only be listened to but obeyed. 'The implanted word can only flourish in the soil of obedience.'[13]

*The illustration he uses, verses 23-24*

James turns to an illustration that both says something about the absurdity of such an approach to Christian living and perhaps also hints at the reason for the problem. The illustration he uses must be amongst the best known parts of his writing. Imagine, he says, looking in a mirror and immediately forgetting what you've seen. Mirrors would, of course, have been much less common and less clear in his day than ours. To see oneself was likely to have been a more memorable experience then than now when we can virtually rely on seeing ourselves in a mirror whenever we want to. Yet we still look in the mirror with a view to doing something about what we see there! We tell ourselves, 'I must comb my hair'. Or, 'I must have a shave'. Or, 'I must put on some make-up'. A few minutes later we may forget all about it: the comb never gets picked up, the shaver lies unused and the cosmetics never get opened. Off we go, happily into the day looking a dishevelled mess! Anyone who did this regularly would be regarded as in serious need of help. If it was because they really had an extreme short-term memory problem, we'd soon line up some treatment.

Yet, this is what we do much of the time with the word of God. We listen, even agree, and promptly forget what it's all about and go on living as if no word from God had been received.

There may be more to it than even this. The mirror may have been deliberately chosen by James to say to us that God's word not only tells us what to do but shows us what we are like. The word of God reveals our true condition, points to our sin and the darkness of our lives within, as well as giving us a prescription of how to amend our lives and live righteously before God. So, it may not only be that he points out the inconsistency that lies between our knowing and our doing but is pointing out that the word of God shows us some uncomfortable truths about ourselves, truths we may wish to avoid or deny. It is a powerful image.

*The solution he proposes, verse 25*

So, what does he propose? He proposes that we give serious attention to the mirror – 'the perfect law that gives freedom' – and follow through on what we see in it. James has no doubts about the continuing role of the law for the Christian believer. It is a 'royal law'[14] and it expresses what God wants of us.[15] Furthermore, as he mentions here, obedience to it, made possible through the work of Christ, leads to lives that are blessed. He calls it a 'perfect law' because it is one of the 'perfect gifts' from above he has referred to earlier, in verse 17. It partakes of God's moral perfection and flawless being. So it is not to be set aside lightly.

Nor should we want to do so since, far from cramping us, the law is the means by which we can experience freedom. We can readily understand that when it comes to traffic laws. We may sometimes wonder about a particular regulation but we know fundamentally that the law of the road is good. If no law existed, stipulating, for example, which side of the road we were to drive on, a good many more accidents would occur than do. If no law existed interpreting the meaning of traffic lights for us and instructing us to obey them, there would be a great deal more loss of life at road junctions than there are. We know the law gives us a true freedom rather than a pseudo-liberty on the road. So it is, on a much grander scale, with the law of God. It is not given to cramp our freedom or restrict our enjoyment of life. It is not to be viewed as a series of negative prohibitions. Rather it is the means by which we can live life to the full and experience a genuine freedom in our upward relationship to God, our outward relation to others and even our inward relationship with ourselves. That's why the great preacher and theologian P. T. Forsyth once wisely claimed that, 'the first duty of every soul is to find not its freedom but its Master.'[16]

Psalm 19:7-11 is an extended meditation on just these issues, highlighting both the perfection of the law and its beneficial effect in our lives.

[7] The law of the LORD is perfect, reviving the soul.
   The statutes of the LORD are trustworthy, making wise the simple.
[8] The precepts of the Lord are right, giving joy to the heart.
   The commands of the LORD are radiant, giving light to the eyes.
[9] The fear of the LORD is pure, enduring for ever.
   The ordinances of the LORD are sure and altogether righteous.
[10] They are more precious than gold, than much pure gold;
   they are sweeter than honey, than honey from the comb.
[11] By them is your servant warned; in keeping them there is great reward.

True religion, then, is about the law. It is about putting it into practice, not just hearing it. But we must be careful how we teach and interpret it for God's intention is that it should liberate, not enslave, his redeemed people, and enable them to grow as fully human and complete persons.

## 3. The practice of social righteousness, verses 26-27

### *The Old Testament background*

James turns to a particular aspect of God's liberating law as he reaches the climax of his description of religion that is acceptable to God 'as pure and faultless'. He highlights the need to look after 'orphans and widows in their distress'. The care of widows and orphans was not a secondary or peripheral issue as far as the Old Testament law was concerned. Widows and fatherless children were two of the most vulnerable categories of people in a society where the father was the breadwinner and which had no formal, centralized social welfare provision. Their plight is illustrated in the moving story of Ruth; the plot of which revolves around the way in which she was in special need of support, security and protection as a Moabite woman, after the death of both her father-in-law and her husband. It tells us of the way in which her bleak prospects were overcome through the action of the kinsman-redeemer. But that was only a particular example of a general problem. How were bereaved women to find support in a patriarchal society in which men provided for their wives? How were insignificant children to survive in an adult-oriented society which considered them unimportant?

The answer was that they would survive if the covenant people of God took seriously what the law said and acted upon it. Negatively, Exodus 22:22 forbade taking advantage of a widow or an orphan. Other sayings, both in the law and the prophets, thundered against anyone who neglected or abused those who were vulnerable and marginalised in society, especially widows and orphans.[17] Positively, their needs were to be taken into account and provision made for them. Deuteronomy 14:28-29 and 26:12 instructed the children of Israel to bring and store up the tithes of their produce every three years for the support of widows and orphans, as well as the Levites and immigrants and others who had no obvious means of economic support. It was a message the prophets were to repeat constantly as, for example, Zechariah did in saying. 'This is what the Lord Almighty says: "Administer true justice, show mercy and compassion to one another. Do not oppress the widow or the fatherless, the alien or the poor." '[18]

The reason for the stress on caring for the vulnerable is twofold. First it flows from the character of God himself. Psalm 68:5 proclaims him to be 'a father to the fatherless, a defender of widows'. It then tells us that this is 'God in his holy dwelling', that is, what God is like when he is at home; what he is by his very nature. Psalm 146:9 says something very similar. If this is what God is like, then we, his followers, must be like it too.

The second reason given for this stress in the Old Testament lies in Israel's own experience. They had once been slaves in Egypt. Now they were free and enjoyed the blessings of the Promised Land. But the experience of Egypt was forever to be seared into their consciences. Given what they had gone through they should never wish to oppress those who were weak and powerless among them, be they aliens, strangers (ethnic minorities), servants, widows or orphans. If they did, then just as God had once heard their cry, stepped in to deliver them and judged their oppressors, so he would step in to rescue those they oppressed and punish them.[19] Rather they should behave towards them with compassion and generosity, remembering that all they had received in their prosperity they received because of the promise and grace of God, not because they had any right to it, nor because their own hands had worked for it.[20]

James develops this last point a step further. Genuine religion is not only to 'look after orphans and widows in their distress' but also 'to keep oneself from being polluted by the world.' The impurity which concerns him is not ritual impurity but ethical impurity.[21] The pollution by the world which concerns him is not the environmental pollution of chemical emissions but the pollution of our minds and spirits by the worldviews and systems which ignore the living God and bow instead at the altar of unworthy idols. The Old Testament frequently connected unethical behaviour with idolatrous worship. It was when people forsook the living and true God of Israel that they started to act unjustly, lack compassion, live immorally and even sacrifice children.[22] Not even Solomon, the wisest King Israel ever had, escaped the trap.[23] And if he fell, who are we to be so sure we won't? We need to keep ourselves uncontaminated by the mindsets which leave God out of account.

### The contemporary application

It would be easy for us to say that James' definition of pure religion no longer fits our contemporary world. Since 1947 Great Britain has operated a welfare system which provides benefits for those in need, like widows and orphans. And most states in the Western World have some form of system in place to provide support for their most vulnerable citizens. So, isn't this now the job of the politicians? Hasn't the problem been solved? Has it anything to do with religion any longer?

To take this attitude would be to fall into the most wooden and literalist of interpretations of James' teaching. Even if the particular plight of widows and orphans is adequately catered for (and there is some evidence that it is not), there are surely still many marginalised, disadvantaged, powerless, vulnerable and inadequately cared for people who need our compassion and practical support. Compassion alone, as James would surely tell us, is not enough. It's action that counts. If, and it is a big 'if', widows and orphans are not in need, then plenty of those who struggle with physical disabilities, mental ill-health, lonely old age, rejection from their families, or, who are single-parents with demanding kids, or members of racially-abused ethnic minorities could do with our applied compassion. There are still many vulnerable people in our society for whom the biblical widow and orphan can stand as symbols. The state does not have the resources to deal with all the needs in our society. Even if it did, care for the vulnerable remains a religious duty before it ever becomes political obligation. It is about our standing before God, not just about whether or not we want to spend our taxes in a certain way.

Such teaching should lead churches to set up some programme of community action and individual Christians to get involved in some form of voluntary service, in addition to taking initiatives in the political arena to secure a more compassionate society. We need to remember that we cannot cure every problem of our complex world, any more than the state, with all its massive machinery and resources, can. We should not berate ourselves if we cannot do everything. But we can quietly start somewhere. As churches we might identify one issue or one group of vulnerable people where we can do something to make a difference. Given the need these days for large resources and high standards of professionalism to meet the requirements of the law in anything we do, we might particularly consider whether it is better for us to engage in a joint church project. When we pull together we can often accomplish what it would be very difficult to achieve on our own.

Fortunately, we have no need to reinvent the wheel in this area. There are a number of publications which can guide us, schemes which are already up and running to inspire us, and many have experience which can help us avoid some mistakes and learn some positive ways forward.[24] Thank God for what Christians are doing in drug rehabilitation schemes, care for young single mums, in providing for asylum seekers, in housing projects and unemployment schemes. Thank God it is happening both through national agencies and in local communities. But there is more which could be done and none of us can sit back complacently, congratulating ourselves that others are doing the work on our behalf, so we need not bother.

Some will react negatively to this teaching. They believe evangelicals are called to preach the gospel, not to engage in social amelioration. Others can do that. What we have that is unique to us is the gospel. So let's leave others to improve the world while we rescue people from it for eternity. The origin of this view goes back to the start of the twentieth century and it seems that some evangelicals have a short memory. During the eighteenth and nineteenth centuries evangelicals had an enviable track record in social action as well as evangelistic preaching.[25] The names of Wilberforce who campaigned to abolish the slave trade, Shaftesbury who worked to improve the social and educational condition of the poor and mentally ill, and Barnardo who established orphanages stand out as exemplary of the evangelical tradition. But they are not alone. C. H. Spurgeon not only preached but founded orphanages for both boys and girls. F. B. Meyer had several social action schemes going when he ministered in Leicester, including a prison gate mission to help ex-offenders and a wood-chopping scheme to provide employment for young men. William

Booth, of course, combined social action and evangelistic preaching perfectly.

In the United States the evangelical commitment to social action was just as secure until the early twentieth century. Revivalist preachers did not demonstrate an indifference to people's real-life situations in this world. Far from wanting merely to rescue people out of the world they were fully engaged in improving their lot in this world. Charles Finney, for example, took a strongly anti-slavery line and, with his colleagues at Oberlin College, was engaged in radical, direct action to illegally secure the freedom of many. In his famous *Lectures on Revival* he not only set out the spiritual dynamics of a revival but names support for slavery as one of the major obstacles to it. 'Revivals are hindered when ministers and churches take the wrong ground in regard to any question involving human rights', he wrote.[26] And he called slavery an 'abominable abomination'.

D. L. Moody is the one who is often blamed for the attitude that evangelicals should only be concerned about people's souls rather than their bodies. It is claimed, he was only concerned with preaching the gospel and rescuing people from the wrecked vessel of the earth for eternity. Since the vessel was bound to sink, why bother doing anything to improve it? But that is to misrepresent him. He set up a range of educational institutions among which were the schools at Northfield and Mount Hermon for the poor who could not afford to pay for education elsewhere. He was among the first to educate women. His schools were always racially integrated and included a fair number of Native American Indians in them. In the words of one of his biographers Moody 'was decades ahead of most educators.'[27]

After those days, in the early part of the twentieth century, evangelicals largely turned their back on this heritage and forsook the biblical balance of fulfilling both the great commission to preach the gospel[28] and the great commandment to love their neighbours.[29] They replaced it with the unbiblical one-sided emphasis on preaching the gospel and withdrew from social involvement. This 'great reversal', as it has been called, was understandable, but wrong. It was partly a reaction to some who had overdosed on social action at the expense of preaching the gospel and seemed to believe that they could bring in the Kingdom of God on earth by their own political and social action.

The church had become theologically liberal and enfeebled in its impact. In the face of this, evangelicals retreated into their ghettos and comforted themselves with sticking to a 'spiritual' gospel. The spectre of the social gospel still haunts some.

Fortunately, for the most part, times have changed. In particular, since the Lausanne Congress on World Evangelisation, held in 1974, evangelicals have begun to rediscover their mislaid social conscience. Clause 5 of its Covenant expounds the subject of Christian social responsibility and having done so concludes, 'The salvation we claim should be transforming us in the totality of our personal and social responsibilities. Faith without works is dead.'[30]

James would have said 'Amen!' to that. The rediscovery of our social conscience and our renewed involvement in compassionate social action is not a matter of political correctness in response to current opinion, but a matter of biblical faithfulness in response to the timeless revelation of God's will. One cannot be religious in a way that pleases God solely by cultivating personal holiness, important though it is. One certainly cannot be religious by the imposition of rules and regulations, for God's law is liberating. But above all, one cannot be religious if one neglects the needs of the vulnerable and the disadvantaged in society. For, 'Religion that God our Father accepts as pure and faultless is this: to look after orphans and widows in their distress and to keep oneself from being polluted by the world.'

Authentic Christian religion, then, is a far cry from contemporary popular understandings, or rather misunderstandings, of religion. It is not about being superior, causing war or imposing morality on others. It is about the cultivation of character which is Christlike and free from evil. How, then, can there be any room for pride, hatred or violence? It is about law, but not a law that curtails freedom. Rather it is about a law which liberates us into freedom. And it is not about baptising the *status quo* or justifying the position of the rich and the powerful. It is about caring, practical action on behalf of the weak and the vulnerable. More religion of that sort would delight the heart of God. And the world would be a better place for it. It could do with more religion if it was like that, not less.

The following poem, written by homeless person and handed into a Shelter office, says it all, with moving eloquence.

I was hungry,
and you formed a humanities group to discuss my hunger.
I was imprisoned,
and you crept off quietly to your chapel and prayed for my release.
I was naked,
and in your mind you debated the morality of my appearance,
I was sick,
and you left me alone to pray for me.
you seem so holy, so close to God
But I am still very hungry – and lonely – and cold.[31]

# 5

# Words and How to Control Them (1:19-21; 3:1-12; 4:11-12; 5:12)

**The continuing power of words**

**The need to control our words, 1:19-20, 3:1**

- ♦ Who?
    - Everyone
    - Teachers
- ♦ Why?
    - The will of God
    - The judgement of God

**The difficulty with controlling our words, 3:2-12**

- ♦ The tongue's astonishing impact
- ♦ The tongue's corrupting energy
- ♦ The tongue's stubborn resistance
- ♦ The tongue's ready duplicity

**The means of controlling our words, 1:21, 3:8, 4:11-12; 5:12**

- ♦ Admit defeat
- ♦ Take action
- ♦ Use help
- ♦ Get real
- ♦ Practise integrity

## The continuing power of words

We are frequently told that words have lost their power today. We no longer even live in the age of the picture. We live in the age of the image. If a picture was worth a thousand words, the image is worth a thousand more. Messages can be conveyed, atmospheres generated, products sold, appetites whetted and understandings reached by the use of the image. Who needs words?

The truth is rather more complicated. Words still have tremendous power to make or destroy. If we think that words have lost their power I suggest we ask Edwina Currie, Gerald Ratner, Glen Hoddle or Jeffrey Archer what they think. Edwina Currie was an agriculture minister in the British Government when her unguarded comments about salmonella poisoning devastated the egg industry overnight. She's no longer even in Parliament, let alone in government (although she is a popular, if outrageous, broadcaster). Gerald Ratner once owned a prosperous chain of jewellery stores when he voiced the opinion, to a meeting of the Institute of Directors at the Royal Albert Hall, that what he sold was 'total crap' and he couldn't understand why anyone bought it. You'll not find a Ratner jewellery store on any of Britain's high streets now. Glen Hoddle was the England Football Manager when unwise comments about the disabled which mixed political incorrectness with orthodox Hindu belief led to his dismissal. Out of football management altogether for a time he now manages a Premier League team, Tottenham Hotspur, but no longer England. Jeffrey Archer was the darling of the Conservative Party, an untouchable peer of the realm. But he told lies in court and has now exchanged the ermine of the House of Lords for the prison garb of a house of correction.

Words still matter. They still have power. We do not need the public stories to convince us since we know to our personal cost how influential words still are. Most of us have said something in a moment of haste we did not mean about someone else. The 'word has got out on the street' and we've tried to withdraw it. But the damage is done. Once spoken, the word cannot easily be recalled. They seem to have a life of their own. Listen to the way Ben Okri sees it:

It sometimes seems to me that our days are poisoned with too many words. Words said and not meant. Words said *and* meant. Words divorced from feeling. Wounding words. Words that conceal. Words that reduce. Dead words.

If only words were a kind of fluid that collects in the ears, if only they turned into the visible chemical equivalent of their true value, an acid, or something curative – then we might be more careful. Words do collect in us anyway. They collect in the blood, in the soul, and either transform or poison people's lives. Bitter or thoughtless words poured into the ears of the young have blighted many lives in advance. We all know people whose unhappy lives twist on a set of words uttered to them on a certain unforgotten day at school, in childhood, or at university.

We seem to think that words aren't things. A bump on the head may pass away, but a cutting remark grows with the mind. But then it is possible that we know all too well the awesome power of words – which is why we use them with such deadly and accurate cruelty.

We are all wounded inside in some way or other. We all carry unhappiness within us for some reason or other. Which is why we need a little gentleness and healing from one another. Healing in words, and healing beyond words. Like gestures. Warm gestures. Like friendship, which will always be a mystery. Like a smile, which someone described as the shortest distance between two people. [1]

When it comes to words, Ben Okri and James the Elder walk hand in hand. James introduced the subject in the menu he set out in chapter 1 and explores it in some depth in chapter 3. He returns to it twice more in the chapters which follow. From the number of mentions it gets, it was obviously a very important issue for him. The emphasis may, on first reading, seem strange to us. But in the context of his day it would have seemed even stranger if the topic had not been fully addressed. Traditional Jewish wisdom involved a great deal of teaching about speech, perhaps because they were much more of an oral culture than we are. But perhaps we are the poorer for not dealing with the issue since, as he points out, the ramifications of what we say and how we say it, for good and ill, are massive.

## The need to control our words, 1:19-20, 3:1

*Who needs to control their words?*

Everyone, 1:19

James had two audiences in mind in what he says about words. First, we are all included. 'My dear brothers and sisters, take note of this: *Everyone* should be quick to listen, slow to speak ...' This is not advice for a select few. We may not find the advice easy but most of us know we need it. It is no accident that God has designed us with two ears and only one mouth but we usually function as if he made us the other way round. We are often too quick to jump in with our opinion. Loose speech, as James hints, is often connected with the expression of anger because we just let fly with whatever is inside us instead of being disciplined both in what we say and how we say things. The old war slogan 'Careless talk costs lives' still holds. And its message applies far more widely than ensuring that we don't let secrets slip out when we are in conversation with enemy spies! Words have such power: power either to build up or to wound. Once spoken, they are irretrievable. The rabbis had a saying: 'Three things come not back, the spent arrow, the lost opportunity and the spoken word.'[2] I doubt that there will be many of us, if any, who do not need to listen carefully to what James teaches on the tongue.

Teachers, 3:1

As well as having everyone in his sights, James also has a particular group, the teachers of the church, in focus. To be a teacher was an honourable aspiration. Jesus had been called a teacher[3] and they had an important role in the early church and are regularly picked out for mention in the letters of the New Testament.[4] In all probability they did not occupy a formalised position in the church; nonetheless they were gifted by the Spirit, occupied a significant role and were recognised by the church as people of understanding who should be heeded. In some respects they were the successors to the rabbis who were the guardians of the Jewish tradition. The onus on Christian teachers was to expound the teaching of and about Jesus and apply it faithfully to the circumstances of their hearers. Their duty was much more demanding than merely serving as a guardians of the truth. They also had a duty to serve as models of the truth. How could they teach in the name of Christ if their teaching style lacked humility, crushed the weaker members of the church, abused power, used unclean language or fell short in integrity? Since teachers particularly use words as their means of teaching, what James says about speech is especially relevant to them. Teachers, then, had a huge responsibility both in what they said *and* how they said it. Paul said something very similar to Timothy. He talked about only giving responsibility to people to teach if they were 'qualified to teach'.[5] It is plain from the context that he was not thinking in terms of the level of their knowledge about the faith alone. Knowledge is required of Christian teachers but so too is character.

All this leads him to suggest that people should not rush into the role of the teacher. Potential teachers should approach the role with some fear and trepidation for their responsible positions will lead them to be judged more rigorously in the end. In the light of this it is surely no accident that James introduces his major discussion about speech by referring to them, even if he does not intend his comments to apply to them alone.

*Why do we need to control our words?*
Having already said that one reason why James is dealing with this topic is because no syllabus of moral or spiritual instruction in his day would have been worth its name if it had not included it, he goes on to tell us some other reasons why it matters. Some psychologists may look for hidden motives to explain his preoccupation with the subject. Was it that he had been ridiculed by teachers himself at an earlier age and was determined not to let others be treated in that way? Perhaps. But the reasons James gives for its importance are theological rather than psychological.

First, it has to do with the will of God for our lives, 1:20
What God desires is that we should live 'a righteous life'. Paul, again, says something almost identical to the recently converted Christians at Thessalonica. He tells them, 'It is God's will that you should be sanctified (made holy)'.[6] Paul then applies it to the sexual life of the

new believers and tells them that to 'please God' they need to learn sexual restraint and marital faithfulness. James says that purity in our speaking is just as important as purity in our sexual behaviour. We may please God enormously by restraining our sexual urges but unless there is a comparable ability to restrain our undisciplined tongues we shall still be living contrary to his will. Although one can see the reason, both on biblical and contemporary grounds, for the church's stress on sexual morality, it has sometimes been at the expense of a more fully-orbed picture of what God requires in our lives. We can all unfortunately picture Christian leaders who would be far too inhibited in the sexual area to put a foot wrong but who can gossip for ever, be sharp and ungracious in their conversation and less than truthful in the way they speak. Failure to control the tongue is offensive to God, just as adultery or other sexual misdemeanours are. Every sin matters to God. If, then, we seek to do his will, we shall react with as much horror to the sins of the tongue, like lying, boasting, gossip or slander, as we shall to theft, murder or adultery. Our aim is surely a life that pleases God in every dimension.

Secondly, it has to do with the judgement of God on our lives, 3:1
When James addresses leaders he introduces a second motive for being concerned about our speech. Leaders, no less than anyone else, are accountable to God. In fact, we 'know that we who teach will be judged more strictly.' Some teachers assume that they are above the tests which will apply to others. They set the examinations, they don't sit them! But spiritually-speaking, nothing could be further from the truth. Those who allow themselves to be in a position where they influence others will carry the burden of that responsibility. They will be held accountable for the discharge of their calling.

If it is true that 'careless talk costs lives', then the careless talk of teachers costs even more lives. On the one hand, teachers have enormous capacity for good. They can encourage, illuminate, develop and instruct. They can see people grow in understanding and gifts. They can solve problems and show a way out of difficulties. They can enable people to grow to maturity in Christ. On the other hand, how much damage teachers can inflict if they are not conscientious. The harsh words, the broken promises, the ill-prepared and inept lesson, the rash claims, the ill-founded teaching, the heresy, the hypocritical stance – all these and more can do damage to the growth of God's people. Sadly one knows the truth of this only too well. A number of my contemporaries in Christian leadership have gone off at tangents and started preaching error, or have gone off the rails in their personal lives and caused enormous harm to those who had respected them and learned from them. Bewilderment, confusion and backsliding follow. And Satan has a field day.

John Chrysostom (347-407) became one of the outstanding pastors of the early church, but he initially resisted the invitation to become a bishop. When asked why he was so reluctant he argued, with irresistible logic, that no one would consider pulling any old person out of the crowd, turning them into a military dignitary and insisting they head up a great army. It would be stupid. Turning to another illustration, he said they would be foolish to entrust a fully-laden merchant ship into the hands of an inexperienced sea captain like himself, 'Lest I should sink the ship.' But in that case, as he points out, the only loss would be a material one. In the church, by contrast, the loss caused by inept or inexperienced handling of people will be eternal.[7] No wonder James writes, 'Not many of you should become teachers.'

Spiritual leaders have immense privileges. But they, even more than ordinary teachers, are in a position of trust with a duty of care. One day they will be called to account for their stewardship. Jesus warned: 'what you have said in the dark will be heard in the daylight, and what you have whispered in the ear in the inner rooms will be proclaimed from the roofs.'[8]

Words matter because we should want to do the will of God and because we should want to avoid the judgement of God.

## The difficulty with controlling our words, 3:2-12

Concern about speech is never far from the surface in James' letter. Luke Johnson points out that he refers to self-justifying speech (1:13), flattering speech (2:3-6), careless speech (2:16) and superficial speech (2:18); with even more references coming later in the letter. But it is in 3:1-12 that the topic of speech moves centre-stage again.[9]

After the initial warnings and headline attention-grabbing statements in 1:19, James develops his thinking by giving us a rigorous and recognizable analysis of why it is so difficult for most of us to control our tongues. Elsewhere the Bible sets out the positive blessing which the tongue can prove to be. Proverbs 16:23-24, for example, describes pleasant words as 'a honeycomb'. Proverbs 25:11 states, 'A word aptly spoken is like apples of gold in settings of silver', which captures the wonderful blessing that words can be to others when we get them right. But James knows that so often we don't. We get them wrong. It is this negative side of the equation which is his chief concern as he explores the issue further in 3:2-12. Four aspects concern him.

*The tongue's astonishing impact, 3:3-5*
The first thing we must come to terms with is the power of such a small member of our body. The tongue has an astonishing impact, for good or ill. Proverbs puts it like this: 'the tongue has the power of life and death.'[10] A Japanese proverb stresses its negative potential: 'the tongue is but three inches long but can kill a man six foot high.' While the wise Jewish apocryphal book of Ecclesiasticus said, 'The stroke of the whip makes marks in the flesh, but the stroke of the tongue breaks bones. Many have fallen by the edge of the sword, but not so many as have fallen by the tongue.'[11] All acknowledge that its effect is out of all proportion to its size. The tongue gives us evidence, if we needed it, that we do not have to be big to have a mega impact. In fact, James reminds us, there are examples of that very point wherever we turn. He mentions three:

A small bit can guide a strong, wilful horse.
A tiny rudder can steer a large, storm-tossed ship.
A little spark can trigger a raging forest fire.

James has an interesting way of expressing himself in this third illustration. Twice he uses the same Greek word (*hēlikos*) but rightly when we come to translate it we translate by two opposite, and apparently, contradictory words. First we use it to mean 'great' (a great forest fire) and then we use it to mean 'small' (a small spark). How can this be? The word *hēlikos* draws attention to the size of something, in either direction. So it can be either very great or very small, but it's never average. His words have a nice symmetry about them. The smallness of the tongue is balanced by the largeness of its impact. What is noticeable about the tongue is its size, whether that is its actual size or the size of its impact. In both respects the tongue is *hēlikos*.

Buried in the middle of these three illustrations James mentions that the tongue is particularly capable of making 'great boasts'. Don't we know it? What we use the tongue for most is to brag. Nobody has ever got as great a bargain as we have. Nobody has ever had such a difficult time as we face. Nobody has ever done the job as well as we do. Nobody has ever had the experiences we have. The tongue is a willing co-conspirator in our sin. When Jerome commented on this verse he pointed out that this was exactly the devil's problem. 'The devil did not fall because he committed theft, murder or adultery; he fell because of the tongue. He said, "I will scale the heavens; above the stars. I will set up my throne, I will be like the most high" ' (Is. 14:13-14).[12] Given the astonishing impact of the tongue and the way it serves us as a willing instrument of sin, we need to be very careful in how we train it.

*The tongue's corrupting energy, 3:6*
It is the tongue's role in corrupting the whole of us which concerns James next. 3:6 is actually quite a difficult verse, although the thrust of it is clear. The tongue has the power to defile everything. It reminds me of an incident on a Christian houseparty some years back. A heating pipe carrying oil in the kitchen split and ruined a great deal of food. Even the food and drink with which it did not actually come into contact was affected. For days everything tasted and smelt of oil! James' illustration is different. He describes the tongue as a fire and, just as a fire contains many evils as it rampages on its destructive way through a forest, so the tongue is 'a world of evil among the parts of the body'. Calvin spoke of it as 'a slender portion of flesh (which) contains the whole world of iniquity'.[13] Having described what it is, James tells us what it does. It affects the whole person and direction of one's life. It is not a discrete part of the body which we can deal with in isolation from the rest of us. What it says affects our total being.

But the most serious element of his critique is to name where the tongue gets its fuel from. The source of the tongue's destructive power is to be traced to 'hell'. By hell, James means Gehenna, the rubbish tip outside of Jerusalem which was perpetually on fire as it was fuelled day after day by the refuse of the city.[14] Manton, as so often, expresses the meaning graphically. The fire is 'from hell, that is from the devil, who is the father of lies, the author of malice and virulency, and doth by the tongue, as a dextrous instrument or fit servant, transmit lies, and slanders, and strife, for inflaming and enkindling the world.'[15] The way we so often use the tongue – for boasting, gossiping, criticising, chattering, wounding or lying – demonstrates all too clearly where its source is to be found, namely, in hell itself.

### The tongue's stubborn resistance, 3:7-8

The old slogan on the ice-cream van used to read: 'Our ice-creams are always licked but never beaten.' Unfortunately it is not easy to lick the tongue at all, let alone beat it. The illustration James now summons to make his case comes from a comprehensive review of the animal kingdom. Using the four traditional categories of creature he refers to animals of the land, birds of the air, reptiles of the earth and creatures of the sea and suggests that in each of these domains people have managed to bring creatures into submission and tame them, restraining their naturally wild tendencies. The farm and the circus, the zoo and the aquarium, the home and the show ground bear witness to the truth of his words. But human beings find it much harder to do the same with the tongue. The tongue resists being tamed more than any animal. It is true, as Churchill reportedly said, that, 'The power of man has grown in every sphere except over himself.'

The reason for its resistance lies in its restless character. It is, in J.B. Phillips' words, 'always liable to break out, and the poison it spreads is deadly.'[16] The image is of the frightening rapid movement of a snake provoked to self-defence or the darting tongue of the viper as it strikes its victim. Indeed, that may be precisely what James had in mind, for his words seem reminiscent of the psalmist who prayed for deliverance from his enemies since they 'make their tongues as sharp as a serpent's; the poison of vipers is on their lips'.[17]

### The tongue's ready duplicity, 3:9-12

A fourth and final devastating criticism is mounted against the tongue. We have seen that throughout his letter James is concerned about double-mindedness. Here the same concern transposes itself into double-tonguedness. The problem which concerns us here is the tongue's astonishing ability to speak two languages simultaneously. If the two languages were a simultaneous translation – both meaning the same thing – it would be miraculous. But the difficulty is that they are a simultaneous mistranslation with the two languages voicing diametrically opposite sentiments. Our tongues cause us both to voice praise to God and to curse people. This is a worse situation than Mr Talkative in Bunyan's *Pilgrim's Progress*. At least he was a saint when abroad and a devil at home. Our tongues succeed in being both saintly and demonic concurrently.

To engage in this continuous double-talk has serious spiritual implications. Consider what such speech implies. First, it *desecrates God's human image*. The people we curse are people who have been made in the image of God.[18] To curse them, therefore, cannot be something which is just between us and them. It is necessarily something which is between us and God. Since all men and women are made in the image of God there are no human beings whom we can curse with impunity. Those of other races, colours, genders or cultures are all made in the image of God and deserve to be treated with the same respect as we are careful to demonstrate in our approach to God. Even our enemies and persecutors are made in his image and so we should respond to their provocations not with cursing but by calling down blessing on them.[19]

Secondly, double-talk *disobeys God's holy will*. The blunt fact is that 'this should not be'. There can be no possible excuse for it. No reason can be invented which would justify it. Complete truthfulness, unwavering integrity, wholesome vocabulary, thankful praise and encouraging words are all declared to be what God would want from us. Never once are we instructed to lie, deceive, speak half-truths, be duplicitous or destructive in our use of words. These run counter to God's morally perfect character and cause him displeasure. The manner of our speech, as well as our conduct, should be governed by the way God himself addresses us.[20] Isaiah 53:9 says of the suffering servant that 'there was no deceit in his mouth.' Jesus was that suffering servant. And since that was true of him, it should be true too of us.[21]

Thirdly, double-talk *defies God's natural creation*. It is unnatural to speak in this manner. Creation itself cannot behave in this manner, so how clever of us to be able to do so! No water spring can simultaneously produce sweet and sour water. No tree can bear two different types of fruit at once. So, how is it that we human beings can speak gracious, truthful and encouraging words whilst at the same time using the same tongue to speak harmful, deceptive and destructive words? Perhaps Jesus gives us the clue. In Mark 7:21-23 Jesus details an ugly catalogue of sin including some which find their expression through the tongue, like deceit, slander and arrogance. These he says, 'come from inside and make you "unclean".' What we say arises out of what is really inside us. It reveals what we truly think about someone, or something. Like the water of the spring, it comes from deep within. Like the fruit of the tree, it grows from the life within. Hence an apple can't grow naturally on a peach tree, nor an orange on a plum tree. What's inside is what comes out. So, the malice, slander, swearing and expression of unbelief are actually revealing to others the state of our hearts. That makes our abuse of the tongue even more serious than we generally accept it to be. It not only has the potential to destroy good human relationships but also to show how poor is our relationship with God.

In summary, James warns us of the significance, strength, stubbornness and slipperiness of the tongue. It is no easy thing to master.

## 3. The means of controlling our words 1:21, 3:8, 5:12

Given his devastating critique what hope does James give us? Since the tongue is such a difficult beast to tame, how can we set about it? Or is the situation hopeless? James' letter gives us a number of scattered clues.

### *Admit defeat, 3:8*

The first step to controlling the tongue is a paradoxical one. We must admit our inability to control it. 'No one can tame the tongue.' Unless we understand the depth of the problem we shall be tempted to think that we can sort it out all too easily. We will resort to sticking plaster solutions when more major surgery is needed. In this respect we need to become like members of Alcoholics Anonymous who know that there is no hope of freedom from their addiction unless first they admit their slavery to it. And even when progress has been made they never see themselves as more than 'recovering alcoholics'. The day they begin to assume they have conquered it is the day they begin down the path to addiction again.

When we recognise the enormity of the problem then we shall be open to turn to others for help. This was what the psalmist experienced. In Psalm 39, he began confidently, asserting that he would not respond to his attackers in a spiteful way but would muzzle his speech and avoid sins caused by the tongue. He soon learned, however, that his silence meant he was bottling up strong emotions within himself which he could not contain, at least in any healthy way. So, he is driven, by verse 7, to look for a power beyond himself to help. 'But now, Lord, what do I look for? My hope is in you.' He begins to see that the opposition he experiences is really an instrument of God's discipline and this new understanding of what was happening drives him to renew his relationship with God which had grown distant. In that restored relationship he would come to discover both renewed emotional health and the secret which would enable him to control his tongue.

### Take action, 1:21

Dependence on God does not absolve us from taking action ourselves. They are not in opposition to each other. Indeed, it is our dependence on God which enables us to take constructive action. Without the Holy Spirit's powerful energy in our lives our action would be futile. Christians run into problems when they fail to keep these two aspects of their Christian experience in balance. Those, on the one hand, who leave everything in God's hands and take no practical action for themselves are in fact avoiding the plain commands of scripture and consequently fail to carry through the transformation of character which God longs to see in us. In some cases they become escapist and tend towards mysticism. Those who, on the other hand, take all the responsibility on themselves end up with a gospel of works rather than grace and frequently also end up stressed because they are quite incapable of bringing about change in their lives unaided.

Where does James tell us about our human responsibility? He

does so when he first introduces the topic of the tongue in chapter 1 when he invites us to get rid of 'all moral filth' from our lives. Perhaps the best commentary on this, though, is to be found in Ephesians 4:20-32. In that passage Paul shows a special interest in the tongue mentioning lying, angry speech, unwholesome talk and slander all within a few short verses. His concern is not only that the misuse of the tongue demonstrates personal spiritual immaturity but that it destroys corporate Christian fellowship. Nothing is so regularly destructive of Christian community as an undisciplined tongue. But he sets this very practical discussion in an astute theological framework. He tells the Ephesians that they are to 'put off the old self', one characteristic of which is an uncontrolled tongue and 'put on the new self' of Godlikeness, righteousness and holiness. In other words, there is action for them to take, something for them to do. But it is only possible for them to do that because of what they have learned about the work of Jesus.[22] It was through him that they were able to renew their minds and think in different ways. Without Jesus, that would have been quite impossible. Without the gospel of Jesus, the command to take action would be nothing other than despairing moralism. But through his grace and given his Spirit's power within, change is possible. We need to take responsible action to work in cooperation with him.

*Use help, 1:21*

There is a third dimension to his advice. Resources have been given to us to help us in this battle which we should exploit. In 1:21 James tells us the answer to the problem of our words lies in the power of God's word – 'the word planted in you, which can save you'. The word of the gospel is a life-producing force within us enabling us to produce fruit of which otherwise we would be incapable. His word is a word of truthfulness, graciousness, righteousness and holiness. So it produces truth, grace, righteousness and holiness in us. Our words may kill and maim but his words are always life-giving.

Although 'the word planted in you' may strictly apply to the gospel it is capable of wider application to the whole word of God. So, one of the best commentaries on James' meaning is to be found in the Psalms. Psalm 119 is a long meditation on the life-giving properties of the word of God. Consider, for example, verse 11. 'I have hidden your word in my heart that I might not sin against you.' Or, verses 41-43, 'May your unfailing love come to me, O Lord, your salvation according to your promise; then I will answer the one who taunts me, for I trust in your word. Do not snatch the word of truth from my mouth, for I have put my hope in your laws.' Or consider the positive use, expressed in verses 171-172, to which the Psalmist wishes to put his tongue. 'May my lips overflow with praise, for you teach me your decrees. May my tongue sing of your word, for all your commands are righteous.' Here are three aspects, among many others which could be listed, of the value of God's word in controlling our words. First, it protects us when we face temptation by instructing us in what is right. Secondly, it directs us away from exacerbating a hostile situation by causing us to put our trust in God. Thirdly, it fills us with the knowledge of God and the wisdom of his ways, causing us to be so taken up with declaring his glory that we do not have the energy to use our tongues for sinful purposes. As we seek to control our tongues God has made resources available to us. We need not battle against this tiny warring member of our body as if we are a beleaguered remnant of an army in defeat. We can battle against it with confidence.

Why is it, then, that we are so reluctant to use the resource God has given us? David Gill has a passion for building moral character. He writes about how Christians can become good. And he comments, as many others have done, that 'Biblical illiteracy is a tragedy for our civilization.' But then he adds, 'but it is a *scandal* as well as a tragedy for biblical people. Reading, rereading, discussing and mulling over these stories, personally and in the community of faith that "owns" them, is a crucial exercise in character formation.'[23] To refuse to use the resources which God has placed in our hands is a scandal. We're crying out for help in this area, we know we should control the tongue more than we do, but we neglect the very tool of transformation God has given us. Meanwhile we search for solutions in other directions. It is to fling God's 'good and perfect gift' of his word back in his face. Reading, meditating, learning, discussing, practising, taking seriously, giving priority to his word is indeed a way to conquer the tongue.

*Get real, 4:11-12*

The subject of speech surfaces once again at the end of a meaty section in the letter, 4:1-10, where James insists his readers need to sort out their relationships. They're falling out with each other, becoming friendly with the world, being too tolerant of the devil and consequently distancing themselves from friendship with God. Firm action, repentance and humility are called for to correct the situation urgently. Having called for humility he now gives a number of examples of their arrogance, the first of which concerns what they say about other people. His plea is that we should 'not slander one another'. Rather than having a narrow focus, the word James uses shows he has a whole range of harmful speech in mind. *Katalaleō* literally means 'I talk someone down'. Mitton explains, 'It means speaking of others in a way calculated to lower them in other people's estimation, and speaking of them in their absence, when they have no opportunity to defend themselves or correct untrue statements.'[24] It is, therefore, highly destructive of Christian fellowship.

How does James help us to stop speaking in such disparaging ways? His cure is simple. 'Get real', he says. Think more deeply about what you are actually doing when you speak like this. To speak like this means you are happy to set yourself up as a judge of others and as superior to the law itself. Which law does James have in mind? It is probably the 'royal law', which he has mentioned in 2:8, the law which enjoins us to 'love our neighbours as ourself.' The reality is that, rather than being greater than the law, you are subject yourself to the law and to the 'one Lawgiver and Judge'. 'Do you really want to speak,' he implies, 'in ways which will add further charges to the indictment you will already face in the divine court of justice? Surely not. Best, then, to avoid speaking in a derogatory way of others and remember your true position.' All life in the here and now needs to be lived in the light of future judgement.

James ends this short section with a sharp, sarcastic and devastating question.[25] To speak like this of others is sheer folly. 'Who on earth do you think you are?' Come on, get real.

*Practise integrity, 5:12*

Having engaged in a number of negative comments about the tongue James' final comment sets out a positive way forward. He stresses the importance of the point with his opening words, 'above all'.

It was a common custom among the Jews to use an oath both in court and in everyday conversation to support promises made and assure the listener of the truthfulness of what had been said. Even God himself was said to swear oaths.[26] In some cases the swearing of oaths was commanded by the law.[27] Since the sacred name of God could not be used in the swearing of an oath the Jews found all sorts of circumlocutions for it and swore instead by things in heaven or on earth. But the use of oaths had soon become devalued and they were often used frivolously. The Pharisees, in particular, had developed a hierarchy of oaths; a way of explaining how some oaths were more important than others and why certain oaths were not binding at all.

It was this practice Jesus referred to in the Sermon on the Mount.[28] He pointed out that swearing an oath in the name of heaven, or earth, or Jerusalem in no way lessened the solemnity of what one was doing since heaven was 'God's throne', earth, 'his footstool' and Jerusalem, 'his city'. So, although the name of God may not be spoken he could not be separated from the terms which had been deliberately chosen as a way around directly referring to him. The oath, therefore, should still be binding. But since people used them so casually, Jesus advocated that it would be better to have done with them completely. Rather than swearing elaborate oaths, his disciples should be known for their simple integrity. If they said, 'Yes', they should mean it. If they said, 'No', they should mean that too. No further elaboration or support should be needed. How much simpler life would be if people told the truth and stuck to it. All the elaborate system of oaths would be rendered obsolete.

It is these words of Jesus to which James is alluding in 5:12, even though he doesn't say that's what he is doing. Christian believers, he says, should be known for their truthful speaking. They should not resort to the sort of words most of us have found to our cost in insurance documents. There we frequently discover too late a clause in the small print which means we don't receive the payment for the item lost or stolen we thought we were due. The very purpose of our taking out the policy in the first place seems frustrated. Our words should not be like the neatly-qualified and complicated language of legal contracts which covers every option and rules out the delivery of what seemed a straightforward promise. Instead, we should use plain language on which others can depend and be sure that the value they have is their face value.

James calls, once again, for Christians to model integrity – a theme which has been his constant refrain. The best thing for Christians to do to use the tongue for the blessing of others is to speak the truth and stick to their words.

Far from being yesterday's issue, James writes about a subject of continuing personal importance and of crucial significance for the harmony and growth of any fellowship. The tongue can be employed for God's glory, to encourage and build up fellow members, to speak truth in love and announce the gospel. Or it can be employed for our glory, to put others down, to be economical with the truth and peddle lies. Even those of us who desperately want to use it for the former purposes struggle to do so. The tongue is a perverse member of our bodies. But with God's help, recognising our need and using the means he has given us, even the tongue can be brought into submission. Maybe there is no more persuasive apology for the gospel than when a man or woman who had a destructive tongue begins to change and control it.

# 6

# Law and How to Keep It
## (2:8-13)

**1. Law is the basis for present conduct, 2:8-11**

- The source of the law
- The focus of the law
- The unity of the law
- The result of the law

**2. Law is the basis for future judgement, 2:12-13**

- What the law requires: mercy
- What the judge assesses: mercy
- What the Lord demonstrates: mercy

More than one spiritual revolution occurred in the 1960s. They were all responding, in very different ways, to the changing cultural climate of the time. There was the theological revolution which occurred through the writings of radical theologians like John Robinson, then Bishop of Woolwich, who, in his book *Honest to God,* declared that our image of God must go. God was not to be thought of as 'out there' but 'in here', the very ground of our being. There was the ecclesiological revolution expressed in such diverse ways as the Jesus People who formed love communities and Jimmy and Carol Owen's *Come Together* which rediscovered the fun and relational dimensions of church. There was the charismatic revolution which rediscovered the experiential dimension of the Christian faith and restored a misplaced Holy Spirit to the Trinity. Then, there was the moral revolution which occurred through the rise of situation ethics and through the teaching of Joseph Fletcher.[1]

Joseph Fletcher, an American Episcopalian, who taught ethics in a theological seminary in Cambridge, Massachusetts, tried to steer a middle course between legalism (an approach which derives its ethical decisions from law) and antinomianism (an approach which rejects law as a basis for moral decisions). For Fletcher the only commandment which was absolute was the command to love. Other laws might guide one into understanding how love could be applied in certain situations but they were not to be invariably enforced. They had no universal significance. They were merely ways in which the people who had lived before us had thought that love would work out. Only the particular situation could determine how to exercise love.

Fletcher's was a pragmatic approach where people came before principles and where relativism was given free rein. Whether an action was good or not depended, he argued, not on whether a law advocated or forbade it, but what the intention of the actor was and what consequences ensued. The rightness of any action could only be determined by the situation in which the action took place. On this basis it is possible to argue that in some situations adultery, and even murder, are justified.

The use of extreme examples seemed to provide clear and convincing evidence to support his argument. The law says it is wrong to murder. But, given that Hitler orchestrated the Holocaust and caused untold damage through the Second World War, would it not have been 'right' to murder him and save Europe from untold misery? Such examples are, however, a little naive. The legal dictum 'hard cases make bad law' applies to ethical discussion as well. The 'law' found in the Bible is not nearly as superficial as the stark contrast presented above implies and there is a complex framework of law which helps one distinguish between the law which prohibits murder[2] and the right of the state to punish evil.[3] Situation ethics assumes that people are basically good and will wish to make loving choices and that they have sufficient knowledge on the basis of which to make that choice. It is a very optimistic view of our human condition.

James simply would not have understood this desire to drive a wedge between law and love. In John's writings there may be an implied contrast between the age of the law and the age of grace.[4] In Paul there appears sometimes to be a sharp contrast between law and grace.[5] Given the specific issues each is addressing both John and Paul have a point. But John's stress on obedience to Christ's commands[6] and Paul's insistence that the law still has a crucial role to play in our Christian lives[7] should make us careful not to prise them apart too much. When we face such apparent inconsistencies in the Bible we must begin with asking what the writer means by 'law' and 'grace' each time it is used. The writers may not always be meaning exactly the same thing, even if they're using the same words. That alone explains how to resolve many apparent contradictions. They are contradictions on the surface only.

For James, the issue is abundantly clear. Law and love stand shoulder to shoulder. There is no need to contrast them. Law is a good thing because it is an expression of the will of God. In 1:25 he described the law as 'the perfect law that gives freedom'. In 4:12-16 he returns to it to argue that if we slander a brother or sister in Christ we are putting ourselves above the law, rather than living humbly under the Lawgiver. His fullest exposition of law, however, is to be found in 2:8-13 where he underlines his already robust teaching about the sin of judging people by their social standing or the size of their bank balance. By contrast to the way they are behaving the law calls them to demonstrate impartial love. What more does he have to say here about law?

## 1. Law is the basis for present conduct, 2:8-11

*The source of the law, verse 8*

The law is 'royal' because it is decreed by God the King. It bears his authority and carries the stamp of his person on it. It is a law promulgated by 'our glorious Lord'.[8] It is the law of his kingdom. It is not a law arrived at by social consent in a public referendum, nor by the will of a democratically elected Parliament. It is neither the will of a constitutional monarch, nor of a self-elected dictator. It is the will of a sovereign, creator God who has revealed it to us. His authority is personal, not an impersonal statute; real, not an imaginary pretence; unchanging, not uncertain like public opinion; and good, not arbitrary and ill-thought-through like much human law which brings harmful, if unintended, consequences in its wake.

If this is so, we have a special and inescapable obligation to fulfil it. As citizens of a heavenly kingdom nothing should delight us more than implementing the wishes of our monarch.

Where is this law to be found? James says, it is 'found in scripture'. Much ink has been shed over precisely what scripture he had in mind. At least five possibilities have suggested themselves:[9] the whole Old Testament or a selection from the Old Testament law book; just Leviticus 19: 18, which he quotes; the teaching of Jesus; the law as personified and fulfilled in Jesus; or, a combination of both the Old Testament and the teaching of Jesus. In deciding between those interpretations two things need to be borne in mind. First, James is not likely to have been writing with the precision required of a postgraduate theological seminar at the Cambridge University School of Divinity. He is likely to have been writing practically and intuitively.[10]

Secondly, it is clear that he has a special affinity with one central chapter of the Old Testament law, namely Leviticus 19. Here he refers to Leviticus 19:15 and 18 but his dependence on that chapter is much wider than that. There are 'certainly four, and possibly six further verbal or thematic allusions to Lev. 19:12-18' in James.[11] It seems that James is strongly shaped in his thinking by this chapter and that he deliberately set out to use it in his letter. Leviticus 19 is a crucial chapter, a charter for community care, social justice and respect for all individuals. But it is obvious that James would have seen it also as a window on to a wider law, the centre but not the circumference of the law. A few sentences later he selects two of the ten commandments from Exodus 20 and Deuteronomy 5 to illustrate his point. So it is the more general Old Testament law that he must have in mind.

But there is more to be said. Jesus referred to Leviticus 19:18 more than once in his teaching.[12] On one occasion it gave rise to his telling the parable of the Good Samaritan.[13] He also mentioned the specific commandments to which James refers in this section.[14] James would surely have been familiar with that. If so, by referring to the law he is not locking himself into the Old Testament but is referring to a combination of the Old Testament and the teaching of Jesus. It is the wider sweep of Scripture which is the royal law to which we must pay attention.

*The focus of the law, verse 8*

Doesn't this emphasis on law imprison us in a legalism from which Christ came to set us free? Did not Paul say, we 'are not under law, but under grace'?[15] Are not Paul and James, then, contradicting each other? The answer to each of these questions is an emphatic, 'No'! The way in which Paul was speaking of law is different from its use here in James. In Paul's argument, to be under the law is to place oneself under the authority of the law as the means of our salvation. If we do that, he argues, then we become slaves to it all. If we fail to keep one little bit of it, we're sunk as far as salvation is concerned. But we're not under the law in that sense. Our salvation is a gift of God's grace and so we're free from the tyranny of attempting to obey it as an entry ticket to heaven. But Paul knows as well as James that the law is holy and good[16] and that it has a continuing role in the life of the believer. Once we have received grace and start living by faith, it continues to function as a useful guide to how we should live in practice. Indeed, in Galatians, where he most strongly emphasises the need for grace, Paul quotes the very same command from Leviticus 19:18 to make the very same point as James.[17]

The second, and more obvious reason in the context, why law is not imprisoning is because of how James (and Paul) view the law. The law is about love. It is primarily a way of giving expression to the meaning of love. If you love someone then the most sensible way in which you can put that love into practice is by keeping the commandments. It is not love to lie to them, to steal their wife, to take away their life, to cheat on them in the marketplace, to be disrespectful to them if they suffer some disability, to pass them by if they need help and it lies within your own hands to offer it.

Take the Sabbath command as an example.[18] Many regard it as oppressive and legalistic. They have some reasons for doing so because that is how the Pharisees of Jesus' day and many latter-day Pharisees too have interpreted it. Some who are more knowledgeable may even point out that it is the only one of the Ten Commandments not to be explicitly endorsed in the New Testament, while Jesus seems to undermine it in his insistence on eating and healing on the Sabbath day.[19] This last point is, of course, a misunderstanding. Jesus is not contradicting the Sabbath principle by his actions. Rather he is exposing the folly of the overzealous interpretations imposed on it by the religious leaders which have led to the law being distorted. And he was quite right to do so, for a key aspect of the law as originally intended was the need to provide vulnerable workers with some protection against oppressive employers. The powerful were not to exploit the weak by insisting they work seven days a week, twenty-four hours a day. They were entitled to some rest, some space. It was a principle enshrined in God's creation of the universe. And the religious leaders had turned this great charter of freedom into an instrument of oppression. But pared back to the original, this command was an expression of a loving way to deal with others just as much as any of the other commands.

We too easily view the law as negative. In reality, the law as given by God (rather than as interpreted subsequently by us) secures our freedom and guides us as to how to live so that societies can function in a harmonious and healthy way. There is no community in anarchy.

This positive perspective on the law explains why in numerous Psalms David rejoices in it as a treasured possession. He celebrates it as perfect and able to revive the soul, as trustworthy and able to make the simple wise, as right and a cause of joy, as radiant and leading to vibrant life.[20] In Psalm 119, his extended meditation on the law, he boasts, 'I will walk about in freedom, for I have sought out your precepts.'[21] He sees no conflict between freedom and obeying law; rather the reverse.

The mistake of the situationist, which we mentioned at the beginning of the chapter, is to pull asunder what belongs together. Love and law both certainly need interpreting and sometimes the application to particular situations is hard. But they fundamentally belong together. The one is an expression of the other. 'What God has joined together, let no man put asunder.'

### The unity of the law, verses 9-11

We talk of 'the long arm of the law'. By that we mean we cannot escape justice easily. When we do wrong, the law will eventually catch up with us and find us out. Just today as I write these words a man has been found guilty in an English Court of a murder that he committed thirty-two years ago. A DNA sample taken from him recently for another purpose established his guilt in the murder of a child all those years before.

James equally recognises the law has a long arm, but by it he has something rather different in mind. The law has a comprehensive claim on our lives and breaking it at one point, however trivial, puts us on the wrong side of the law and makes us lawbreakers. 'For whoever keeps the whole law and yet stumbles at just one point is guilty of breaking all of it.' That sounds harsh and legalistic, especially if the word 'stumble' is meant to indicate something of the weakness of our flesh. But a moment's reflection will help us see the sense of it. The law is not like an examination paper where candidates are invited to 'answer four questions out of twelve', with the choice being left to them. You cannot compensate for failure (or ignorance) in one area by doing well in another. It's much more like a car windscreen or, at least, car windscreens as they used to be, as I recall from bitter experience. A small stone hits it just at one point and the whole windscreen shatters, causing the driver a sudden and total loss of vision. Break the law at one small point and the righteousness you have constructed is shattered completely. The law is a unity. To break it at one place is to be on the wrong side of it altogether. The speeding driver is on the same side of the law as the serial killer; the minor opportunist thief on the same side of the law as the career fraudster. They're all on the wrong side!

The reason why this is so important is that we all have a natural tendency to seek to justify ourselves. We protest that, though we may not have kept this particular part of the law, we've done well elsewhere. To say that though we disobeyed this particular command we kept the rest of it is no defence. We're just as guilty as those who have broken the law on a massive scale. We both deserve the label 'lawbreaker'.

The central figure in Nick Hornby's novel *How to be Good* is Kate. She is a doctor who does a great deal of good but then has an extramarital affair. As she struggles to come to terms with what is going on in her life she muses, 'I'm a good person. In most ways. But I'm beginning to think that being a good person in most ways doesn't count for anything very much, if you're a bad person in one way. Because most people are good people, aren't they?'[22] She protests that she's not bad enough to sleep with someone during working hours, only outside them. But, even so, being a doctor, all the good she does can't make up for the one bad thing she has done, even if it was after hours. Kate puts her finger on the very thing James is saying.

James illustrates the point, in verse 11, by selecting two laws as examples. Several reasons have been suggested as to why he latches onto these two. Hilary of Arles said they were chosen because they 'deal most closely with loving and hating one's neighbours.'[23] But it could equally be that these were the two laws most relevant to the pagan context, or that they were chosen because Jesus speaks of them first in the Sermon on the Mount or that they relate most clearly to the actual situation in the church.[24] He imagines a conversation in which someone says, 'Well, though I've committed adultery, I've never murdered'. The unspoken implication is that therefore the speaker feels adultery is less serious than murder and so he, even though an adulterer, is a better person than a murderer. James will have none of it, and rightly so. Both the adulterer and the murderer have disobeyed God's law and so both are equally culpable lawbreakers. In this light, none of us has any reason for pride. We all stand on level ground as those who somewhere or another at some time or another have broken God's law. We may be among the religious and respectable. Our sins may be more socially acceptable than those of others. But we're lawbreakers nonetheless.

We may be comfortable with the logic of James' position, so far. But we will probably not be so comfortable with his application. The particular reason he spends time on this issue is that his readers are breaking the law by their discriminatory practices in church. These verses arise out of the story of the rich man and the poor man who go to church and the different way in which they are treated (verses 1-7). The rich man is warmly welcomed and given a seat of honour. The poor man is ignored, insofar as it is possible to do so, and told to sit on the floor or even to act as a footstool. An earlier section looked at several reasons as to why such discrimination on the grounds of social status is wrong.[25] But in these verses James alludes to an additional reason why it is wrong. The law of the Lord forbids such prejudicial behaviour. Not only is the whole tenor of the law against it, as can be seen from the way the people of God are commanded to treat aliens, slaves and the economically vulnerable who live among them, but the law specifically prohibits it. Leviticus 19:15 says, 'Do not pervert justice; do not show partiality to the poor or favouritism to the great, but judge your neighbour fairly.' What was forbidden in the courts was being practised in the church which should surely have exhibited a higher standard of holiness not a lesser one. So, James' readers may well be priding themselves on leading moral lives, on neither committing adultery nor murder. But they have no reason for arrogant complacency. In behaving as they do in church they are breaking the law of God. In failing to show love to all, without regard to their social standing, they have become lawbreakers, just as surely as if they had committed adultery or murder. It may only appear a tiny hole in the 'windscreen' of the law. But it has shattered it all, for the law is a unity.

*The result of the law, verse 12*

In verse 12, James builds a bridge between what he has said about the law as the basis of our present conduct and what he is about to say about the law as the basis for our future judgement by reminding us of the purpose of the law. He repeats what he has already said in 1:25. The law is not given by God to impede us, stunt us, imprison us or destroy us but rather to give us freedom. Without law there can be no freedom. As Campbell Morgan once put it, 'As a room is no room that has no walls, so liberty is no liberty that has no boundaries.'

Common sense tells us it is so. My freedom to drive safely on the roads depends on my obeying the rules of the road and on other drivers doing the same. If I want the anarchy (not freedom) of deciding which side of the road I want to drive on, or whether I stop at green traffic lights and go on red ones, each time I get in the car then I am not likely to live long. The law against breaking and entering similarly produces a measure of security for my property. The law against murder ensures a degree of security in my life. We welcome each of these laws because they have the effect of producing freedom. We do not protest that they are unnecessarily restrictive and legalistic. They restrain our natural anarchic instincts, our unbridled desire to possess what is not ours, and our murderous thoughts. And we welcome them because the restraint leads not to less freedom but to more. So it is with the law of God. It is given that we might live freely in relation to him, to our neighbours and, even, live at peace with ourselves.

As Christians we have freedom in Christ.[26] But it is a freedom not to do what we like but what God likes. It is a freedom to love and to serve, not to spend our liberty on ourselves.[27] And there can be no greater freedom than that.

## 2. Law is the basis for future judgement, 2:12-13

Two shifts of focus now follow. First James turns from a consideration of the present to a consideration of the future, although he spells out the connection between them. They are part of a continuous story. How one lives now will affect how one is judged then. Then he turns from a focus on the law to a focus on judgement. But, again, there is an obvious connection between them. Those who break the law end up in court and stand before the judge awaiting sentence. Even those who keep the law are sometimes assessed before a tribunal and rewards or punishments meted out according to their performance. Law leads somewhere. It leads to judgement. Throughout his letter James is concerned with judgement. He returns to it regularly[28] and with a sense of urgency. Verse 12 may well be translated 'as those who are about to be judged' rather than just 'those who are going to be judged' one day. Why the sense of urgency? Because he wants to shape a community which is not only ready for judgement eventually but whose members have taken the implications of that judgement on board so seriously that they live in the light of it now. One of the best ways of doing that is to remind people that judgement could indeed take place at any time. We will not necessarily have any warning about it, nor the opportunity to revise for it and prepare ourselves at leisure. We must live ready for it today.

So what is the basis of the judgement that we will one day face? It is 'the law that gives freedom'. Again Paul and James are at one. We are saved by grace, and grace alone. The threats of hell and eternal death have been removed from us by the death and resurrection of Christ. Nothing can undo that. The believer who walks in companionship with Jesus has nothing to fear. But there is, even so, a judgement we face. Paul talks of our 'appearing before the judgement seat of Christ' to receive what is due for the things done in the body whether good or bad.[29] Here, James spells out what the good things and the bad things are to which Paul refers. They relate to the theme of 'mercy'.

Even more important is that James and Jesus agree. Here James is only expressing in a more abstract and summarised form what Jesus had taught in the parable of the sheep and the goats.[30] In that parable Jesus had looked ahead to the coming judgement and explained that the basis for determining our future destiny would be whether we had fed the hungry, refreshed the thirsty, housed the homeless, clothed the naked, nursed the sick or visited the imprisoned. Failure to do these things when possible was the basis on which people were consigned to 'the eternal fire prepared for the devil and his angels.'[31] Jesus' primary concern is that we must do these things to our Christian brothers and sisters. But, though the parable doesn't say so, it is surely right to assume that he does not want us to limit such action to them alone but to extend it to those outside the believing community who are in need as well. In serving these people, he tells us, we will actually be serving Jesus himself.

Some Christians have interpreted Jesus' words as teaching a gospel of works. But it is not so. Bruce Milne has recently pointed out just how many notes of grace flow through the parable. The righteous receive the gift of eternal life not because of their works but as an 'inheritance prepared for them since the creation of the world'.[32] Inheritances are not earned. They are freely bestowed. So, salvation is a gift from God which is received because of his electing grace. The deeds, then, cannot earn salvation. Rather they are 'actions of overflowing and uncalculating kindness which are the natural fruit of hearts which have themselves received grace.'[33]

It is in this wider context that James' words should be read.

## What the law requires: mercy

We live in a hard world. Mercy is hard to find. We are taught from earliest days that we get what we deserve. There's no such thing as a free lunch. We have to pay our way, earn our keep. People won't make allowances. They'll judge by strict standards. Law will be held up to condemn, to point out failure, to remind us we're not good enough, we don't measure up. It was always so. The context in which James' readers lived was one where envy was rife and people evidently demanded their rights and were prepared to fight to get them.[34] There was little grace in the system. Indeed, if there was no God to whom people were accountable there need be no grace in the system. We can live for 'number one.'

But God's law operates on an entirely different plane. As we have seen throughout this passage, it requires us to show mercy and to practise love.[35] We are not to assume that the poverty of the shabby man who comes into church is his own fault, still less that it is a punishment from God. We must see them through the lens of mercy. Even if it were his own fault, as a person made in God's image and a person for whom Christ died, the future is redeemable. So, mercy is called for so that the grace of God might begin to take effect in his life.

Churches are not very good at viewing people through the lens of mercy. We tend to err on the side of strict morality, of middle class values, of people getting what they deserve. We tend to be like Job's comforters. If you're in that mess you must have done something wrong to get you there. We tend to be Jonahs who don't really like the gospel of grace and think it profligate of God to forgive those who have so blatantly sinned. That is why he disobeyed God in the first place and refused to preach in Nineveh and, why, once he had done so with the result he feared, he sat grumpily under a tree and longed to die. God should not have been so merciful! But as Thomas Carlyle's poem, 'You Jonah', says so incisively, God is not about to give in to the Jonahs of this world.

> And Jonah stalked
> to his shaded seat
> and waited for God
> to come around
> to his way of thinking.
>
> And God is still waiting
> for a host of Jonahs
> in their comfortable houses
> to come around
> to his way of loving.[36]

Our way of thinking ... his way of loving.

Philip Yancey tells the story of Johnny Cash visiting a maximum security prison and asking an inmate who was serving life for attempted murder to tell him what the song 'Amazing Grace' meant to him. He received the surprising reply: 'I'd been a deacon, a churchman, but I never knew what grace was until I ended up in a place like this.'[37]

The law leads us to act mercifully. The gospel compels us to preach mercifully. The church is called to live mercifully. Mercy must characterise all we are and do. If it doesn't we're in trouble when we stand before the judgement seat of Christ, as James goes on to explain.

*What the judge assesses: mercy*

At this judgement tribunal, we will be judged by the standards we have used in judging others. It follows, therefore, that if we have not been merciful to others, the Lord will not be merciful to us. Again, James is only repeating in different words what his brother had so clearly taught. Jesus told the story of the unmerciful servant who judged others much more severely than he was initially judged himself. In the end he was judged by his own master by the same harsh standards that he had used against others, with drastic and unwelcome consequences. It would have been better for him to be merciful.[38] Jesus not only taught this truth in stories but in plain statements too. The only difference between James and Jesus is that while James puts it negatively to warn us, Jesus put it positively to inspire us. In Jesus' words, 'Blessed are the merciful for they shall be shown mercy.'[39]

At this judgement tribunal, it will not be our knowledge, our position, our activism, or our rectitude which will be uppermost in the judge's mind – but our indiscriminate compassion.

Again we must ask: does that mean we're ultimately saved by our good works? Not at all. There's a step in the argument here which James takes for granted which explains why being merciful is so important when we stand before our judge. In commenting on this passage, Douglas Moo explains the issue in the same way in which we saw Bruce Milne had done in reference to the parable of the sheep and the goats. It is not because we have reached a certain standard of mercy that we receive a favourable judgement but that our merciful attitudes and actions 'count as evidence of the presence of Christ within'.[40] It is what mercy demonstrates about our relationship to God that is really crucial. And it is with God's mercy that James concludes this section.

### What the Lord demonstrates: mercy

James concludes, 'Mercy triumphs over judgement!' It's a fine sounding phrase but it is problematic and puzzling. Whose mercy triumphs? It cannot be ours, since, as we have seen, our acts of mercy are not sufficient to remove the wrath of God from us. So it is surely God's mercy that triumphs over his otherwise negative judgement on our lives.

Again, caution needs to be exercised in what we make of that lest we interpret it in such a way as to pull the rug out from under all that James has said up to now. Is he saying that ultimately God's mercy gets the better of his judgement? If so, isn't he saying that at the end of the day you don't have to demonstrate mercy to others because God will forgive you anyway? If mercy ultimately and always triumphs, why bother? Why not let it take its course?

True believers could never countenance such a slipshod argument. True believers, united to Christ, long to see the image of Christ formed within them. They will then seek to imitate Christ in their lifestyles. Hence, we can never be unkind, unmerciful or sinful in any other way, and presume that God will forgive us. God forbid that we should treat his grace so cheaply.

Yet it remains true that when we stand before God the judge it is his mercy that triumphs in our lives. For all our shortcomings, over which we grieve, we are forgiven because Christ has already stood in our place, borne the wrath of a righteous God on our behalf, and arranged through his cross for us to experience the mercy of God, not his judgement. So mercy really does triumph over judgement.

It is in the very nature of God to be merciful. From earliest days he revealed himself to be, 'The Lord, the Lord, the compassionate and gracious God, slow to anger, abounding in love and faithfulness, maintaining love to thousands, and forgiving wickedness, rebellion and sin.'[41] He is the God who is 'kind to the ungrateful and the wicked'.[42] Hence the call of Jesus, reiterated by James, to 'be merciful just as your Father is merciful.'[43]

Listen to the thoughts of John Chrysostom about mercy in his commentary on this passage:

Mercy is the highest art and the shield of those who practise it. It is the friend of God, standing always next to him and freely blessing whatever he wishes. It must not be despised by us. For in its purity it grants liberty to those who respond to it in kind. It must be shown to those who have quarrelled with us, as well as those who have sinned against us, so great is its power. It breaks chains, dispels darkness, extinguishes fire, kills the worm and takes away the gnashing of teeth (Mark 9:44-48). By it the gates of heaven are open with the greatest of ease. In short, mercy is a queen which makes men like God.[44]

Law and love should never be divided for the law is about love. When we exercise love we keep the law. When we obey the law we act in love. And if we do this, we shall have nothing to fear from the judgement.

# 7

# Faith and How to Prove It
## (2:14-26)

**James and Paul: a celebrated debate?**

**1. James exposes an empty claim, 2:14-17**

- A question
- An illustration
- A deduction

**2. James opposes a false division, 2:18-20**

- A hypothetical objector
- An irrefutable response
- A theological principle

**3. James disparages a fruitless faith, 2:21-26**

- The example of Abraham
- The example of Rahab
- The example of life

Some years ago I took part in an evangelistic mission in a small town in Northern Ireland. Not long after I arrived I was sitting with one of the elders of the church in the front room of his house. The room had a commanding view of the main street and he seemed to know everybody who lived there and passed his window. More than once he commented, 'There's Audrey. She runs the grocers. She doesn't come near us now but she did once. Years ago she went forward at a meeting. She's got a testimony. She's saved.' 'There's Andy, he serves petrol at the local garage. He was converted ten years ago at a mission and was baptised shortly after. But he quickly dropped away from church and doesn't profess faith now. Still, never mind, he's got a testimony. He's saved.' 'There's Jack. I remember the night he responded to the Gospel appeal. He's been in trouble with the law and is divorced from his wife. He wouldn't want to admit now that he got converted. But, no matter, he's got a testimony.'

To this brother, apparently, the only thing that mattered was getting people to 'make a decision for Christ' at some time in their life and then they were in the Kingdom. It didn't matter what they did subsequently, whether it was good, bad or indifferent spiritually. They were on their way to heaven. To all such people James has one simple devastating message to convey in this passage. 'Faith without works is dead.' To speak as if such people had faith was sheer fantasy. Perhaps they never really had it. But if they did, it had died long ago.

James obviously felt strongly about the issue for, in what might be considered overkill, he drives his readers three times in these verses by different roads to the same destination. Each time he arrives at the one conclusion which he repeats using remarkably similar words (verses 17, 20 and 26). There is no point in claiming to have faith unless you prove it by your works. Faith which isn't able to provide evidence that it is a lively faith by the good deeds it produces must either be stillborn or, if it ever did briefly flicker into life, is dead already. It is a completely phoney faith that has nothing to do with the genuine article.

### James and Paul: a celebrated debate?

Many have presumed, on the basis of what James writes in this section of his letter, that he is in conflict with the teaching of the apostle Paul, and is perhaps even explicitly voicing disagreement with him. Paul emphasised that faith and faith only, not works or obedience to 'the law', was the basis for our being justified by God and receiving the Holy Spirit. One particularly fine summary of the gospel he preached so tenaciously stressed just this: 'It is by grace you have been saved through faith – and this not from yourselves, it is the gift of God – not by works, so that no-one can boast.'[1] It was a belief he expounded most fully in Galatians and Romans but many of his other writings also show how vigorously he opposed any who thought they could be justified by works. His stance resulted in his being opposed throughout his ministry. His footsteps were dogged by other so-called Christian teachers who said that it wasn't that simple. They argued that keeping the Jewish law and doing other 'works' were essential in addition to faith for salvation.

According to Galatians 2:12, even the Apostle Peter had a disagreement with Paul over the issue. At one point Peter seemed in full agreement with Paul's way of preaching and had accepted the radical implications contained within his gospel of grace. The practical outworking of Paul's gospel meant, among other things, that circumcision was no longer an indispensable rite of initiation into membership of God's people, that Jews no longer needed to eat separately from Gentiles, nor to observe the many Jewish food regulations which the Old Testament and its subsequent interpreters had imposed. Apparently Peter and Paul were in harmony on these matters (at least as focused in the issue of sharing the same table as Gentile believers) 'until certain people came from James'.[2] When these emissaries of the leader of the Jerusalem church arrived Peter (and Barnabas) recanted of the liberty they had been enjoying and reverted to submitting to the demands of the Jewish law on themselves and others. Here, then, is supposed evidence of a disagreement between James and Paul. Was James' recurrent soundbite that 'faith without works is dead' a caustic remark aimed at Paul and his followers? Or, conversely, did Paul write several of the purple passages in his letters to correct the error he saw in James? Was there an irreconcilable antipathy between them?

Some want to rejoice that such diversity is found in the New Testament and use it to argue against what they regard as the imposition of a crippling straightjacket of orthodoxy. Diversity, they say, is to be welcomed. They see it as integral to early Christianity and believe that there was 'no single closely defined Christianity or Christology (that is, the doctrine of Christ) in the New Testament'.[3] But scholars who take that approach often end up with a minimalist view of what New Testament Christians had in common and are in danger of dissolving the New Testament into almost irreconcilable fragments. The New Testament may exhibit diversity on some issues but not on something as fundamental as this and for the most part what is surprising is the substantial unity which it manifests, given the diversity of personality, background and culture of those who composed early Christianity.

The older view that here we see two giants of the New Testament in conflict has certainly been modified in recent days, even if not altogether laid to rest.[4] It is largely recognised that one cannot accept that this is a picture of simple antagonism and that there are several adequate ways of explaining the apparent differences. The writings are written at different times, to deal with different problems, and to address different audiences. Therefore, it would be surprising, even suspicious, if they were written in identical terms. Once this is taken into consideration the element of conflict significantly diminishes.

Furthermore, by the key words – which are, 'faith' and 'works' – James and Paul do not mean the same things. Regarding faith, Paul, some say, is primarily concerned about faith which is the foundation of the Christian life.[5] It may be this kind of faith which James refers to in 2:19 where he declares it to be 'Good'. He clearly has no desire to downplay the importance of such faith elsewhere in the letter. Indeed, in 2:5 he has said that it is those who are 'rich in faith' who will inherit the Kingdom. Certainly, nowhere in the passage under consideration does he disparage the need for faith as the basis for salvation. James' concern is rather with the quality of faith of supposedly mature Christians, the ongoing faith of a developing Christian life.

Then regarding works, Paul uses it to mean 'works of the law', whereas James never uses that term and has something much more like charitable acts in mind. The sort of works James refers to seem, in fact, to be the very ones Paul himself commends when he talks about 'faith expressing itself in love.'[6] Douglas Moo provides us with a particularly clear statement of this sort of position. He writes, 'The difference between Paul and James consists in the sequence of works and conversion: Paul denies any efficacy to pre-conversion works but James is pleading for the absolute necessity of post-conversion works.'[7]

In a fresh and extensive examination of the issues, which is easily the most helpful discussion of recent times, Richard Bauckham[8] has questioned more fundamentally the way in which we typically approach the whole debate. James has usually been made to defend himself because primary importance has been given to the writings of Paul either because they are considered to be historically or theologically of greater importance. But this assumption, Bauckham claims, is unjustified as a true understanding of the canon suggests. Both James and Paul should be read in their own context and for their own merits, not placed in some form of pecking order of spirituality.[9] He also points out that if James was trying to undermine Paul's position on faith he does not make a very good job at it. The chief issues which were at stake, such as circumcision, eating with Gentiles and the other food laws are not even raised by James. That is surely very curious if he really was in debate with Paul. Rather, James' focus seems to lie elsewhere.[10] If we set James' writing in the context of other Jewish writings on the subjects he covers he makes much more sense. We do not have to posit a debate with Paul to explain them.[11] Significantly, Bauckham points out, there are some remarkable similarities of language between what James writes about Abraham, in 2:21-24, and what Paul writes of him in Romans 4:2-3. But since they were both drawing on the same Jewish literature and Jewish understanding about Abraham, even if using it to their own purposes, that should not surprise us.[12] The differences, then, can easily be overestimated between them, while the similarities can be underplayed. Bauckham explores just how much else James and Paul actually have in common. Their approach to wisdom and status, which Paul deals with in 1 Corinthians, is remarkably similar and their view of Christ has more in common than is often supposed. Ironically, even on the law they can sound very alike.[13] His conclusion is that if there is a disagreement between them it is on the surface only, as when James says 'people are justified by what they do and not by faith alone'.[14] The greater reality is that they are totally complementary in practice.

Given these arguments, though there may still be some rough edges between James and Paul, surely we can agree with Alec Motyer who concludes that, 'the supposed conflict is entirely imaginary.'[15] The 'faith only' position which James wishes to expose as a sham is not the 'faith only' position promoted by Paul. The faith which Paul advocated was living and genuine, but that which James criticised was decidedly dead and bogus.

The problem with the supposed controversy between James and Paul is that people get so excited about it that they fail to take note of what James actually says. So, having in part cleared the rubble of theological controversy out of the way, we can now turn to what James actually writes and hear his message on its own terms. His argument is developed in three phases, each of which climaxes with the words 'faith without deeds is dead', or words to that effect.

## 1. James exposes an empty claim, 2:14-17

*A question, verse 14*

Verse 14 sets out the headline question which the rest of this section seeks to answer. 'What good is it, my brothers and sisters, if people claim to have faith but have no deeds? Can such faith save them?' The question follows naturally from what James had been saying earlier. The immediate verses before – about the nature of pure religion (1:27), the need for love to be impartially put into practice in the church (2:1-8) and for anything that falls short of total obedience to the law to be amended (2:9-13) – prepare the way for a discussion of the nature of true faith. The logic of all that he taught to this point is that real faith must express itself in active works. And now, the formal argument supporting what he has been saying is to be set out.[16] The question James asks, then, is a rhetorical one which clearly invites the answer, 'No'. To reply in any other way would make a nonsense of what he has been saying, or perhaps suggest that we haven't grasped his practical teaching.

Careful note should be taken of the fact that James assumes we have a need for faith. It is to misread him grossly if we think he is offering us some false antithesis: that we can be *either* saved by faith *or* by works. The question is not that at all, but about what kind of faith it is we possess – 'can *such* faith save them?' Salvation here may refer to 'the final deliverance from sin, death and judgement in the last day',[17] rather than our initial deliverance from those enemies. In James salvation often has a future emphasis about it.[18] In the previous verse he had been talking about judgement, so his eye here might well be on our ultimate salvation. But the contrast he draws is not between the introductory faith required for initial salvation and the persevering faith required for ultimate salvation so much as the contrast between effective and ineffective faith, whether it be at the start or the end of the Christian life.

The 'deeds' which James has in mind would be largely the acts of charity, such as alms-giving and the provision of hospitality, which were characteristic of the piety of Old Testament and the Jewish religion. However, his use of Abraham and Rahab as examples show that he has something wider in mind than just those kinds of acts.

So the basic starting point is that faith which is merely a public profession or a mental assent to doctrine is an inadequate faith. If it gives no evidence of life in the actions of the one who claims it, it is a useless faith which cannot possibly result in salvation.

*An illustration, verses 15-16*
To leave students with an abstract problem, especially when the answer is a foregone conclusion, is unlikely to teach them much and certainly not to lead to transformation of life. So, as a good teacher, James grounds his question in a concrete situation so that it will have the desired impact. He makes use of his graphic powers of description once again and asks us to envisage a situation where fellow believers who are in obvious need because they lack the very basic necessities of life – clothes and food – come into contact with other believers who are, equally obviously, in a position to help them. And yet, instead of receiving practical help all they get is a mouthful of pious platitudes: 'Depart in peace. Keep warm, keep fed.' The words of the Jewish blessing which the devout pronounce sound spiritual enough but they are a thin cover-up for their failure to act. They speak of grace but even as the words come out of the mouth the speaker fails to minister

grace. How can they 'go in peace' when the truth is they will 'go and freeze to death' and 'go and die of hunger'? They may feel blessed but in reality they will still be very vulnerable, their bodies unclothed and their stomachs empty.

It was just this sort of situation which Bill Hybels witnessed, Sunday after Sunday, in the church where he grew up, which motivated him to seek to build a church which would model true Christian community. Week-by-week he saw rich Christians in his home church shake hands with those who were really struggling financially and in other ways. He heard them say nice things to each other, but the rich never lifted their hands to help the poor. Hybels testifies that he never set out to build one of America's largest mega-churches at Willow Creek. He set out to build a church that functioned according to the biblical mandate of community, based on the pattern of Acts 2:42-47. He sought to model a church where the poor got more than a cold handshake but where goods were shared and all were cared for in practical ways.

After thirty years in Christian ministry I can thankfully tell the other side to this story. I have seen well-off Christians give their money and much else besides to the poor time and time again. They have done so at inconvenient times and at great cost to their own comfort and sometimes their own families. They have crossed the social divides few others would traverse in the name of ministering the love of Christ. And I honour such people. Yet the church can be very schizophrenic. As well as knowing of wonderful acts of kindness, I also know that it can manifest an indifference to the needy which is callous. Some of its members can be cruelly aloof from those in need and even justify their insensitivity on so-called biblical grounds. The error James illustrates is sadly still all too real.

*A deduction, verse 17*

It is much harder to resist James' point when he confronts us with a concrete example as he does in this illustration than if he left it just as an abstract theological proposition. When he tells it like that then we can only make one deduction. The faith of such hardhearted people is 'dead.' It is not only that it doesn't show any outward signs of life. It is dead on the inside too.[19] It cannot bear fruit because, like a tree that has been afflicted by some fatal disease, it no longer has any life left in it. The point is that God doesn't measure faith by what we say. Nor is he open to be persuaded no matter how much we engage in verbal protestations that we believe. As Robert Wall has aptly put it: 'God measures true devotion by the book and that book requires action.'[20] QED. The claim to a living faith is an empty claim. It is as empty as any claim I might wish to make on the throne of England since I've not a drop of royal blood in me. This claim to faith has no warm blood in it either. Faith like this is dead.

## 2. James opposes a false division, 2:18-20

The target of empty faith is now re-presented in the form of barren faith whose infertility is brought about because something is missing from the soil in which it is nurtured.

### *A hypothetical objector, verse 18*

The second cycle of the discussion starts with the introduction of an imaginary sparring partner. He poses an objection to the straightforward deduction James has made, in verse 17, that faith by itself without accompanying works is dead. There is no reason to suppose that there was any actual person who voiced such an objection in the church. There may have been. But it is much more likely that James was just adopting a familiar strategy among those who engaged in theological and philosophical argument, that of positing a hypothetical dissenter so that he can refute him. To rebut any objections raised would strengthen the case he wants to make all the more.

So what is the objection to what James has said? The debater suggests that James' view is too exclusive and demanding. It is surely possible, he argues, that people can specialise when it comes to religion. Some people, perhaps the super-spiritual whose orientation in life is other-worldly, exhibit faith whereas others are good, down-to-earth, practical people who demonstrate their beliefs by what they do rather than by exercising the more spiritual aspects of their religion. Must faith and deeds really stand or fall together? Cannot individuals major in one *or* the other? Do they really have to have both?

The argument is not as hypothetical as it might at first seem. There are two variations of it which are frequently met today. On the one hand there are good, hard-working, salt-of-the-earth type people who will tell you all about the good works they do for the community – the charity collections, the meals on wheels, the hospital car service, and the running of voluntary organisations – who also tell you that they've no time for church, or prayer and can't be bothered with the Bible or understanding Christian truth. They have deeds. Practical Christianity is their creed. On the other hand there are good evangelicals who not only have faith – they genuinely do believe – but live a life of punctilious faith. They are scrupulous in their observance of the prayer meeting and the worship service, but they have little time to do anything beyond the religious activities of the church. They know a thing or two about theology and go the second mile in attending Bible conventions. But they would certainly not want to soil their hands by being involved in doing anything in the community by way of good deeds. Indeed, if they engaged in such activities they lie awake at night anxious that they were trying to get to heaven by their works rather than by trusting in God's grace alone. So, the hypothetical objection is not so remote from our experience as it may at first seem.

### An irrefutable response, verses 18-19

The objection gives James the opportunity to enter a full and devastating reply. First James invites his interrogator to show him what 'faith without deeds' looks like. He'd be happy, he says, to respond in kind and would be glad to show the objector what his living faith looks like. It can readily be seen by what James does. How else would you know faith was there? Was there another way in which the reality of faith could be made visible?

But even before his opponent is able to utter the first syllable of a reply James brushes him aside, sweeps on his way and provides an answer to his own question. He gives us an illustration of what faith without works looks like, and it is not a flattering one. He has seen an example of such faith before, he says, in ... the demons. They have faith in a cardinal doctrine of orthodox religion. They believe, at least in the sense that they mentally assent to it, that 'there is one God'. And that is the very basis of Jewish and Christian monotheism. It had been proclaimed since Deuteronomy 6:4 which the Jews recited frequently and which, in Jewish tradition, became known as the

*Shema'*. It expressed the fundamental truth of their religion. 'Hear, O Israel: The LORD our God, the LORD is one'. The same truth of the oneness of God was reasserted time and again in the New Testament writings as well.[21] The demons knew it to be true and believed it for real. The implications of it made them shudder. Perhaps James recalled the story of Jesus casting out the Legion of demons who had taken up residence in the man who lived in the tombs in the region of the Gerasenes.[22] When Jesus approached him they were said to have shrieked at Jesus and to have begged him not to hurt them. They knew that they were powerless in comparison with him and so they trembled in his presence. And rightly so, for they know that if there is one God then the master they serve, who seeks to usurp God's throne, is doomed, and they along with it. They shudder, then, not as a sign of worshipful awe but in terror at the thought of the coming judgement.[23] They shake in fear at the thought of God's merciless judgement.[24] But it makes no difference to them. Their belief does not lead them to exercise repentance. They show no amendment of life. Their belief is merely a mental assent, not a wholehearted trust and it only serves to compound their guilt.

It is hard to think how James' conversation partner could adequately reply to this. The claim James makes about demons is obviously true and the implications James draws out seem to be based on a flawless logic. That being so, James is justified in turning his sarcasm on his interrogator. 'Good for you', he mocks. 'Your position means you are on a level with demons. It's great company you keep.' One of the earliest commentators on James, Caesarius, Bishop of Arles (470-543) pushed the logic of James' statement one step further when he wrote: 'The apostle says that a man who believes and does not act has the faith of demons. If that is true, imagine the fate of a man who does not believe at all.'[25] True, but that is to go in a direction James does not take us. James' point is about those who claim to have faith, indeed, an accurate belief system, but one which doesn't make any difference to how one actually lives. To paraphrase Leslie Mitton, we need not only to possess an accurate theology but let that accurate theology possess us.[26]

### A theological principle, verse 20

His sarcasm continues as he brings this section to a brief climax. He calls his sparring partner an empty (*kene*) person, that is one who is empty-headed (hence the NIV translates it as 'foolish'), void, barren and unproductive. The latter is a particularly good way to nuance the translation of what is in James' mind, for the essence of his conclusion is that not only is his protester empty but the faith he claims to have is barren as well. It is incapable of yielding any fruit because it has no life within it. Once again, the same conclusion has been reached by another route: faith without deeds is useless because it is dead. James would save them from possessing a fruitless faith.

The theme of fruitfulness, and its lack, is one that runs throughout the New Testament. Paul in particular seems haunted by the idea that his preaching might prove worthless and he gains great encouragement when there is evidence to the contrary.[27] He also encourages his converts not to receive the grace of God 'in vain'.[28] James' concern is similar. It is not sufficient to say that all scripture requires is that we believe the right thing, or have faith and go on trusting regardless of there being any evidence of it. The consistent message of the apostles is that faith should bear fruit. If it doesn't, we have every reason to ask whether it is not a false faith.

Just as God is one, united and indivisible being[29] so faith and fruit are indivisible. To suggest we can specialise in the one without bothering about the other is nonsense and anyone who advocates it is 'out of his mind.'[30]

### 3. James disparages a fruitless faith, 2:21-26

Having used first a contemporary illustration and then a logical argument to expose those who wish to pretend that faith can exist independent of any deeds, James now comes at the issue a third time; this time using historical, biblical examples as the support for his position. The startling thing is the examples he chooses: Abraham and Rahab.[31] Perhaps there is nothing very surprising about his first choice, Abraham. As the great patriarch of the nation of Israel and one who was famed as an exemplar of what it meant to live faithfully it would, indeed, have been surprising if he had not been mentioned. But to pair him with the relatively unknown Rahab is a different matter.

While some try to discover similarities between them, as for instance in the way they offered hospitality to strangers, it would seem that the precise point James wants to make is that they were so different and yet both illustrate the same principle; namely, that they were declared to be righteous because of what they did. The clues are in the text to suggest that James chose them because of their dissimilarity to each other, rather than their similarity. Abraham's story occupies many chapters in the Bible. Rahab's tale is briefly told. They were social opposites. Abraham, a Jewish male, was respected as the 'father' of the Jewish people. Rahab, a foreign woman, was 'a prostitute.' Given what James had written earlier about the need for the Christian church to be non-discriminatory, the choice of Rahab is a stroke of genius.[32] If, then, the principle holds for these very different people, then it must hold for all. So, what does he say about them?

*The example of Abraham, verses 21-24*
The key incident in Abraham's life on which James focuses is the offering of his son Isaac in sacrifice to God, as recorded in Genesis 22. But it is chosen as a choice example among many other acts of obedience which could have been selected. Philo called it 'the greatest of Abraham's works' and it was a frequent cause of devotional and theological reflection among Jews.[33] There could be no greater test of Abraham's faith than this. All his life Abraham had been promised an heir. Eventually, when Abraham and Sarah were well past child-bearing age and beyond any reasonable expectation that they would be able to become natural parents, God kept his promise and Isaac was born. To be asked, therefore, some years later, to offer the young man up to God as a sacrifice was as ultimate a demand as God could make of Abraham. What was God doing? It was as if, Joyce Baldwin comments, God had suddenly put his promises into reverse gear; as if applying the reverse thrust of an aeroplane engine when it comes into land. You've been flying happily in one direction all this time and suddenly life is thrown into the opposite direction.[34] Was God about to wipe out all that had been accomplished, leaving it all the more improbable than it was before that he would be able to keep his promise and give Abraham and Sarah yet another child?

We want to raise a multitude of questions about it and enter a storm of protest against it.[35] We want to question the morality of God. What sort of a God is it who demands such a sacrifice? But that is not James' purpose. He wants to shed light on one very simple point. Whatever the apparent absurdity of the request, Abraham obeyed. So, James deduces, Abraham was a man in whom faith and works were in perfect harmony with each other. He uses a wordplay in the Greek to bring out that perfect harmony more clearly than our English translations permit. Abraham's faith worked with (*synergei*) his works (*ergois*). And his obedience led to a faith which was perfected or completed. Without it, Abraham's faith would have been deficient and still in need of being seasoned. What better illustration could there be of the truth James had set out in 1:2-4 than this? Abraham's faithful obedience to God through all the trials and tribulations which littered his tortuous path led him to 'be mature and complete, not lacking anything.' Faith that had not been subject to such testing inevitably would not share in the level of development achieved by a faith that had persevered against all odds.

Two results followed from Abraham's obedient action. First, he was awarded the status of being righteous in God's sight, and, secondly, he was awarded the title of 'God's friend'. The first is stated on the authority of Genesis 15:6.[36] The second is stated on the authority of Isaiah 41:8 and 2 Chronicles 20:7.

The first means that he was shown to be in a right relationship with God because of the actions he undertook. The issue is not how to acquire faith but how to distinguish a genuine faith from a phoney faith. Abraham's faith was proved to be authentic because of what he did. This is not to be confused, as we have seen, with the issue Paul deals with where he was contending against those who claimed to be made right with God on the basis of their doing works of the law, that is by getting circumcised, submitting to ritual washings or eating only kosher food.

The second meant he enjoyed a special intimacy with God and the sort of relationship which James, a little later in his letter (4:4), is going to accuse his readers of lacking. So many of James' themes come together in the way James refers to Abraham. Luke Johnson summarises them well, as follows:

Abraham, then, represents above all the person of faith who is *not* double-minded, who truly thinks and acts according to the measure of God .... But Abraham was a 'friend of God' because he measured by God's measure. He viewed the world as an open system in which God gives generously to all without grudging (1:5) and is the giver of every good and perfect gift (1:17) and to the humble gives a greater gift (4:6). If God gave Isaac, then God could give another gift. Abraham's willingness to give back to God what God had given demonstrated and perfected his faith and revealed what 'friendship with God' might mean.[37]

Having set out the case James, in verse 24, turns like a lawyer in a courtroom to make a direct plea to the jury which, in his case, is made up of his readers. All that he has said leads only to one conclusion, does it not? People are not only justified by faith, indispensable though that is as James agrees, but also 'by what they do'.

*The example of Rahab, verse 25*
And so to the very different example of Rahab. Some might argue that Abraham was a special case. What had he, the father of the race and special friend of God, in common with ordinary people? James seems to be aware of the possibility of such an objection and that it might undermine his argument. So he goes right to the opposite extreme to illustrate that the principle holds no matter who is involved. However you measure it, Rahab was both wicked and foreign. She had no special privileges because of her race, nor any special intimacy with God. Someone further removed from Abraham it would be difficult to imagine. But 'the contrast is deliberate and provocative, carefully chosen for maximum effect.'[38] Yet, for all their differences, they have one thing in common. Both Abraham and Rahab acted in such a way as to demonstrate they had believed in the living God and believed in him as the ultimate reality who governed their lives. He was more real to them than the circumstances and people around them. That's why they acted in ways which the world might consider absurd in the extreme. Consequently, we are justified in claiming that it is faith and deeds combined which meant these two were counted among the righteous. Together they form pretty inclusive book ends. Anyone can surely find a place somewhere between them.

The story of Rahab is told in Joshua 2:1-24. Two Israelite spies were on an espionage mission deep in enemy territory when rumours of their whereabouts came to the ears of the king of Jericho. He immediately dispatched soldiers to seize them from Rahab's house where they were said to be hiding, as indeed they were. She bravely misled the soldiers and set them off on a wild goose chase, not only saving the lives of the spies but ensuring that the intelligence they gained would be put to good use not long afterwards when the tribes of Israel crossed the Jordan and, by a somewhat unusual strategy, engineered the fall of Jericho. Rahab risked her life to save the spies. But she did so, as Joshua records, because she believed in their God, not the gods of Jericho. She professed that it was their Lord who was 'God in heaven above and on earth below.'[39] Except for her faith, her action made no sense. Because of her faith she could not really have acted in any other way.

So both Abraham and Rahab took great risks and acted in potentially dangerous ways because they believed in a living God. The value of Abraham's action lay essentially in his relation to God. It resulted in this verdict on his life: God said, 'Now I know that you fear God, because you have not withheld from me your son, your only son.'[40] The value of Rahab's action lay in her rescuing of men. Lives were saved and victory in battle was assured. The Bible's verdict on her was, 'By faith the prostitute Rahab, because she welcomed the spies, was not killed with those who were disobedient.'[41] Both Abraham and Rahab demonstrate that faith *and* works justify.

*The example of life, verse 26*
For a third time, then, James repeats his proposition by way of a conclusion. The only difference in how he puts it this time is that he expresses it in the form of a similitude, an 'as ... so' saying. 'As the body without the spirit is dead, so faith without deeds is dead.' The example of life itself illustrates the fundamental point he has been making about spiritual life. Faith cannot exist without works any more than a body can be alive without the spirit, or steam can exist without water, or a desert can exist without sand, or a kleptomaniac can exist without stealing, or Pavarotti can exist without singing. They are inseparable.

The sledgehammer of James' threefold approach has surely had its effect. To maintain that one can have faith without works is an empty claim. To contend that faith and works can exist independent of one another is to trust in a false divide. To assert that faith is adequate on its own regardless of deeds is to live a fruitless life.

Martin Luther may not have thought much of the letter to James. But, ironically, he summed up its crucial message in his preface to the Epistle to the Romans.

> O it is a living, busy active thing, this faith. It is impossible for it not to be doing things incessantly. It does not ask whether good works are to be done, but before the question is asked, it has already done this, and is constantly doing them. Whoever does not do such works, however, is an unbeliever. He gropes and looks around for faith and good works, but knows neither what faith is nor what good works are.[42]

It would seem that James and Luther were not so far apart after all. Faith is not genuine unless it is a working faith.

# 8

# Relationships and How to Handle Them
## (4:1-10)

## 1. Relationships within the fellowship, 4:1-3

- Where they go wrong
- Why they go wrong

## 2. Relationships with the world, 4:4

- Friendship with the world: why it matters
- Friendship with the world: what it shows
- Friendship with the world: where it leads

## 3. Relationships with the devil, 4:7

- The command we must obey
- The condition we must fulfil
- The confidence we may have

## 4. Relationships with the Lord, 4:4-10

- Friendship is intended
- Grace is provided
- Humility is required
- Integrity is essential
- Reverence is imperative

The major problem of our day is our inability to make relationships. People are crying out to belong. They have a thirst for community; a thirst which never seems to be satisfied. We live in a culture of advanced individualism. The old means by which people formed relationships have broken down and, as yet, new ones have not replaced them. The blessing of family life was that it knocked off the rough edges and taught people to get along with one another. It was the crucible of character where much that matters in life, like trust, sympathy, sociability, loyalty, responsibility and attachment was learned.[1] Many relationships within the family now are like flat-pack furniture. We put them together, let them continue a precarious existence for a period, but then dismantle them and replace them whenever it suits us.

Relationships in other areas of life are undergoing a transition as well. Neighbourhoods are changing. Many people do not know the person who lives next door. They are just as likely through the Internet to know someone on the other side of the world better than a person who is physically close. Team games have been relegated to a secondary place behind sports which test the skills of individual competitors. Sports and social clubs have given way to consumer-orientated health and fitness centres where people have substituted having a personal trainer for playing in a league. Voluntary associations which demand a continuous involvement, like youth clubs, the Scouts and the Girl Guides, are struggling to recruit leaders. But charitable causes in which members can participate in their own time and according to their own preference, like the National Trust or the RSPB, have no difficulty in recruiting members.

Why are relationships so difficult to forge and maintain? Is it just that we are undergoing a period of massive social and moral change and we don't yet have the maps to show us the way to build them in the new, frontier world? Partly. But we should not underestimate the difficulty of building healthy relationships in any age or in any culture. James 4:1-12 is all about relationships. His concern is not a social analysis of why they are difficult but a spiritual analysis. His insights apply no matter what the time or place because he's dealing with fundamental things about human nature. The true battle lies there if we are to construct nourishing relationships. And he tells us that it is not relationships as such that is important but relationship with whom that matters.

## 1. Relationships within the fellowship, 4:1-3

The stark opening words of chapter 4 come as something of a shock. The previous chapter had ended on a note of peace but here we are suddenly plunged into the din of war.

*Where they go wrong, verses 1-2*

The Christian life is one of warfare but, sadly, we're often fighting the wrong enemy. Instead of fighting the world and the devil, topics to which James will come shortly, we're often found fighting each other in the church, the so-called 'fellowship' of Christ's people. The church ought to be the place of unity, harmony, understanding and forgiveness. It should be the place where we listen to one another and bear one another's burdens.[2] The peace of Christ should reign.[3] Instead, the church James knew was full of 'fights and quarrels' and I know a few churches like that too. Aggression ruled, not peace.

The 'fights and the quarrels' were probably literal physical altercations, or, at the very least, violent verbal disputes full of harsh, arrogant and judgmental words. Some have found evidence in these words that the church was situated in a 'Zealot-infested' area and that the members of the church had once been Zealots and still reacted to injustice in typically volatile and violent Zealot ways.[4] The Zealots formalized their existence as a party in AD 67-68 but existed in embryo well before that. They rejected the complacent response of Israel's leaders to Roman aggression – and especially to their defiling and pilfering of the temple – and chose to wage war on Rome instead. It led to a civil war and eventually to the reconquest of Palestine and the sack of Jerusalem by the Romans.[5] While the suggestion of the Zealot background does make sense of some of the letter and the issues it addresses, most scholars question this position. They both doubt the date which would be required if the letter was written against a Zealot background and the need to be that specific in this particular case. The aggressive behaviour mentioned here might well have been expressed by Zealots, but it is by no means confined to them.

Beneath the calm surface of oceans or lakes there sometimes lies the deadly killing machine of a nuclear submarine. Relations in church can be like that. On the surface all seems calm. But only a little below lies combativeness, power politics and belligerence which, given a little provocation, will cast off restraint and strike. Even in the most well-controlled of situations it occasionally breaks surface. I know of fist fights in a few British churches (mercifully not many) and of table thumping and shouting in others. In 'nice' middle class churches in Britain we would expect outwardly aggressive behaviour to be severely restrained. We're taught to bottle things up (not always healthily). But elsewhere it's different. A friend I visited in the interior of Brazil told me how guns were regularly brought to church meetings and brandished around by the young converts who had been brought up in a wild west type of area. Today we might account for such behaviour by referring to our social situation, our psychological make-up, or our personal upbringing. But if James' analysis of where the problem comes from is right, while it might be triggered by these, it is caused by something else. If the root of aggressive behaviour is spiritual, as he contends, then sadly it might show itself in the church anywhere, anytime, regardless of the particular situation; until, that is, the members of the church learn the lessons he will go on to teach.

### Why they go wrong, verses 2-3

The description of their sinful behaviour, in verse 1, gives way to the diagnosis of its cause in verses 2-3. Where does all this aggressive speech and behaviour originate? Rhetorically he asks, 'Don't they come from your desires that battle within you?' We are people of 'passion' – a more accurate translation of the word James uses for 'desire' (*hēdonē*) – passions of a destructive and negative kind. And those passions are hard to restrain. They 'war against our soul'[6] and are 'permanently on active service,'[7] causing us to be torn apart within. The believer lives a life of perpetual civil war against sin. Yet believers do not live this life despairingly, for we have all the resources of the risen Christ available to us as well as the assurance of ultimate triumph. The battle is real nonetheless and we are called to fight it with all our might. We shall get nowhere in our conquest of sin unless we recognise the reality of the battle within. 'Victory is ours not for the taking, but ours for the winning', as Alec Motyer says.[8]

Even outside the church there is recognition of the truth of these words. Jonathan Glover, in his history of morality, comments on how much of 'twentieth century history has been an unpleasant surprise'. The advent of nuclear weapons has taken us into a new league as far as warfare is concerned. But then he quotes Albert Einstein who puts his finger perceptively on the real issue: 'Nuclear weapons have changed everything, except our modes of thought.'[9] The truth is that the cause of war, fighting and quarrels, both within the church and outside in the world, lies not in external causes but deep within our flawed and fallen human natures. It lies on the inside of us. It lies in the hateful thoughts, the vengeful attitudes, the murderous inclinations, the covetous intentions, the 'will to power'.[10]

James shows how foolish and destructive such unbridled passions are, especially when there is another way. 'You do not have because you do not ask God. When you ask you do not receive because you ask with the wrong motives, that you may spend what you get on your pleasures.' Immature children think they can catch God out. 'Can God do anything?' they ask. 'If so, can he give me a new bicycle, or my dad a Ferrari?' When God fails to produce the goods, they quickly and erroneously conclude that God is not omnipotent after all. Such children have a thing or two to learn about prayer. James' readers weren't much more mature than this. If they bothered to ask God at all, which they often didn't because they supposed that the answer lay within their own (violent) hands, they asked him for things which indulged their own passions. They should have known differently.

The fact that you are making the requests to God should cause you to exercise a certain restraint on what you ask for. You cannot ask him to aid you in some sinful design. 'A good and gracious God simply doesn't reply to petitions motivated by self-centred commitments; such prayer is idolatrous, even blasphemous, because it renders God as a mere provider of pleasure rather than as a sovereign covenant partner.'[11] Such prayer insults his integrity, impugns his holiness and contradicts his grand design for believers, which is that they should be holy. Coming into the presence of God should purify our motives, reveal to us our own errors and self-centredness, and make us selective in our requests. In his presence certain petitions are unmasked as absurd. To pray them should make us blush. Take the prayer of John Ward MP, to which John Blanchard refers:

> O Lord, thou knowest that I have mine estates in the City of London, and likewise that I have recently purchased an estate in the county of Essex. I beseech thee to preserve the two counties of Middlesex and Essex from fire and earthquake; and as I have a mortgage in Hertfordshire, I beg of thee likewise to have an eye of compassion on that county. As for the rest of the counties, thou mayest deal with them as thou art pleased.[12]

We laugh at such barefaced cheek. Yet some of our prayers are not much better. If prayer changes anything, as it does, the first thing it ought to change is the pray-er. As we come to ask anything of God we should realise the need to check our motives and adjust our agendas, so that our will comes into closer conformity to his. Only then can we truly pray 'in the name of Jesus'.

Relationships within the fellowship would have been altogether different if only God had been brought into the picture, instead of being left out of the church. Then the relationships would have been characterised by love, not war; peace, not hostility; forgiveness, not resentment; unity, not fragmentation; and, a working for the common good, not selfish ambition.

## 2. Relationships with the world, 4:4

They may not be friends with one another, but they are friends with the world. And that is the cause of much of the problem.

### Friendship with the world: Why it matters

Luke Johnson has made out a good case that this verse is the key verse in the whole of the letter.[13] Throughout the letter James writes in terms of strong contrasts and dualities. We live at war or in peace. We show meekness or anger. We forget or we remember the word of God. We are unstable or mature. We are foolish or wise. We display folly or wisdom. We speak a curse or praise. But here is the underlying contrast which is the foundation of them all. We are either friends of the world or friends of God. But we cannot be both.

What he teaches assumes greater significance if we understand the nature and importance of friendship in the ancient world. To become a friend was to relate to someone well beyond the level of casual acquaintance or occasional agreement. 'To be friends meant above all to share: to have the same mind, the same outlook, the same view of reality.'[14] So, to be a friend with the world was to share the outlook of the world, to live according to the mindset of the world, to be sucked into its worldview. To be a friend of the world therefore inevitably meant (and still means) that they were choosing 'to live by the logic of envy, rivalry, competition and murder.'[15] That's the way the world lived outside of Christ. And, sadly, these were the very characteristics which were being exhibited in the church and which were ruining relationships within it. Friendship mattered because it revealed where people's true loyalties lay.

*Friendship with the world: What it shows*
The way they were falling out with each other demonstrated that there was something fundamentally wrong. Relationships in the church were being destroyed because their relationship with God himself was under threat by their friendship with the world. Their envy, jealousy, quarrelling and fighting were driving him out of the church.

It showed what they really thought about life. Two things were evident: they thought that God could not be trusted and that self must be central. In their view, God could not be trusted because, if they had trusted him, they would not feel the need to fight their own corners in the way they did. They would pray and leave God to sort the issues out. If they had really believed that 'the Father of Heavenly lights' did not change but continued to shower 'good and perfect gifts' on his people[16] then they would neither be anxious, nor envious, nor aggressive. Their lives would be confidently entrusted to his care.

Their friendship with the world also betrayed the fact that they still believed self to be central. Their lives revolved around what brought them immediate pleasure, which was most likely either something in the material or the carnal areas of life. They sought this, regardless of its effect on others, or of what it did to their relationship with God. They were the yardstick by which success in life was to be judged. Their behaviour was, in truth, as clear an illustration of practical atheism as could be found.

We should note that in speaking like this James applies a deeper spiritual analysis to their behaviour than we often do. We are content with the pragmatic approach. 'Let's agree with each other because it will be more comfortable that way.' Or we bring in the conflict managers to enable conciliation to take place using the wisdom of secular management disciplines. Or, to be frank, we often flunk the fact of division altogether hoping that if we ignore it, it will go away. Or, we excuse people because that's just human nature and none of us is perfect. But James will not let us off the hook that easily. These are not pragmatic issues. They are spiritual issues. Ungodly behaviour in the church must be challenged. It can't just be ignored. It demonstrates where our true allegiance lies.

### Friendship with the world: Where it leads

If friendship is above all about loyalty it is impossible to be a friend of the world and of God at the same time. Friendship with the world and with God are simply incompatible because God and the world's approaches to life are diametrically opposed to one another. We have to choose. Hence James' strong language. In ringing Old Testament terms[17] and using language reminiscent of Jesus condemning the unbelieving generation among whom he ministered,[18] he addresses them as 'adulterous people'. Just like Israel they were about to prove disloyal, separate from their faithful husband, and go after another partner who they thought would satisfy them more. They had, as Paul put it, 'been promised to one husband' to be presented 'as a pure virgin' to Christ.[19] But they had chosen to stray. The relationship of love and trust is eroded.

No relationship can sustain itself once the allegiance of one of the partners has changed. Inevitably, therefore, James argues, 'friendship with the world is hatred towards God. Anyone who chooses to be a friend of the world becomes an enemy of God.' It is not, as James Adamson explains, 'because God hates him but because he hates God.'[20] The issue is that serious. Friendship with the world leads to unbelief and apostasy and puts one on the wrong side of God.

In much of this passage James is going to tell us how we can cultivate our friendship with God. But before we explore that there is a third negative, unhealthy relationship to which he alludes. That is, our relationship with the devil.

### 3. Relationships with the devil, 4:7

Here the third member of the evil trinity is introduced into the discussion. 4:1 speaks of the flesh. 4:4 speaks of the world. 4:7 speaks of the devil. He's stitched into this ugly picture of quarrelling behaviour in the church just as much as the flesh and the world are. We cannot account wholly for the quite astonishing unChristlike behaviour of many churches simply in terms of the first two members of this unholy threesome. The flesh plays a part and we cannot abdicate our own responsibility for the arguments and blame it all on the devil. The 'world' is very real and its powers of seduction strong. But the cause of our sinful behaviour is not purely environmental. Aligned with the flesh and the world is the fallen angel, the devil, whose ambition is to trip up the saints and have reason to accuse the members of Christ's church of hypocrisy before their God.[21] His fingerprints are all over the ungodly anarchy which characterises the church of James' day, as well as so much of the church of our own day.

How does James say we should handle him?

*The command we must obey*

James gives us a simple command. We are to 'resist him'. We are neither to play with him, trifle with him, compromise with him, nor even sail close to him. We are to have no truck with him. We need to see him for what he is – a fallen rebellious angel, who wants to seize God's throne and is out to ruin God's world and destroy God's church.[22] We are on active service and are called to repel him in every possible way.

This applies not just to the individual believers, as Satan sows the seeds of doubt in their ears about the truth of what God has said[23] and tempts them to sin,[24] but to the church as a body, a corporate organism, as well. The year 1987 proved curiously frustrating for me and the church I was pastoring at the time. The marriages of some of my colleagues were under extraordinary pressure, the church's activities were constantly being side-tracked and precious energy wasted, our evangelistic outreach was subject to perpetual, if silly, frustrations, and a fight broke out in the church when an argument developed between some folk on the church's fringe and responsible people within the church. The more the picture of frustrating events mounted the more we felt we were being harassed by Satan.

Each situation was examined carefully and steps taken to accept responsibility for our part in what was going wrong and amend our actions accordingly. But we were also conscious of a young woman who attended our services and youth activities who made no secret of the fact that she had pledged herself to the devil and was actively praying to Satan, with others, against the church. Many had faithfully tried to love her and had struggled for a long time to show her the love of Christ. But her resistance to the gospel was palpable and the hours of time and energy she was absorbing were an obvious diversionary tactic of Satan. So, reluctantly and taking due precautions, both in prayer and consultation with the lay leaders of the church to secure their commitment to the stance I was going to take, I explained what was happening to the church and publicly banned her from the premises and all our activities. Acts 13:6-12 and 16:16-18, as well as 1 Corinthians 5:13, give some precedents for such action. We took no steps beyond banning her. We were not into medieval witch-hunts. We were simply concerned to protect our own activities and properties and to guard our right to worship and minister without harassment.

Of course, I was accused of being uncharitable. I was told that others would succeed in winning her for Christ, where those who had striven with her until now had failed, if only I gave her a second (actually it would have been more like a thirty-third) chance. But the leaders of the church held their ground. They were not going to give Satan a foothold in the church. And I can only say that resisting him in this way lifted the cloud from the church and more peaceful and fruitful times of ministry followed.

The choice before us is stark. Thomas Manton expresses it in these words: 'Either you must resist him or be taken captive by him. There is no middle course; you can make no peace with him but to your own harm; to enter into league with Satan is to be overcome: he now tempteth, hereafter he will accuse.' Then he adds, 'to resist him, not to yield to him, is the only way to be rid of him.'[25] We should have the courage to obey the commands of scripture more and 'resist him'.

### The condition we must fulfil

There is, however, a condition of which we should be aware if we are to resist him successfully. We must not arrogantly assume that we possess the power to resist him ourselves. It is the sovereign Lord who alone has the power to defeat him and has done so supremely through the cross. We are unable to resist him in our own strength. If we could we would soon become proud of our own spiritual powers and end up falling in the same way in which Satan himself did in the first place.

James does not give us a full account of spiritual warfare here. Other biblical insights, like the way in which Jesus handled temptation[26] and various teachings of Paul, need to be taken into account for that.[27] But James gives us an important hint about such issues. The context of the command to resist the devil is important. It is prefaced by the command to 'submit yourselves, then, to God.' Resistance without prior submission is bound to fail. The devil is not frightened by us, *per se,* but he is frightened by the believer who is fully devoted to the Lord, who is walking closely with God and who is wearing the spiritual armour which God has provided for our equipment.

### The confidence we may have

Providing that condition is fulfilled you may have every confidence that 'he will flee from you'. The reason why we may be confident lies not so much in his own failures and shortcomings, as some have suggested,[28] but in the fact that he has already been defeated at Calvary. The principalities and authorities of our world, including Satan himself, were there stripped of their status, weapons, dignity and power and held up by Christ, like soldiers defeated by the armies of Rome, to public ridicule.[29]

So, while we must not treat him too lightly, since he has real and continuing power, neither must we be too intimidated by him. Some Christians resort to the most elaborate and extraordinary strategies in the belief that only by doing so will he be defeated. Complex spiritual hierarchies are proposed and intricate techniques and rituals are practised. Much of this goes well beyond what the Bible teaches clearly in this area and delves into the realm of mere speculation. Much of it, too, is due to a failure to understand what Christ achieved on the cross and how it is preaching and living the gospel of Christ crucified that is the means of victory in spiritual warfare. They sometimes take Satan too seriously and credit him with greater power than he has. They speak as if it is our task to defeat him, whereas the truth is he has already been defeated by Christ. All we need to do is appropriate the power which is Christ's and live in the light of his gospel.[30]

As Thomas Manton (again) commented, '... we must not fear him; the devil hath no enforcing power, but only a persuading sleight (cunning). Distrustful fear giveth him the advantage. We must manifest our resistance, partly by refusing to commune with him.'[31] In more contemporary words, he can only exercise a power over us if we who are believers in Christ let him. He often does so by pretending to be more powerful over us than he is and we fall for it. We shouldn't. Instead, we should resist him, confidently.

## 4. Relationships with the Lord, 4:4-10
The key to getting all these other relationships right is to get our relationship with the Lord right. If we are in right relationship with him, walking closely in obedience and enjoying his companionship, then we will not want to be fighting in the fellowship, cozying up to the world or fraternising with the devil. They will all both lose their seductive power and be unmasked for the destructive and evil influences that they are.

*Friendship is intended, verse 4*
Perhaps it is stating the obvious, but the obvious is sometimes worth stating. The implication of verse 4 is that God desires our friendship. His purpose in creating men and women was that they should be the ones, out of all his creation, with whom he could converse. Genesis 3:8-9 hints at what the relationship must have been like before it was spoiled by sin. God walked in the Garden of Eden in the cool of the day to spend time with Adam and Eve. Seven generations later, Enoch epitomized friendship with God. He 'walked with God' 300 years and 'then was no more, because God took him away.'[32] They must have got to know each other very well during that time and enjoyed each other's company to have been companions that long. Enoch must

have been moulded by God during that time and learned to think the way God would think and derive pleasure at the doing of God's will. Such intimate friendship was rare. James speaks of Abraham as 'a friend of God'.[33] Moses spoke to God 'as a man speaks to his friend.'[34] But in Christ, what had been an exceptional experience until his coming was to become the common experience of all believers. He came that we might no longer be merely God's servants, obeying him but without intimately knowing him, but that we might be his friends.[35] The reconciling work of Christ on the cross results not just in an end to hostility between God and us but with a closeness of relationship and enduring friendship which should go on blossoming until we enter finally into his presence.

*Grace is provided, verses 4-6*
Our difficulty is that God is not alone in seeking our friendship. Others, as we have seen, would like to cultivate our friendship too, especially the powers which shape the world, and they are skilled in the art of seduction. What is more they have a powerful ally in their attempt to woo us. The seductive forces of the world conspire with our own fallen natures and, in doing so, render our powers of resistance even weaker. That, I take it, is the meaning of verse 5.

In the original, verse 5 is unclear. The problem arises because it is not obvious whose 'spirit' lives within us. Is it our human spirit or the Holy Spirit? The words flow more satisfactorily if it is a reference to our human spirit. If so, James is pointing once again to the power of intense 'envy' with which we all have to grapple as fallen creatures, which he has already mentioned as characteristic of the folly of the world (3:14-16) and as destructive in the fellowship (4:1). A further reason for taking it this way is that 'envy' (*phthonos*) is not a word which is connected to God anywhere else and since it has negative connotations it seems inappropriate to ascribe it to God's Holy Spirit. Even so, while acknowledging the difficulties, some connect verse 5 not to the verse before – as an explanation of why we find it natural to be friends of the world – but the verse which follows – as an explanation of why we can receive more grace – and see that it is a reference to God's jealousy for his people and his desire to prevent them from being seduced by the world. They argue that this is how

God spoke of himself to Israel[36] and that he is unlikely to be less protective of the affections and interests of the children of the new Israel.[37]

If it is the human spirit which is meant, then James' point is that we find the combined overtures of the world system and our unregenerate natures hard to resist. But there is a strength available to us to help us stand our ground against them. We may not be able to resist but God is able and he 'gives us more grace' as we have need. As the power of the temptations are ratcheted up, so is his grace. It is always equal to our need. Grace is a powerful force. 'It is,' says Philip Yancey, 'the only force in the universe powerful enough to break the chains that enslave generations. Grace alone melts ungrace.'[38] And grace alone can enable us to resist being lured away from our friendship with God and committing adultery with the world.

### Humility is required, verses 7, 10

Our stress on being friends with God contains the danger that we might think of it as a partnership of equals. That, most of the time, is what friendship is. If it isn't, it is more likely to be a relationship of patronage than friendship. But our friendship with God can never be a relationship between equals. To think that it could be would be presumptuous and would destroy it. If we are to cultivate friendship with God we must remember our place. James makes the point in two ways. In verse 7 we are told to 'submit' to God. And in verse 10, we are told to 'humble' ourselves before God. Verse 7 is the heading for what follows. Verse 10 is the summary of what has gone before. What does it mean?

* It means to listen to God, in order that we might know what his will is. That requires stillness, prayerfulness and adopting a habit of reading the Bible.

* It means to bow before God, in heart and attitude, not just in action. It is to inwardly agree with God, adopt his agenda, take his side and seek his glory.

* It means to seek God, rejecting the proud path of self-sufficiency and recognising our constant need of him.

* It means to obey God, putting his commands into action in our lives.

* It means to be used by God rejecting our concerns with self, rather than to use God for our own ends and comfort.

David Wells, in typically robust fashion, criticises contemporary evangelicalism for its view of God. He claims: 'We have turned to a God that we can use rather than a God we must obey; we have turned to a God who will fulfil our needs rather than to a God before whom we must surrender our rights to be ourselves. He is God *for* us – for our satisfaction...'[39] If so, God has few friends in the contemporary church, for there can be no friendship with God apart from humble submission.

### Integrity is essential, verse 8

James returns to his favourite theme in describing the next aspect of how to foster our friendship with God. To do so, integrity is needed, through and through. Three parts of us are pressed into service as he explains what he means. He refers to our hands, our hearts and our minds. Our hands need to be clean. Our hearts need to be pure. Our minds need to be single. Our hands symbolise our outward actions. We cannot use our hands to make shady deals, to retaliate aggressively, to behave immorally, or shake hands with the world if we want to be friends with God. Our hearts symbolise our inner attitudes. Some of us are clever actors. We manage to control our outward behaviour whilst continuing to sin inwardly. People think we're saints because we never do anything wrong. But our hearts may be far from God. Our minds symbolise our wills, our intentions and ambitions. Here we need to rid ourselves of any trace of double-mindedness. To be in two minds about being a friend of God is to ensure that we shall never be his true friend.

Integrity, then, needs to be evident throughout our lives, in behaviour and attitudes, in actions and thoughts, in public and private, in the external and in the internal aspects of life.

*Reverence is imperative, verse 9*

Just when you think James is getting near to allowing us to enjoy friendship with God, he fires another gloomy bombshell into the discussion. Sounding like a grumpy Old Testament prophet he thunders out that we should 'Grieve, mourn and wail. Change your laughter into mourning and your joy into gloom.' Why so?

James has grasped what few of us have these days, namely, the awesome holiness of God and the awful depravity of sin. Our temptation is to pass too quickly from his invitation, in verse 8, to seek cleansing from God into enjoying a renewed relationship with God as our friend. A cursory self-examination, a quick moment of confession, a short announcement of absolution and we think everything is fine. 'Of course God will forgive us. That's his business.' At least, that's what we think deep down. But that's cheap grace. It is why few of us really experience the grace of God in all its richness. To experience the grace of God truly means to linger over self-examination and genuinely sense how unworthy we are. It is to mourn over sin and grieve that it is so inimical to our relationship with God and so offensive to his person. It is to seek forgiveness without presumption. True repentance involves genuine sorrow for sin.

David Wells has put his finger on the failing of the contemporary church in this regard once again. He writes:

> The fundamental problem in the evangelical world today is not inadequate technique, insufficient organisation, or inadequate music, and those who want to squander the church's resources on bandaging these scratches will do nothing to staunch the flow of blood that is spilling from its wounds. The fundamental problem in the evangelical world today is that God rests too inconsequentially upon the church. His truth is too distant, his grace is too benign, his gospel is too easy and his Christ is too common.[40]

Short-cuts to friendship with God will fail. They will leave us searching for what we have not found, famished and undernourished in our relationship. The only way to friendship with God is to let God be God.

Friends have a powerful impact on the way we live. Peer pressure on the child at school exerts a powerful influence on the clothes they wear, the language they speak and the habits they adopt, often to the horror of their parents who wonder who this stranger is who has come to live among them. Emerging teenage friendships exercise a powerful influence over those who fall in love. The telephone bill goes up, the bathroom is suddenly occupied for an interminable time and the teenager always appears to be somewhere else but home. When friendship turns into committed marriage the consequences are even more transforming. The child moves out of the home and accepts responsibility for their own decisions and bills from then on (theoretically!). Friendships shape us.

Spiritually we have the choice of being a friend of the world or a friend of God. Be careful who you choose as a friend, for the consequence of the choice will be massive. And, like the two poles of a magnet, they are mutually opposed to each other. You cannot be a friend of both.

# 9

# Tomorrow and How to Face It
## (4:13-16)

**1. The attitude James opposes** 4:13

- Arrogant presumption
- Misguided priorities

**2. The folly James exposes** 4:14

- Our ignorance
- Our fragility

**3. The wisdom James proposes** 4:15-16

- The will of the Lord and our speech
- The will of the Lord and our decision-making
- The will of the Lord and our attitude

It was just another Tuesday morning. Young financial executives, aged 33, would have woken up to 1716 of them in their lives. As they made their way to work that morning, not one would have expected anything different. But the date was Tuesday 11th September, 2001. It was the day which changed America.

Claudia Robichaud, who worked for Marsh and MacLennan, had gone into work in the World Trade Center in New York early. In spite of that putting her in a bad mood, she recalled, 'it was a beautiful morning, really sunny and clear.' The early start meant she stepped out to get some breakfast. It was then she heard an explosion, looked up and saw the result of the two planes flying into the twin towers. The London *Times* quoted her as saying, 'It's too early to make sense of it all. It seems so incredibly strange. This morning I was sitting at my desk talking with my colleagues, drinking coffee, but now there's nothing there: no office, no work, no company – it's all gone forever.'[1]

At 8.47 a.m., the clocks stopped, the meetings halted, the panic spread, the priorities changed and thousands were blasted into eternity.

James might well have said that he tried to warn us. Centuries before, he had written, 'Why, you do not even know what will happen tomorrow. What is your life? You are a mist that appears for a little while and then vanishes.'

We know he is right, in theory. But it often takes a personal jolt to convince us that it is more than theory. His words are etched deep into my memory because of one such jolt. My wife was expecting our first (and only) child. She was in hospital experiencing a difficult pregnancy when one Friday morning, while I and my close colleagues in the denomination's national office where I was then working were having our weekly prayer time together, we were interrupted. It was our custom to follow a set Bible reading plan and the reading that morning was these verses from James. No sooner had the words got out of my colleague's mouth than the telephone rang and one of our secretaries apologetically called for me to come to the phone. It was the hospital. Could I go immediately? My wife was losing the child and she needed me to be there. In fact, when I got there, they told me the child was likely to be born alive within the next couple of hours, but because he was so extremely premature I would soon need to take a decision and instruct them as to whether I wanted them to try to preserve his life or not. The quality of life, they said, would be highly questionable. In the goodness of God, and due to the skill of the doctors, the child remained in the womb until he was born, still very premature, but healthy. For the next eight weeks, though, everything went on hold. Life was lived in suspended animation. We really never did know what a day would bring forth. I have good reason to know from personal experience, as do so many other people, that James is talking sense.

In this section of his letter James introduces three illustrations of human arrogance. He has called his readers to humility before God (4:10). Lest they should fail to grasp his meaning he follows his call up by giving three illustrations of the way we demonstrate conceit in our lives. We do so by self-righteously slandering others (4:11-12); by self-confidently forecasting our futures (4:13-17) and by self-contentedly exploiting the poor (5:1-6). It is the second of these we now explore.

His teaching about the uncertainty of tomorrow may be brief but it is no mere cliché soundbite. It has depth to it and is full of spiritual wisdom. There are three facets to it. There is something he opposes, something he exposes and something he proposes.

## 1. The attitude James opposes, 4:13

The people who exhibit this particular form of arrogance seem to be merchants who travel from city to city doing business. They may well be in the circle of rich people who are causing grief to the poorer believers about whom James is so concerned. But even so his strictures are not limited to them. There are two aspects of their mindset which he opposes. First, he opposes their arrogant presumption and, secondly, he opposes their misguided priorities.

### *Arrogant presumption*

With total confidence they announce, 'Today or tomorrow we will go to this or that city, spend a year there, carry on business and make money.' They show not the slightest flicker of doubt about their ability to chart the course of their own lives, not just in the short term but for the next year or so. Life is all planned out. Their career is mapped out in front of them and the cartography is of their own making. They're the ones in charge, or so they think. It makes good sense, they'd argue, to plan the future rather than just drift into it. That's what makes a good businessman. Efficiency, forward projections, new targets, reaching fresh goals, forever moving forward – that's the name of the game. They're self-important people. They're self-sufficient people. That's why they're successful. It is why they've got on in the world and why they're are not stuck in some pokey parochial hole like their less ambitious relatives. They have wide horizons and they can shape their futures.

While we can recognize and laugh at the 'yuppies' who openly brag about their tomorrows in exactly these kind of words we need to concede that you don't have to be a 'yuppie' to fall into precisely the same false mindset. Alec Motyer points out that the terrifying thing about the boastful attitude to which James is objecting is that, 'it is all so ordinary'. It seems so natural to speak in these terms. His conclusion is that 'when James exposes the blemish of presumptuousness, he expresses something which is the unrecognized claim of *our* hearts from time to time.'[2] Our plans may be less ambitious, our goals more mundane, but our confidence that tomorrow belongs to us is just the same.

### Misguided priorities

The second factor which worries James in this sentiment is just as significant: it is what it reveals about their misguided priorities. Not only do they ill-advisedly feel that they control the future but the purpose to which they put the future is also highly questionable. They see the primary objective of their lives as making money. To create wealth may well be a legitimate activity before God, given certain qualifications, as we discussed in chapter 3. But James is no lover of the rich because those important qualifications were studiously ignored by the rich he had to contend with. Their money was being made by oppressing the poor and then being spent on lives of obscene self-indulgence. And that was wrong.

As so often in this letter, one wonders if the words of Jesus were ringing in James' ears. In Luke 12:13-21, Jesus tells the parable of the rich fool. His harvests had been abundantly successful and served him well. His solution was to build bigger barns to store his grain. One might think he was making a sensible business decision. Was expansion not an obvious necessity? What else was he to do? To do nothing would be to waste wonderful resources. The opportunity needed to be seized. Why, then, does God call this man a 'fool'? Because his wealth led him wrongly to assume he could control his future. He said to himself, 'You have good things laid up for many years.' How did he know he had 'many years' left? His wealth had seduced him into spiritual lethargy as his soliloquy, 'take life easy; eat drink and be merry' demonstrates. But he was ignoring one important fact. He was not in control of his future. God was. God therefore had the right to say to him the words that took him by surprise: 'This very night your life will be demanded from you'. Significantly God added, 'then you will get what you have prepared for yourself.' His priority in this life had been to make money. But money was not the currency that mattered in the life to come. After death he would find his investments were worthless. If he had really been wise and taken the really long-term view, there were other priorities in which he should have been investing all along. Only then would his eternal destiny have been secure.

The merchants whom James has in mind had clearly never heard the parable or, if they had, registered its meaning. Our lives hang by a thread. They are not ours to control. We do not know the day of our departure. We dare not assume that we will have 'many years' left to prepare ourselves for the time when we will stand before God. The only truly sensible course is to live now and to live every day with the right priorities, the priorities which will serve as a good investment for eternity.

The summer of 2001 will never be forgotten by me and my colleagues at London Bible College. We will remember it not just because of 11th September when the twin towers – the arch symbols of the money-making machine of Western capitalism – were suddenly and unexpectedly destroyed; which in itself is a desperately sad but powerful demonstration of James' teaching. We had other reasons for remembering it too. That same summer, just a few weeks earlier than that fatal day, a former student on his way to work in the City was involved in a traffic accident and seriously injured. He was thought to have sustained permanent injuries and brain damage. In the goodness of God, though still far from completely healed, he has made a better recovery than anticipated. A few weeks later another former student, who had only that summer been awarded his Ph.D., drowned on holiday while swimming with his son. For many years he had been a missionary in South America and was just about to throw himself into a new and significant work at a missionary training college in England. One worked in finance, the other in mission. Both lives abruptly took totally unexpected turns. But both were ready for eternity because the one who worked in the City, no less than the one who had worked on the mission field, had heeded the warning of the rich fool and had his priorities right before God. Both had shaken off spiritual apathy and both were investing for the kingdom. You can be rich and still build up spiritual capital, though Jesus warned it was hard.[3] It all depends on priorities.

## 2. The folly James exposes, 4:14

The presumptuous arrogance and misguided priorities he denounces are not only wrong but stupid as well. James gives us two reasons why it is absurd to live by them. First, there is our ignorance. Secondly, there is our fragility.

*Our ignorance*

Far from being able to plan the coming year, or the development of our long careers, the reality is 'we do not know what will happen tomorrow.' Our ability to see the future is as short as the present moment. Yesterday, as the saying goes, is a spent cheque. Tomorrow is only a promissory note. All we can be sure of is now. We may confidently boast of what our futures hold, and others may be taken in by it, but the truth is that what we parade as sophisticated knowledge cloaks massive ignorance. The fact is, we just don't know what tomorrow holds.

Even the experts haven't a clue. Governments throw millions of pounds into research and statistics to inform them of the future only to discover, when the future arrives, how inaccurate those forecasts are. Totally unexpected events on the international scene can throw the best-made plans of stable democracies into chaos. Bryan Wilson, the doyen of sociologists of religion in Britain, confessed recently at a conference that sociologists had a deplorable track-record in predicting the future. They missed totally, he lamented, the moral and social revolution that swept Britain in the sixties. Other 'experts' have been equally mistaken: from the Astronomer Royal who declared that space travel was 'utter bilge' not long before it happened, to Margaret Thatcher who famously said, 'No woman in my time will be Prime Minister or Chancellor or Foreign Secretary – not the top jobs.' Ten years later she became Prime Minister. If the experts can't predict tomorrow with any accuracy, what hope is there for us?

Recognizing our ignorance about the future need not paralyse us into irresponsible inactivity, as it has some. On the basis of this teaching some have failed to plan and refused to take sensible decisions with regard to the days ahead. They will neither invest in education to prepare themselves for good employment, nor take necessary financial decisions to provide adequately for their families when they die. Such short-sightedness, however, is to miss the point. Planning is positively commended elsewhere in the Bible. Proverbs, for example, pours scorn on the lazy person who doesn't anticipate the need to plough his field and sow his seed in the autumn and so looks in vain for a harvest which doesn't exist in the spring.[4] A little forward planning would have avoided that embarrassing situation. Planning is both sensible and laudable. The issue is the spirit in which the planning is done. Proverbs is as alert to this, as is James for whom it is the central point.[5] Make your plans by all means. But do so with humility and fully aware that whether those plans come to fruition or not depends totally on God. In the words of Proverbs, 'Many are the plans in a human heart, but it is the Lord's purpose that prevails.'[6]

This accent on the uncertainty of life used to be the hallmark of evangelical preaching. Life was uncertain and at any moment, for a whole variety of reasons, it might end. It was therefore urgent that people got right with God and walked in constant harmony with him. Like many others I suppose, as a youngster I reacted with some degree of cynicism to such claims, forgetting that for those who had lived through the recent war the claim would have been all too real. But in my experience on the whole, people did not come to unexpected and premature ends. Now, of course, with the greater experience of age I see it very differently. The sudden plane crash, the unplanned road accident, the unforeseen disaster at sea, the uncontrolled collapse of a building, the unknown illness which suddenly strikes, the random freak of nature, innocently being caught in the web of other people's violent conflict, being in the wrong place at the wrong time, and life can be abruptly cut short. The television news records it all the time. But the truth is more personal than that. The truth is that I have known personally so many people who did not know what would happen tomorrow. If they had they would have handled life differently. As a pastor, I have grieved with too many families, buried too many friends, and been taken by surprise too often to dismiss James' words as one of those things that pious preachers might be expected to say. His words are for real.

We have to admit that our knowledge is so extremely limited that it is foolish to pretend we know anything with certainty about our futures. The best futurologists and statisticians who use their calculations to predict what will happen next consistently get it wrong. Those who should know have a lamentable track record in forecasting the future. So who are we to be confident we can be sure of tomorrow? Why do we keep up the pretence and speak with such conceit? It is a self-deception we can ill-afford.

### Our fragility

Our ignorance is compounded by our fragility. In case we are tempted to think that such things always happen to other people but not us, James bears down upon us and asks us to consider how secure our own lives are. His conclusion is that we are 'a mist that appears for a little while and then vanishes.' Like the mist at sea in the early morning we've disappeared completely before coffee time – at the most a passing blip in the great sweep of history. Life is 'transient, short-lived and insecure'.[7]

The Bible makes the point over and over again, pressing first one and then another image into service to do so. Life is as momentary as a breath,[8] as temporary as a cloud,[9] as fleeting as an evening shadow,[10] and as impermanent as the grass or as a beautiful flower.[11] The picture of the short-lived flower is one which James has already used in his letter, in 1:10-11, when commenting on the fate of the rich. But here it is the destiny of all who are in mind. Rich and poor alike share the fragility of their common humanity.

The Psalmist said our bodies have been fearfully and wonderfully fashioned.[12] He was right. When we think of the wonder and complexity of our bodies we readily acknowledge the magnificent achievement of our creator. It takes years for human beings to begin to copy small parts of them and engineer replacements which are not half as good as what God imagined and created in the first place. But with that insight we can also begin to see part of the problem. Our bodies are such complex systems that many things can go wrong with them. Our bodies are such delicate systems that, in spite of their robust capacity to recover after illness, they can easily run into difficulty. Our bodies are such degenerative systems that even if we survive into old age they will wear out sooner or later. Built-in obsolescence was true of our bodies before it was true of our cars and our washing machines. No one has yet discovered the secret of eternal youth. Our bodies are such contingent systems that we depend totally on God's daily grace to continue our existence.[13] We are fragile.

Our ignorance and our fragility should breed a genuine humility within us that stops our boasting about tomorrow.

In the light of such truths, how should we live?

## 3. The wisdom James proposes, 4:15-16

James suggests a way of handling the future which is both wiser and more realistic. The self-important folly which many exhibit should be replaced in the lives of believers by a conscious awareness that our lives are in God's hands.

*The will of the Lord and our speech*

First, he suggests we need to cultivate this conscious awareness of God by adopting the right language and speaking often of 'the will of the Lord'. So, James recommends that we should preface announcements of our future plans by saying, 'If it is the Lord's will, we will live and do this or that.' To speak like this regularly will serve to remind us of the one who is really in control of our lives and of our own limited powers to manage our futures.

The question arises: are we really to speak like this? Does he really expect us to go around saying it every time we say to someone,

'I'll meet you for coffee tomorrow morning?' Is he really saying we should verbalise our dependence on God every time we speak of our futures?

Calvin, no doubt speaking for many others, thought not. He argued that it was not repeating the formula that mattered but fixing the principle which was James' concern.[14] I have a certain sympathy for this view. For years in the church where I grew up I endured an elder adding the words *Deo volente* (Latin for 'God willing') to the notices. The sad fact was that one suspected that the programme he announced probably would happen regardless of whether it really was the will of the Lord or not! The phrase can become a meaningless formula, glibly spoken, something akin to a superstition. Even so, I do not think we should be so hasty in dismissing the value of actually saying the words, at least more often than we are generally accustomed to doing these days. Let me explain.

Language is a vital component in the way we make sense of the world. It helps us to describe the reality we experience, to organise it into some sort of wider framework and converse with others about it. Language is an essential to our sharing the objective world with others. But language does more than that. It also has an impact on what we subjectively experience. Its power extends to shaping the way we see things. Language can either undermine or reinforce the meaning we give to our experience.[15] So, to use a commonly mentioned example, in Britain we only have one word for snow because it is not a great part of our experience. One word is sufficient. We have a good laugh when we are told by those running our railways that the trains are late because 'the wrong kind of snow' has fallen on the tracks and caused delay. To us, it is simple. Snow is snow. But the Inuit have many different words for snow. Snow is a much greater part of their experience so they have a much richer vocabulary to describe it. But their richer vocabulary not only helps them describe what they see but actually to see the snow with eyes altogether more finely tuned than those of the average inhabitant of Britain. Their vocabulary not only describes the world they see but also helps them to see it with different eyes than those of others backgrounds.

The Bible knows the importance of language if a faith-filled interpretation of the world is to be maintained. The annual Passover meal was an important time for every Jewish family when the story of Israel's deliverance from slavery in Egypt was told year after year. Fathers were instructed to tell their children the meaning of the meal. Children were encouraged to interrogate their fathers as to its meaning and to expect a full and verbalised answer in reply.[16] Similarly, the Psalmists were consistently encouraging Israel to tell the story, to express their praise, to pass it on from one generation to another, and proclaim God's goodness among the nations.[17] Typical is the command to 'Tell among the nations, the Lord reigns.' It was vitally important to them that the story be articulated and not just taken for granted. Failure to say it in words would mean that sooner or later their whole identity would be lost, the reality of who God was and what God had done would be forgotten. Then other realities, which were much spoken about, would displace him.

We are, I believe, in danger as Christians if we resort to taking some Christian truths for granted and not expressing them. There is a danger in speaking only in matter-of-fact, ordinary, even secular ways which leave the living God out of vocabulary. What we take for granted today we forget altogether tomorrow. The less we say grace before a meal, for example, the less we will remind ourselves that our food is provided by God and the more we will come to think that it is really provided by the supermarket. Of course, the moment we stop to think about it we know that God is our provider. But that's the point. Unless we say it, we're not likely to stop and think about it.

So it is with regard to our future. The less we say, 'If the Lord wills...' the more we will come to assume that our lives are ours to fix and plan. The more we say, 'I have decided...', 'I plan...' 'My intentions are...'; or, more impersonally, 'It worked out like that...'; or, even worse, 'Fate decreed', then the more we exclude God from our mindset until he drops out of the picture altogether. The language we speak simultaneously reflects and shapes our worldview. If we don't say it perhaps we don't believe it. If we don't say it perhaps although we might believe it today, we won't believe tomorrow.

Thomas Manton argued that we should say the words for two reasons. First, because such explicit expression of God's providence was good for us; and secondly, because we find frequent examples of it in the writings of Paul who should serve as our model.[18] If the early Christians did it, there is probably a good reason why we should do it too. Manton's insights are not to be lightly set aside. We may think that we make the decisions and that the future lies in our hands but our lives are in truth being steered, all unseen, by the great shepherd of our souls. He guides, he provides, he protects. To speak, then, explicitly of 'the will of God' is a testimony to the providence of God, a providence which cannot be defeated and ought not to be neglected.[19] All that we do depends on his divine will and we need regularly to remind ourselves that it is so.

### The will of the Lord and our decision-making

There is another aspect to saying 'if it is the Lord's will'. Not only does it remind us of our dependence on God but it makes us conscious of whether or not what we are proposing to do is in conformity with the will of the Lord. It is certainly possible that the phrase can become a meaningless ritual. But it is more likely that speaking of the Lord in this way will make us question how closely our lives are achieving God's intention for them.

In the Bible, God's will primarily refers either to his sovereign will or his moral will.[20] His sovereign will is always accomplished. His moral will determines the paths in which he wants us to walk. So, to do God's will is essentially to obey his law. This means living both in our relationships with others and in our own personal characters in conformity with what he has revealed to be his plan for us. Psalm 40:8, for example, puts it very clearly. 'I desire to do your will, O my God; your law is within my heart.' A string of Bible verses, such as Psalm 143:10, Isaiah 30:21, Matthew 6:10, Mark 3:35, Ephesians 5:17, Colossians 1:9 and 1 Thessalonians 4:3, confirms this picture. So, the will of God in the minds of the biblical writers is not first and foremost about whether they were to wear red or green socks that morning (which is to trivialise guidance) but whether they would choose to live a righteous life (with all that is wrapped up in that expression) before God that day.

Living a righteous life before God will, in fact, result in some very practical decisions regarding day-to-day guidance. Take the following examples. God made us to work in his world. To work is to participate in worship of him, not to endure something until we can escape it at the earliest moment to go and sing praise songs in church. Since work was part of God's original creation design for us, we should not lounge around in bed all day, nor indolently fritter away the hours doing nothing. God is a God of righteousness. We cannot therefore engage in dishonest activity, tell lies to sell products, or do business which will harm others. God is a God with a heart for the less privileged. We should therefore shun any job which requires us to exploit the weak and the vulnerable. God is a God of purity. We cannot therefore earn our living by participating in the sex trade. Being conscious of the will of God limits our choices and begins to give us directional guidance regarding what business we engage in and decisions to take.

If we take God out of our vocabulary, we may well end up taking him out of our decision-making. If we do that, our decisions will be less well-grounded and may well end up being less worthy of him.

*The will of the Lord and our attitude*

More fundamental than the words we say, but not unconnected, is the question of the attitude we hold. James ends this paragraph in his letter by returning to the way people actually behave in church, rather than the way they should behave. As he observes the way they conduct their lives he sees them to be full of arrogance and egotism. The truth is that his readers omit any reference to the will of God not because they don't want to be seen to mouth some empty pious claptrap. The truth is that they don't say these words because they don't really believe them. Their vanity shows through. They really believe they are in charge of their lives and their futures and that they have the right to determine what they will do tomorrow. And, assuming they're like many people we know in the church today, their language probably suffers from a great deal of inflation to boot. They probably claim they are going to achieve all sorts of things which everyone knows is sheer fantasy. They probably won't deliver on half the boasts they make. Then they will be unmasked as the fools they really are.

James' concern, however, is not to save them from embarrassment. Far from wanting to spare their blushes, their words should cause their cheeks to turn a bright day-glo red. James' concern is not that their words are misguided or immature. His concern is that their words are 'evil'. To boast in this way means that they are putting themselves centre stage and therefore casting God out of the central place he alone should occupy in our lives. Such self-centredness is the essence of sin.[21] Their worldview really squeezes God out. It reveals whose friend they really are and they are not friends of God. That's why it is evil. Such talk reveals the speaker to be a functional atheist.[22] It's not just unwise. It's sinful.

Professor Tasker's conclusion on the matter is, I believe, still apt half a century after he penned it. Admitting the danger of the words becoming an empty ritual he wrote:

> For the most part, however, Christians today do not give sufficient expression to this sense of man's utter dependence upon the will of the transcendent God; and they might profitably ask themselves whether their refusal to say 'God willing' is really due to a horror of hypocrisy or to a failure to acknowledge the supremacy of God.[23]

For James the key issue is the integrity of our hearts. Do we really believe, through and through, that we are totally dependent on God and that God is in control of our lives and that they are safe, left in his capable hands? If so, there is no room for pride. Rather, we should show humility and shun every trace of arrogance. We should recognize ourselves for the small creatures we are before the awesome majesty of our creator God. We should know that humility here and now means that we will be exalted in his presence in the future.

Mentioning God's will in conversation is no guarantee that our attitude will be right. But it is more likely to encourage us to think aright than if we never mention it at all.

In our English Bibles chapter 4 ends with another verse (verse 17) which appears to be at best only a loosely attached appendix. After a clear and tightly-knit argument James adds, 'So, then, if you know the good you ought to do and don't do it, you sin.' In fact, it is not as disconnected a comment as it seems. James has already spoken at length of the danger of listening to the word of God but not doing it.[24] Here he echoes this earlier warning.

As a wise pastor he knows that there would be plenty of people in the congregation who would applaud his words warmly, tell him what a great preacher he was, heap praise on his wisdom, and then do nothing about what he has said. I remember Bill Hybels once telling the story of preaching on fidelity in marriage one Sunday morning. On his way home his mobile phone rang. It was a member of his congregation who congratulated him fulsomely on the sermon he had just preached and then told him that he was going to break up from his wife. Apparently he had not made the connection! Nor sometimes do we. 'Yes, James, that was a brilliant sermon on facing the future. And by the way, have I told you my plans ...?' To hear God's word and then fail to live by it is to sin. One sin compounds another. To the sin of boasting we now add the sin of omission and that, put in other words, is the sin of disobedience.

No wonder James wants to warn us urgently about the judgement we face.

How, then, should we face the future? We need not face it apprehensively, nor fearfully. We should not face it indifferently, nor apathetically. Above all, we dare not face it arrogantly, nor self-confidently. Instead we must face it humbly, trusting in God. If we do we can face it as a wonderful adventure, conscious that though it may be full of surprises, some of which we might not have chosen for ourselves, God knows best.

> How good is the God we adore!
> Our faithful, unchangeable friend:
> His love is as great as his power
> and knows neither measure nor end.
>
> For Christ is the first and the last;
> His Spirit will guide us safe home:
> we'll praise him for all that is past
> and trust him for all that's to come.[25]

# 10

# Prayer and How to Use It
## (5:13-20)

**1. The inclusive nature of prayer,** 5:13

♦ In times of pressure
♦ In times of pleasure

**2. The healing potential of prayer,** 5:14-16

♦ The role of the elders
♦ The role of every member

**3. The spiritual dynamic of prayer,** 5:14-16

♦ Anointing
♦ Faith
♦ Confession
♦ Righteousness

**4. A biblical model of prayer,** 5:17-18

♦ The humanity of Elijah
♦ The fervency of Elijah
♦ The effectiveness of Elijah

**5. The practical outworking of prayer,** 5:19-20

According to a well-circulated piece on the Internet[1] our experience of prayer in the day of 'voice mail' is probably something like this.

When you pray, this is what you might hear:

Thank you for calling my Father's house.
Please select one of the following four options...
Press 1 for requests
Press 2 for thanksgiving
Press 3 for complaints
Press 4 for all other enquiries

In response you might hear the following message:

All the angels are helping other callers right now.
Please stay on the line.
Your prayer will be answered in the order in which it was received.

Having stayed on the line, you then might hear:

In you want to speak to:
Gabriel, press 1
Michael, press 2
For all other angels, press 3.
In you would like King David to sing a Psalm for you, press 4.
To find out if a loved one has been assigned to Heaven, enter his or her NHS number.
For all reservations in my Father's house, press the letters J O H N followed by the number 3 1 6.
For all answers to nagging questions outside the instruction book (e.g., about dinosaurs; the age of the earth; creation; where Noah's Ark is, etc. etc.) wait till you get here.
Our computers show that you have called once already today; please hang up immediately.
The office is closed for the weekend, because the Principal is busy in His house. Please call again on Monday after 9.00 am.

James' teaching on prayer is mercifully somewhat different! How glad we should be that God is personal. He does not respond to us as a disembodied voice, constrained by the limits of a pre-programmed machine. He hears exactly what we say, meets us where we are and responds to us according to his grace. That's the essence of this final section of James. Many read it as a manual for a healing ministry. But to do so is to extract the one part which refers to healing from a wider discussion of prayer and consequently gain a distorted picture of what James is teaching. These verses cover many different aspects of our prayer life.[2]

## 1. The inclusive nature of prayer, 5:13

Prayer is not to be reserved for special occasions, and even less for those occasions where we are up against it and, unable to cope ourselves, feel the need to cry out to God. It is to cover the whole spectrum of life, from its most positive experiences to its most negative aspects, and to include the humdrum and mundane affairs of life *en route*. James tersely identifies the two extremes:

*In times of pressure, verse 13*
'Is anyone of you in trouble? You should pray?' Trouble is an all-embracing word for being in difficulty. Paul used it, for instance, to describe his imprisonment. James' letter has been concerned with a number of problems which his readers face including injustice, poverty, broken relationships within the fellowship, the uncertainty of life and sickness. They are all swept up by the word 'trouble'. Whatever the difficulty we should resort to prayer.

In Philippians 4:6-7 Paul expands this thought and presents prayer as the antidote to worry. 'Do not be anxious about anything, but in everything, by prayer and petition, with thanksgiving, present your requests to God. And the peace of God, which transcends all understanding, will guard your hearts and your minds in Christ Jesus.' Paul says, 'Why worry when you can pray?' Contemporary Christians are just as likely to say, 'Why pray when you can worry?' Prayer is one of the greatest untapped resources available to Christian believers today. We tend to make it a last resort – when all else has failed – rather than the first port of call, as God intends. He longs for his children to 'cast all their anxiety on him because he cares for them.'[3] But somehow we don't want to bother him, or don't believe he will be able to do anything about our predicaments.

Sophisticated modern Christians tend to think that Joseph Scriven's hymn is too simplistic and sentimental to be sung these days. His simple-hearted hymn was born of experience. Scriven (1819-1886) had lost his fiancée in a drowning accident at the age of 25. Years later he penned these words as a consolation to his mother on the death of his father. We are the poorer for not singing it, and even more poor for not believing its truth.

> What a friend we have in Jesus,
> all our sins and griefs to bear!
> What a privilege to carry
> everything to God in prayer!
> O what peace we often forfeit,
> O what needless pain we bear –
> all because we do not carry
> everything to God in prayer!
>
> Have we trials and temptations?
> Is there trouble anywhere?
> We should never be discouraged:
> take it to the Lord in prayer!
> Can we find a friend so faithful,
> who will all our sorrow share?
> Jesus knows our every weakness –
> take it to the Lord in prayer!
>
> Are we weak and heavy-laden,
> cumbered with a load of care?
> Precious Saviour still our refuge,
> take it to the Lord in prayer!
> Do thy friends despise, forsake thee?
> Take it to the Lord in prayer!
> In his arms He'll take and shield thee,
> thou wilt find a solace there.

The truth expressed here has been a life-saver to me, and to countless other believers down the centuries.

*In times of pleasure, verse 13*

Some find it relatively easy to cry out to God when trouble surrounds them and threatens to engulf them but are soon tempted to forget him when he answers their plea. But God is to be involved in the pleasures of our lives as much as its pressures. 'Is anyone happy?', asks James. Then, they too should engage in prayer by giving thanks and singing songs of praise. Though 'happy' strictly refers to 'inner cheerfulness', a contented and satisfied inner spirit, it may be taken as a symbol for all the positive experiences of life: the joyful family occasions, the birth of children and grandchildren, the exam passes, the promotions at work, the achievements we accomplish. These are to be celebrated not simply on a horizontal level with one another but in the presence of God as well by singing songs of praise or, to translate James' word more literally, 'psalming'!

To express praise in prayer like this accomplishes a number of things. First, it stops us from treating God as if he is only a heavenly breakdown service to be called in to rescue us when things go wrong. It treats God properly since all the good things we enjoy in life come from him.[4] Secondly, it prevents us from becoming arrogant. It reminds us that all that we have and all that we might achieve is due to his grace and not the result of our own powers. So, praise keeps us humble. Moses warned the children of Israel that when they settled in the land of Canaan they would have to be very careful not to assume that the prosperity they enjoyed was the result of their own work and forget God. The spiritual amnesia which leads to days void of thanksgiving is both tragic and hazardous. It will not go unobserved by the Lord.[5] Thirdly, the expression of praise enriches the positive experiences of our lives still more. C. S. Lewis in his *Reflections on the Psalms* posed the question of whether God was not just on an ego-trip in commanding us to praise him. As he grappled with the issue he came to a new understanding of the value of praise.

> I had never noticed that all enjoyment spontaneously overflows into praise unless (sometimes even if) shyness or the fear of boring others is deliberately brought in to check it. The world rings with praise – lovers praising their mistresses, readers their favourite poet, walkers their favourite game – praise of weather, wines, dishes, actors, motors, horses, colleges, countries, historical personages, children,

flowers, mountains, rare stamps, rare beetles, even sometimes politicians or scholars. I had not noticed how the humblest, and at the same time the most balanced and capacious, minds, praised most, while the cranks, malcontents and misfits praised least. ... I had not noticed either that just as men spontaneously praise whatever they value, so they spontaneously urge us to join them in praising it: 'Isn't she lovely? Wasn't it glorious? Don't you think that magnificent?' The Psalmists in telling everyone to praise God are doing what men do when they speak of what they care about.

Then he adds, 'I think we delight to praise what we enjoy because the praise not merely expresses but completes the enjoyment; it is its appointed consummation.'[6]

Our God truly is a 'God for every circumstance'.[7] Prayer connects us to him just as the correct cable helps to connect our laptops to the mega-resources of the World Wide Web. There we find something for every possible question. In God, the Creator of the cosmos, the one who knows all the intricacies of the World Wide Web and who knows far more than we'll ever discover on the Internet, we find one who is interested in us and, like a Father, one who delights in our talking with him and listening to both our sorrows and our joys.

## 2. The healing potential of prayer, 5:14-16

From prayer and trouble in general James turns to one particular form of prayer and one particular form of trouble. He deals next with prayer in relation to healing. He treats us to the most extended teaching about a healing ministry in the local church to be found anywhere in the New Testament. Jesus, of course, practised healing as a sign of the inbreaking of his kingdom but gave no instruction manual to his disciples as to how they were to practise it.[8] Paul mentions healing as a gift of the Spirit but nowhere does he elaborate his understanding of it.[9] He seems content to accept that illness is part of the Christian's experience without demanding that healing should always or immediately take place.[10] It is left to James, then, to set the ministry of healing within the context of the local church. In doing so he speaks of the role of the leaders in the church and the role that every member can play. While his teaching does not rule out the ministry of healing taking place away from home or through itinerant preachers and spiritually gifted healers, the things he says should make us wonder whether such a ministry is not best carried on in the local fellowship. It is difficult to envisage how the holistic nature of the ministry he advocates can adequately be achieved outside of ongoing relationships in the local church.

### The role of elders, verses 14-15

In these tightly packed verses several features of praying for the sick stand out. First, such prayer should be *requested.* 'Is any one of you sick? *Call* the elders of the church to pray ...' Every pastor is familiar with the situation in which a member of the church goes into hospital insisting to her friends that the pastor is not to be told and then complains that the pastor never came to visit! Pastors are assumed to have supernatural words of knowledge about the circumstances of every member of their church. A call, informing the pastor, might be helpful. But that is not, I think, what James has in mind here. More likely he is encouraging the leaders of the church to behave with wisdom and pastoral sensitivity. Ministry to the sick is not to be foisted on people whether they want it or not. Enthusiastic but inexperienced church leaders have caused untold damage to people spiritually, especially in this area of healing, by intruding where they were not invited and promising in Christ's name all sorts that they should not have pledged. Counsellors are very familiar with the common wisdom that lies behind this advice. If someone is to find healing for their problems, they must first want to be made well. That is why counsellors look for some initiative on the part of their clients (like ringing up to book an appointment) before they will make any moves towards them. It reminds one of the question Jesus posed to the sick man who had lain on his mattress beside the pool of Bethesda, 'Do you want to get well?'[11] This is not to deny that James may have had spiritual factors in mind as well, especially whether faith is present. It is to say that he includes more than that. The whole person is involved in the process, mind and will, not just spirit and body.

Secondly, such prayers should be *corporate.* Church leadership in the New Testament is always portrayed as plural leadership. It is never solo. It may be that James is simply stating an assumption, therefore, that several elders will be involved. But, given our subsequent exaltation of the clergy and their isolation from the common laity it is worth drawing attention to it. Several representatives of the leadership team of the church should be involved. It is an interesting, but tangential, question as to whether these people fulfil defined offices or whether he is referring to the older, wiser and spiritually more experienced members of the church to whom people of the day might have more naturally looked for leadership.[12] They would certainly not have defined the role in the precise ways that we who are the products of a bureaucratic and litigious culture do. It would have been much more fluid. But that must not distract us from the point that the government of the church is always shared.

Thirdly, the prayer should be *expressive*. The words the elders pray are to be given a tangible expression in their actions. To pray 'over' someone implies laying hands on them while you pray. To that symbolic act a second symbolic act, that of anointing with oil, is added. Jesus could heal at a distance and by simply saying a word. But on many occasions he touched those who were to be healed and on one occasion anointed the eyes of a blind man with spittle.[13] The symbols have no effective power in themselves. It is neither the laying on of hands nor the oil which brings about the healing. But, as outward expressions both of the concern of the church and the power of God's grace (a point we will explore more fully later in the chapter) they can stimulate faith. Actions make the words more tangible.

Fourthly, the prayer should be *God-centred*. The prayer is offered 'in the name of the Lord'. Praying for healing is no different from any other sort of prayer. It should conform to our general way of praying and we should not expect God to respond to it any differently than he does to other prayers. So, like all prayer, first and foremost it should be concerned about the will of God and the advance of his glory. In what way will the purposes of God be served in this healing? How will restoration to health be for the greater glory of God? That should be our primary motivation rather than the comfort or convenience of the one who is sick. The miracles of Jesus were not wonders by which he dazzled people into his kingdom or which he did simply to astound the onlookers, as contemporary faith-healers might wish to do. They were signs which pointed to a greater reality and which symbolized spiritual truths about the kingdom.[14] Unless we can ensure that our motives are consistent with the will of the Lord we should be reluctant to claim the name of the Lord in prayer.

The centrality of God in praying for the sick is further underlined by James when he says, in verse 15, 'the Lord will raise you up'. It is neither the elders, nor the rite which heal the sick person. It is the Lord and he alone who does so.

Fifthly, the prayer should be *faith-filled*. 'The prayer offered in faith will make you well.' There are people who were healed by Jesus who do not seem to have exercised personal faith prior to their healing, although in those cases it usually follows. Sometimes, as with the man let down through the roof in Capernaum[15] or the official's son who was healed in Capernaum while Jesus was in Cana,[16] the faith seems to be exercised by others. In spite of the qualifications, however, there seems a general link between faith and healing.

It would be surprising indeed if James had not mentioned faith in this connection. His stress on single-mindedness applies here no less than to the other issues where he applied it. To ask God for healing while being double-minded and full of doubt is no basis for receiving from God. Wholeheartedness is called for. Some churches have taken this to mean that they have to stoke the fires of faith and fan it into a mighty conflagration before a reluctant God will acknowledge it. But that is not quite James' point. It is not the quantity of faith that matters.[17] It is the integrity of faith, however small, to which God responds.

Sixthly, the prayer should be *comprehensive*. Although the subject is unquestionably about physical healing and not some rather vague healing of the memories or spiritual healing, it is with the whole person that James is concerned. His move from praying for physical healing to mentioning the forgiveness of sins is seamless. People cannot easily be dissected so that different aspects of their beings are isolated from one another and allocated to different departments for attention. That is the mistake much modern western medicine has made, as is increasingly being discovered. Even the most ardent materialist recognizes 'psychosomatic' illness. People are integrated, united wholes and the mental, physical and spiritual aspects of their lives all interact with each other. This is not to say that all illness is caused directly by the individual sin of the sick person. To believe that is to fly in the face of Jesus' teaching where he stated there was no necessary connection between them.[18] It is also to have a superficial view of the effect of the Fall since the Fall not only affected men and women but the whole of creation, allowing destructive elements to be unleashed into the system which cause people to be sick and to die. Nonetheless there may be a connection between sin and sickness and the Lord may be using it to bring certain things to our attention to which we would otherwise be indifferent, as Paul told the Corinthians in discussing their behaviour at the Lord's table.[19]

James is saying that one should not minister to people's bodies without taking their spiritual state into account. There are plenty who want to deal only with one facet of people's lives, while ignoring others. Wise pastors will look more broadly. They will certainly never be concerned about the healing of the body while being indifferent to the spiritual condition of the person for whom they pray. Sinfulness and suffering both need healing. The one needs the healing of forgiveness, the other the healing of restoration. Prayer is a vital instrument in bringing both about.

Seventhly, the prayer will be *effective*. James confidently asserts, 'the prayer ... will make you well;[20] the Lord will raise you up.' In my own ministry I have witnessed the truth of these words, as have many others. First and foremost we should rejoice that God does heal in answer to prayer. Even so, we must ask, if James' remark is not too confident? Is he promising what many of us know from experience not to be true? Should he not be more guarded in his pronouncement?

The most helpful comment I have found on this statement is that of Alec Motyer:

> Now how do we understand these unqualified assurances concerning answers to prayer? We know from the word of God and confirmatory evidence in our own lives that these promises are expressed as great affirmations, first to assure us of the generosity of God who will withhold nothing from us that is good, and, secondly, to assure us of the liberty of asking given to us, whereby there is nothing we cannot ask of God. But the one thing these promises do not imply is that God allows us to be stubborn in his presence and insistent on what we think is right.[21]

The truth is that these are not unqualified words. Read in their context the safeguards are there. James knows that not all prayers are answered positively. Some don't deserve to be.[22] Much depends here, as Ralph Martin noted, 'on the motive of the person who prays.'[23] One major condition for the fulfilment of these words is that we pray 'in the name of the Lord.' To do so is to recognise his awesome sovereignty, to bow before him in humility, to appreciate his concerns for our lives are wider than our own, to know that his ways are mysterious and to acknowledge his concern is for our ultimate and eternal, not transient and immediate, good.[24]

*The role of every member, verse 16.*
The ministry of prayer is not reserved for a special class of priests. In Christ's new covenant we are all priests and therefore all qualified to exercise this ministry of intercession and pastoral care. More briefly, then, James mentions the role we all have to play.

First, he says that prayer should be *mutual*. His command is that we should 'pray for each other'. He uses that wonderful New Testament word *allēlōn,* one another. No single word captures the meaning of true Christian community more than this one. We are, for example, to be devoted to one another,[25] to live in harmony with one another,[26] to accept one another,[27] to instruct one another,[28] to serve one another,[29] to be compassionate to one another,[30] to forgive one another,[31] to encourage one another,[32] to spur one another on to love and good deeds,[33] and above all to love one another.[34] Here, the command is to confess to one another and pray for one another. As brothers and sisters in Christ we do not view the church as an hierarchical organisation but as a mutual organism. Members minister to fellow members. They minister just like the elders, even if the elders have more experience or opportunity in fulfilling their ministry. All have a role to play even if the elders have a special gift to exercise.

Since we are all sinners and all forgiven by the same grace that flows from Calvary, there should be no embarrassment in confessing to one another. I do not think that James was saying we should regularly stand before everyone in the church and confess all. That might soon degenerate into a competition as to who was most unworthy, encourage a misguided flaunting of sin on the part of the confessor and encourage an unhealthy voyeurism on the part of some listeners. Perhaps James had something like the old Methodist class meeting in mind or contemporary cell groups where in a small group situation in which people can be trusted confession can take place. We can reveal our vulnerability without it being abused. There is certainly something spiritual and psychologically healthy about holding ourselves accountable, at least to one or two soulmates or mentors in Christ. Confession is only one aspect of the mutual relationship James wishes to encourage but a more comprehensive prayer ministry is in view too.

Secondly, he says mutual prayer should be *purposeful*. We pray for each other 'so that you may be healed.' Honesty would compel us to admit that our motives often fall short of this. From the standpoint of those who pray the truth is that we sometimes enjoy being part of the prayer chain so that we are 'in' on the gossip and because it satisfies our nosiness. From the standpoint of the prayed-for we have to say that some like being the object of prayer because it makes them the centre of attention and brings their problems to the fore, making them feel significant when otherwise they might be ignored. But James is crystal clear. The purpose of asking for prayer and being prayed for is 'so that you may be healed.' The word *iaomai* definitely refers to physical healing. But it is quite legitimate to generalise beyond this, especially in view of the discussion above of the unity of our beings, to say that our objective in prayer should be to see greater and greater wholeness in Christ, spiritual no less than physical until the totality of wholeness is reached. Prayer should not be an aimless meandering in the presence of God where we vaguely ask him to 'bless' those we name. It should be for a real and measurable progress to be made in their relationship to Christ.

Thirdly, he says that the pray-er should be *righteous*. We cannot live in flagrant disobedience to God and then expect him to listen to our prayers when it suits us. James 4:1-3 has already taught us that. We need to live in a right relationship with him as a general matter of course if we are to intercede effectively. In my younger days I heard people teaching this as if James was advocating that perfection was required before God would listen. (Whether I heard them correctly or not is another matter!) He is not advocating perfection or super-sainthood. But he is deterring us from spiritual apathy. If we expect God to answer we must ask what the climate of our relationship with him is like. There may be days when the weather is cold or wet but the general climate may still be warm and sunny. So it must be in our walk with God if we are to be effective in our prayer life.

Lastly, he says that we will then discover that praying can be *powerful*. 'The prayer of a righteous person is powerful and effective.' The vocabulary of power speaks of the inherent strength of prayer and reminds us of what a great untapped resource it is to those of us who struggle in our Christian lives. Alec Motyer comments, 'The most unpromising tracts of land conceal beneath them rich oil wells, seams of gold; grey seas cover deposits of natural gas. This is the picture suggested by the word used – not the unpromising face of the landscape but the immensity of the concealed power.'[35] Beneath the surface of our lives lies all the abundant riches of God who is able to 'meet all your needs according to his glorious riches in Christ Jesus.'[36] Effectiveness speaks of things changing, people being transformed, goals being reached and progress being accomplished.

Prayer is a great God-given resource which takes us deeper and deeper in our relationship with him. We are foolish to ignore it as we seek to prop one another up in our Christian lives. We really ought to try it his way more often.

## 3. The spiritual dynamic of prayer, 5:14-16

Let's review these verses briefly to draw out several important spiritual principles about prayer which have been mentioned in them. They make clear that the mere act of praying is no guarantee of receiving the outcome we want. There is a spiritual dynamic to it which must be respected and which encompasses anointing, believing, confessing and being righteous. Each of them has to do with integrity.

*Anointing, verse 14*

The practice of anointing with oil was widely observed by the Jews and on one occasion Jesus' disciples are reported as having adopted the practice themselves in healing the sick.[37] Although oil was considered to have medicinal properties itself, as the story of the Good Samaritan illustrates, it is not usually for that reason that it was used and that is not why it is mentioned here. It is mentioned here for its symbolic value. Manton summarizes it like this: 'Oil among the Hebrews was a usual symbol of divine grace, and so fitly used as a sign of that power and grace of the Spirit which was discovered in miraculous healing; it was an extraordinary sign of an extraordinary and miraculous cure.'[38] The primary dynamic of prayer, then, is to be a channel of the grace of God. It is to enable his restoring power to flow into people's lives, not to draw attention to the power or effectiveness of the one who prays.

It should be noted that oil was also used for commissioning people for service, whether they be kings or priests. The inference here, then, is that those prayed for and anointed with oil are being restored to active service as priests and kings of the new Covenant. They are not being made well so that they might live self-centred indulgent lives or be indolent in serving God. They are being healed to return to active service.

*Believing, verse 15*
Faith is a vital ingredient in prayer. If there is no faith, there is no point in praying. Unless we believe God will hear us and is able to respond to us, why bother approaching him? Effective prayer is marked by conviction – the sort of conviction one hears on the lips of the Gentile Centurion who asked Jesus to heal his paralysed servant: 'Lord, I do not deserve to have you come under my roof. But just say the word and my servant will be healed.' He did not doubt that Jesus would be willing and able to respond.[39] Honesty compels us to admit that our prayers are often much more like the father of the spirit-possessed son whom Jesus healed. When Jesus spoke to him of the importance of faith in God if one was to see the impossible, he replied, 'I do believe; help overcome my unbelief.'[40] But, as we have already mentioned, consistent with James' wider theme of integrity, it is a prayer of the former not the latter kind that he commends.

Faith, here, as in the teaching of Jesus about prayer and faith in Matthew 17:20 and 21:21-22, means a wholehearted trust in God. This is what distinguishes the healing referred to here from magic or the workings of self-appointed faith healers. The power involved is not an impersonal force. It is the power of a loving God who can do the impossible, especially when his people are totally and transparently dependent on him.

Yet, we must remember that faith though a necessary ingredient if we want our prayers answered is not the only ingredient which determines God's response. Faith on its own is not the complete story. Other things have to be in place as well, such as the factors which have to do with our motivation (which is often suspect), with his longer-term plan (of which we are usually ignorant), and our spiritual good (about which our vision is often very limited). So even with faith there can be no guarantee of the outcome. There is no room for an attitude of presumption which automatically demands 'success'. In recent years many Christians interceded with God and exercised much faith for the healing of two well-known Charismatic leaders, David Watson and, sometime later, John Wimber. But neither was healed. Faith was not absent. But the prayer was not answered positively. Why not? Ultimately we must say we do not know. We must affirm that God did answer but his answers, for reasons which are often beyond us, are sometimes 'no' or 'not yet' as much as 'yes'. Perhaps this is one of those areas where we need not only faith but wisdom – wisdom to know what to pray for. James would tell us that even if we don't know what to pray for in relation to someone's healing we can at least come to God and ask him for direction and wisdom (1:5) so that we can discern his will more clearly.

### Confession, verse 16

Confession is one of the other factors involved if we are to pray so that God hears us. Before coming to God with our shopping list of wants, as if he were the customer service agent at some heavenly supermarket, we need to examine the state of our relationship with God. Even though the Christian is fundamentally cleansed from sin there is still the need for daily confession of sin. During the last supper Jesus spent with his disciples he rose from the table and washed their feet. Typically, Peter protested and said he would never permit Jesus to do such a menial thing to him. Jesus told him that unless he submitted Peter would not belong to him. So, characteristically overreacting, Peter now wants Jesus to give him a full bath! Jesus' reply is interesting. 'Those who have had a bath need only to wash their feet;

for their whole body is clean.'[41] In contemporary terms, you may shower at the beginning of the day and you are fundamentally clean. But during the course of the day you still need to go and wash your hands from time to time. So, in relation to God, the forgiven sinner is fundamentally clean. But there is still the need to clear the sins that accumulate, like dirt, during the course of the day.

Sin can still alienate the believer from God and, unless dealt with, the believer's heart will grow cold towards God and the relationship will eventually deteriorate in a major way. Our relationship with God is like the relationship a couple have in marriage in that respect. Even the most perfect of husbands and wives are bound to offend each other some times. And if they do not deal with those offences quickly they are likely to build up until there are huge issues between them and their relationship grows distant and love wanes. There is of course a difference between that and our relationship with God. In the relationship with God it will always be us who need to confess, not him. But the main point holds. It is not surprising that there is so much unanswered prayer in our churches since there is so much unconfessed sin in our lives.

*Righteousness, verse 16*

Confession and righteousness are two sides of the same coin. To confess sin is to remove uncleanness. To live righteously is to live cleanly. It is to avoid being contaminated by the dirt of sin in the first place. Confession deals with the negative situation. Righteousness portrays the positive situation. Confession is what we do when things go wrong. Righteousness is what we do to prevent things from going wrong to begin with.

Here, then, are four aspects of integrity:

♦ Effective prayer will be marked by integrity in regard to humility. We will not pretend the answer to prayer lies in our own hands. By the laying on of our hands and anointing with oil we will remind ourselves that the source of all answered prayer is to be found only in God and his grace.

♦ Effective prayer will be marked by integrity in regard to faith. We will not be half-hearted or double-minded but will wholeheartedly believe both in the requests we bring to God and in his ability to deal with them.

♦ Effective prayer will be marked by integrity in regard to sin. We will not come to God in pretence, hiding our failures and holding out on him in other areas of our lives. Our relationship with him will be characterised by a rigorous honesty and by the necessary apologies.

♦ Effective prayer will be marked by integrity in regard to living. There will be no disjointedness between what we say and how we live. We will seek to walk in holiness before God and to please him in all things.

## 4. A biblical model of prayer, 5:17-18

If I had chosen to provide a biblical model for what James has been writing, I think I might have chosen Daniel, one of my favourite biblical characters. But he chooses to illustrate his teaching by reference to the prophet Elijah. His choice is better than mine, for one very important reason. Both Daniel and Elijah saw dramatic, measurable answers to prayer. Daniel saw the mouths of lions shut and Elijah saw the prophets of Baal crumple. But Daniel almost seems too good to be true. His faith was unwavering. His practice of prayer was well-disciplined. His wisdom seems to know no bounds. He always seems to know what to do in every situation. He is presented as an almost unattainable ideal. But Elijah, as James says, 'was human just as we are.' And that is why James chooses him.

### *The humanity of Elijah*

The story behind James' illustration is found in 1 Kings 17:1-19:18. Elijah saw some mighty miracles take place in his years of prophetic ministry. He correctly prophesied a three and a half year drought; was miraculously fed by ravens; saw a widow's meagre supply of food miraculously replenished day after day; was instrumental in her son coming back to life after he had died; and was victorious in the showdown with the prophets of Baal on Mount Carmel. He doesn't sound 'human just as we are', does he? But he was. There is more than one indication of his humanity in the story. Right after Carmel this mighty man of God shrivelled up in depression and fled in terror before the threats of a woman whose lackeys he had just trounced. Then, he showed he could be full of self-importance and capable of overestimating his part in the story. 'I am the only one left,' he protested. But it wasn't true. What he needed was a good rest and a good meal. Only then would he see things in a right perspective. He was human, after all, just like the rest of us. It is this very ordinariness of Elijah which makes him such a good illustration for James.

Well-meaning preachers of an earlier day often held up examples of mighty prayer warriors in an attempt to inspire people to pray more. Luther, Wesley, Simeon, Brainerd, McCheyne and many others were pressed into service to prove that long hours in prayer were vital for effective ministry. E. M. Bounds, in a much-admired work whose message still provides a necessary challenge to the shallow spirituality of today's church, wrote, 'The men who have done most for God in this world have been early on their knees. He who fritters away the early morning, its opportunity and freshness in other pursuits than seeking God will make poor headway seeking him the rest of the day.'[42] The difficulty was that such examples, at least as they were presented, were far too idealistic and removed from the lives most of us were compelled to live.

James doesn't make that mistake. His example was a man of failings and passions. He didn't always get it right. His prayer life, as recorded in scripture, was not extensive even if his relationship with God involved a running conversation. His emotional life was up-and-down. Here is a person with whom I can identify and, therefore, from whom I can learn.

### The fervency of Elijah

Although his passionate nature could lead him into trouble it could also prove to his advantage. The same passion he demonstrated in dealing with God's enemies and expressed in his emotional swings he also channelled into his praying. So he 'prayed earnestly'. He didn't just say prayers, he prayed prayers ... really prayed them.[43] His situation demanded that he did so. As Luke Johnson points out he was not praying from a position of obvious strength. 'He was beleaguered and isolated when he prayed.'[44] He had no resources of his own to achieve anything. He was not a power in the land by ordinary standards. He had no armies he could call on. He had no money to throw at the situation. All he had was God. So, unless God stepped in, he was sunk, and all Israel with him. But he predicated his life on his friendship with God and worked on the basis that God would hear him. The beleaguered Christians among James' readers are encouraged to do the same.

### The effectiveness of Elijah

What he prayed for happened. When he prayed for a drought, it came. When he prayed for rain, it came. God heard and responded to his strong prayer not because Elijah had dreamed up some scheme for dealing with wicked King Ahab and his minions who served Baal but because it was in line with his own intentions for Israel. Right at the heart of Elijah's prayer was a concern for the honour of God. When we pray in ways which enhance his honour we are sure to be effective.

## 5. The practical outworking of prayer, 5:19-20

The closing words of the letter seem, at first sight, to be disconnected from what has gone before. But there are a number of connections and there is good reason for James to bring his letter to a close in this way.

The first reason why these verses belong here is because they continue the theme of healing. The same word is used in verse 20 as was used in verse 15 to speak of saving a person. The concern now is not for those believers who become physically sick but those who become spiritually sick by deviating from 'the truth', by which is meant not only correct belief but also right living. The NIV translation 'wander from the truth' rather implies that the person might just have strayed from the truth unintentionally by just meandering away from it. But that is to be more precise than James means to be. Intentional and unintentional deviations are in mind.

In a mature Christian fellowship attempts will be made to restore people who have wandered away, whoever they are and for whatever reason. A surprising number of people do drift from the church, many after many years of experience and responsibility within it.[45] How little effort is invested in getting them back. Many say that when they left no one contacted them, no one visited, no one phoned, no one seemed to care. A number might have been reincorporated into the living body of Christ if only these elementary steps had been taken. As Robert Wall says, 'the vocation of the "user-friendly" church ... is the restoration of the foolish to the way of wisdom.'[46]

The effect of restoring these people will be twofold. On the one hand they will be saved from death, which points forward to the judgement. On the other hand, their sins, however numerous, will be covered over and blotted out of view. Drifting from the fellowship, then, is no light matter. It's not like letting your membership of a political party lapse because you've lost interest in politics nor like failing to renew your subscription at the fitness centre because you hardly ever use it. These issues have eternal consequences. Gregory the Great put it in its rightful perspective when he commented, 'It is a great thing to rescue someone's body when it is on the point of death, how much greater is it to deliver someone's soul from death, so that it might live forever in the heavenly country.'[47]

The second reason why these words belong here is because they make a fitting climax to the whole of James' letter. They are a summons to action. Words alone are not enough. It is good to pray for people who are drifting from the church. But it is not sufficient just to pray. Something practical must be done to restore them. Visits must be made, meals offered, burdens shared, relief given, doubts and loneliness entered into, listening practised, discussions had and questions answered. Active steps to make restoration possible must be taken, not just pious hopes expressed within the walls of the church or down the telephones of the prayer chain. Eugene Peterson's paraphrase puts the emphasis where it belongs. 'My dear friends, if you know people who have wandered off from God's truth, don't write them off. Go after them.'[48]

James is closing the loop. He has virtually come full circle. Early on, in 1:26-27, he wrote that the kind of religion which was acceptable to God was religion which did something, not merely talked about doing something. It looked after orphans and widows. Here now finally it goes after drifters and doubters. It is, then, a fitting climax to the letter because the final words are words of commissioning. Right at the end James says the important thing is to 'go and do'.

# Endnotes

## 1. Introducing James

[1] See *The New Lion Handbook of the Bible,* ed. Pat and David Alexander (Oxford: Lion, 1999) p. 70-73.

[2] Quoted in Richard Bauckham, *James* New Testament Readings (London and New York: Routledge, 1999), p. 117.

[3] 2 Timothy 3:16.

[4] Matthew 13:55; Mark 6:3.

[5] Mark 3:21, 31-34; John 7:2-5. See also Mark 6:4.

[6] 1 Corinthians 15:7.

[7] Galatians 1:19.

[8] Acts. 12:17.

[9] Acts 15:12-21.

[10] Acts 21:18.

[11] A limestone burial box has recently been discovered in Israel which has the words 'James, son of Joseph, brother of Jesus' inscribed on its side. Tests date it to AD 63. André Lemaire, the archaeologist who has recently published the details says the appearance of these three names together is 'striking'. But there could have been twenty men in Jerusalem around that time called James and with a father called Joseph and a brother called Jesus. It is possible that it could be the burial box of the author of this letter but we cannot be certain. If it is, it would be the first physical object from the first century to be found which relates specifically to Jesus.

[12] Bauckham, *op. cit.,* p. 16.

[13] For a full discussion of the various finer interpretations of this phrase see Ralph Martin, *James,* Word Biblical Commentary (Waco: Word, 1988), pp. 8-11.

[14] Peter Davids, *The Epistle of James*, NIGTC (Exeter: Paternoster Press, 1982), pp. 28-34.

[15] Robert W. Wall, *Community of the Wise* (Valley Forge: Trinity Press Int., 1997), pp. 15-16.

[16] Martin, *op. cit.,* pp. lxvii-lxix.

[17] *Ibid.,* pp. lxix-lxxvii.

[18] Sophie Laws, *A Commentary on the Epistle to James* (London: A & C Black, 1980), pp. 22-26.

[19] Douglas Moo, *The Letter of James,* Pillar New Testament Commentary (Grand Rapids: Eerdmans and Leicester: Apollos, 2000), p.25.

[20] Bauckham, *op. cit.,* p. 13. The full argument is developed on pp. 11-28.

[21] *Ibid.,* p. 26.

[22] *Ibid.,* p. 28.

[23] The following is based on *Ibid.,* pp. 29-60.

[24] *Ibid.,* p. 30.

[25] *Ibid.,* pp. 143 and 152.

[26] Luke T. Johnson, *The Letter of James*, Anchor Bible (New York: Doubleday, 1995), pp. 85-87.

## 1. Trouble and how to meet it

[1] *Leadership* IX.1 (1988) p. 36.

[2] John Henry Sammis (1846-1919).

[3] John 9:1-3, 11:1-4.

[4] For example, Matthew 5:10-12, John 15:18-25.

[5] Quoted in Eugene Peterson, *Five Smooth Stones for Pastoral Work* (Grand Rapids: Eerdmans, 1980), p. 51.

[6] *The New Testament in Modern English* (London: Geoffrey Bles, 1960).

[7] Leslie Mitton, *The Epistle of James* (Edinburgh: Marshall, Morgan and Scott, 1966), p. 20.

[8] John 15:11.

[9] Robert Wall, *Community of the Wise* (Valley Forge: Trinity Press International, 1997), p. 48.

[10] C. S. Lewis, *A Grief Observed* (London: Faber and Faber, 1961), p. 36.

[11] Alec Motyer, *The Tests of Life* (London: IVP, 1970), p. 22.

[12] 1 Peter 1:6-8.

[13] Luke 21:19.

[14] Matthew 5:48.

[15] 1 Corinthians 2:6; Ephesians 4:13; Colossians 4:12; Philippians 3:15.

[16] Peter Davids, *The Epistle of James*, NIGTC (Exeter: Paternoster, 1982), p.70.

[17] *Ibid.*

[18] Richard Bauckham, *James*, New Testament Readings (London and New York: Routledge, 1999), p. 177. See pp. 175-183. The word group of perfection, wholeness or completion is found directly in 1:17, 25; 2:8,10, 22; 3:2, 3, 6. Its opposite is to be double-minded (1:8, 4:8) and unstable (1:8, 3:8). Its meaning is very apparent in 4:4.

[19] 2 Corinthians 13:11. See also verse 9.

[20] Alec Motyer, *The Message of James* (Leicester: IVP, 1985), p. 34.

[21] Quoted in *Ancient Christian Commentary on the Scriptures,* XI, ed. Gerald Bray, (Downers Grove: IVP, 2000), pp. 10f.

[22] Thomas Manton, *An Exposition of the Epistle of James* (London: Banner of Truth, 1962, orig. ed. 1693), p. 79.

[23] Genesis 22:1-19. James refers to this incident in 2:21-23.

[24] Judges 2:22.

[25] 2 Chronicles 32:31.

[26] See especially Job 1:6-12.

[27] Mitton, *op. cit.,* p. 47.

[28] Genesis 1:14-18; Psalm 136:7; Isaiah 40:26; Jeremiah 31:35.

[29] Mitton, *op. cit.,* p. 54.

[30] The world and the devil are both mentioned elsewhere in James, e.g., 4:4-7.

[31] Davids, *op. cit.,* p. 83.

[32] Douglas Moo, *James*, Tyndale New Testament Commentaries (Leicester, IVP, 1985), p. 73.

[33] Bray (ed), *op. cit.,* p. 12.

[34] Luke T. Johnston, *The Letter of James*, Anchor Bible (New York: Doubleday, 1995), p. 315.

[35] Motyer, *The Tests of Life*, p. 106.

[36] Exodus 34: 6.

[37] Manton, *op. cit.,* p. 114.

[38] Quoted in John Piper, *Tested by Fire* (Downers Grove: IVP, 2001), p. 72.

## 2. Wisdom and how to obtain it

[1] London: Hodder and Stoughton, 1980, p. 1.

[2] William Cowper, 'The Winter Walk at Noon.'

[3] Richard Bauckham, *James* New Testament Readings (London and New York: Routledge, 1999), p. 31.

[4] *Ibid.*, p. 30.

[5] See *ibid.*, pp. 74-93.

[6] The rest of the paragraph is dependent on *ibid.*, pp. 93-109.

[7] Ruth Valerio, *Globalization: Three information and discussion papers* (Teddington: Tear Fund, 2001), p. 8.

[8] Oliver James, *Britain on the Couch* (London: Century, 1997). The quotation is a summary statement found on the dust jacket of the book. Its substance is depressingly spelled out on pp. 42-127.

[9] Gerard W. Hughes, *God of Surprises* (London: Darton, Longman and Todd, 1985), p. 115.

[10] Peter Davids, *The Epistle of James,* NIGTC (Exeter: Paternoster, 1982), p. 73.

[11] Proverbs 1:7; 9:10.

[12] *Against the World, For the World,* ed. Peter Berger and Richard John Neuhaus (New York: Seabury Press, 1976), p. 10.

[13] Philippians 3:19.

[14] John 8:44.

[15] Bill Hybels, *Making Life Work: Putting God's Wisdom into Action* (Leicester: IVP, 1998), p. 261.

[16] For the latest example of the truth of this claim see Andrew Rawnsley, *Servants of the People: the inside story of New Labour* (London: Penguin Books, 2001). Though Rawnsley details the power hungry ambitions and the factions and personal rivalries of the present government, similar stories could be documented of all previous governments.

[17] Mark 7:20-23.

[18] Quoted in John Blanchard, *Not Hearers Only* (London: Word Books, 1972), Vol 2, p. 148.

[19] Thomas Manton, *An Exposition of the Epistle of James* (London: Banner of Truth, 1962, orig. ed. 1693), p. 304.

[20] Douglas Moo, *James*, Tyndale New Testament Commentary (Leicester: IVP, 1985), p. 135.

[21] 2 Corinthians 11:2. See also Ephesians 5:25-27.

[22] Matthew 5:5

[23] Matthew 11:29.

[24] Evangelical Contribution on Northern Ireland, 1 Brunswick Street, Belfast, BT2 7GE.

[25] Matthew 5:9.

[26] Matthew 11:29.

## 3. Wealth and How to Treat It

[1] See chapter 2, pp. 40-41.

[2] Adapted from William Boice, *Leadership,* IV.4 (1983), p. 87.

[3] See David de Silva, *Honor, Patronage, Kinship and Purity: Unlocking New Testament Culture* (Downers Grove: IVP, 2000) for a full exposition of how the theme affects our reading of the New Testament.

[4] Luke 8:42-48.

[5] Luke 5:12-16.

[6] Luke 7:1-10; 10:25-37; 17:11-19 and Mark 7:24-30.

[7] Luke 7:36-50; 19:1-10.

[8] Luke 14:15-24; 16:19-31; 18:9-14.

[9] Luke 16:15.

[10] Luke 1:52-53.

[11] See Joel Green, *The Theology of the Gospel of Luke*, New Testament Theology (Cambridge: Cambridge University Press, 1995), pp. 76-94.

[12] For details see Ralph Martin, *James*, Word Biblical Commentary (Waco: Word, 1988), pp. 25-26, and Peter Davids, *The Epistle of James*, NIGTC (Exeter: Paternoster, 1982), p. 77.

[13] Thomas Manton, *An Exposition of the Epistle of James* (London: Banner of Truth, 1962, orig. ed., 1693), p. 201.

[14] John Blanchard, *Not Hearers Only* (London: Word, 1972), Vol. 2, p. 45.

[15] J. B. Phillips' paraphrase in *The New Testament in Modern English* (London: Geoffrey Bles, 1960).

[16] Philippians 2:1-11.

[17] Alec Motyer, *The Tests of Life* (London: IVP, 1970), p. 42.

[18] Craig Blomberg, *Neither Poverty Nor Riches* (Leicester: Apollos, 1999), p. 153.

[19] James Adamson, *The Epistle of James*, NICNT (Grand Rapids: Eerdmans, 1976), p. 102.

[20] See note 18 for details.

[21] Ronald J. Sider, *Rich Christians in an Age of Hunger* (London: Hodder and Stoughton, 1977), p. 76.

[22] Psalm 50:10.

[23] Ephesians 1:3-14.

[24] Isaiah 60:5.

[25] Genesis 1:28

<sup></sup>26 1 Timothy 4:4.

27 Matthew 6:24.

28 Matthew 6:25-34.

29 1 Timothy 6:6-10.

30 Richard Foster, *Money, Sex and Power* (London: Hodder and Stoughton, 1985), p. 26.

31 Richard Foster, *Celebration of Discipline* (London: Hodder and Stoughton, 1980), pp. 78-83.

32 For details of this possible setting see Davids, *op. cit.,* pp. 28-34.

33 John Blanchard, *Not Hearers Only* (London: Word, 1974), Vol. 4, p. 19.

34 Genesis 4:1-16.

35 2 Peter 2:13.

36 1 Kings 21:1-24.

37 Adamson, *op. cit.,* p. 188.

38 R.V.G. Tasker, *The General Epistle of James* (London: Tyndale Press, 1956), p. 116.

39 2 Corinthians 8:9.

40 James 4:4.

## 4. Religion and how to practise it

1 *The Times*, October 9, 2001, p. 22.

2 Lesslie Newbigin, *Foolishness to the Greeks* (Grand Rapids: Eerdmans, 1986), p. 117.

3 Amos 5:21-24.

4 John Blanchard, *Not Hearers Only* (London: Word Books, 1971), Vol 1, pp. 146-149.

5 Robert Wall, *Community of the Wise* (Valley Forge: Trinity Press International, 1997), pp. 75f.

6 Timothy Dudley-Smith, *John Stott: A Global Ministry* (Leicester: IVP, 2001), p. 267-68.

7 Luke T. Johnson, *The Letter of James* Anchor Bible (New York: Doubleday, 1995), p. 200.

8 Gregory the Great, *The Book of Pastoral Rule,* Nicene and Post-Nicene Fathers, Vol. 12 (Grand Rapids: Eerdmans, 1894), p. 39. Gregory the Great (540-604) was Pope from 590 onwards and wrote this work in 593. His actual words are, 'For sometimes the meek, when they are in authority, suffer from the torpor of sloth, which is a kindred disposition, and as it were placed hard by. And for the most part from the laxity of too great gentleness they soften the force of strictness beyond need.'

9 Ralph Martin, *James*, Word Biblical Commentary (Waco: Word, 1988), p. 48.

10 Jeremiah 31:33.

11 See, for example, Wall, *op. cit.,* pp. 32, 73.

12 Douglas Moo, *The Letter of James*, Tyndale New Testament Commentaries (Leicester: IVP, 1985), p. 81.

[13] James Adamson, *The Epistle of James*, NICNT (Grand Rapids: Eerdmans, 1976), p. 82.

[14] 2:8-10.

[15] 4:11-12.

[16] P. T. Forsyth, *Positive Preaching and the Modern Mind* (London: Hodder and Stoughton, n.d.), p. 49.

[17] See also, for example, Deuteronomy 27:19; Job 22:9; Isaiah 10:2 and Malachi 3:5.

[18] Zechariah 7:9-10.

[19] Exodus 22:21 typically links their slavery in Egypt to their treatment of 'aliens' but in verse 22 continues to echo the experience of Egypt as a motivation for treating widows and orphans with compassion and justice. Exodus 22:22-24 echoes Exodus 3:7-8.

[20] Deuteronomy 8:1-20.

[21] As also in Paul, 1 Corinthians 5:8.

[22] See, among many other possible references Leviticus 18:1-19:37; Deuteronomy 8:19-20; Isaiah 1:13-17; Jeremiah 32:35.

[23] 1 Kings 11:1-13 and 12:1-9 tell something of his failure to live faithfully to God and the consequent social impact his idolatry, encouraged by his many wives, had.

[24] Among these are Fran Beckett, *Called to Action* (London: Fount, 1989) and Steve Chalke, *Faithworks* (Eastbourne: Kingsway, 2001).

[25] For a brief, but fuller than above, overview see Derek Tidball, *Who are the Evangelicals?* (London: Marshall Pickering, 1994) pp. 177-95. For the story in the United Kingdom see *Evangelical Faith and Public Zeal* ed. John Wolffe (London: SPCK, 1995) and for the United States see Timothy Smith, *Revivalism and Social Reform* (Baltimore and London: John Hopkins University Press, 1980).

[26] Charles Finney, *Lectures on Revivals of Religion* (Cambridge, Mass: Harvard Univ. Press 1960, orig. ed. 1835), p. 287.

[27] Lyle W. Dorsett, *A Passion for Souls: The Life of D. L. Moody* (Chicago: Moody Press, 1997), p. 287.

[28] Matthew 28:19-20.

[29] Matthew 22:37-39.

[30] John Stott, *The Lausanne Covenant An exposition and commentary* (Minneapolis: World Wide Publications, 1975), p. 25. The last sentence is a quote from James 2:20.

[31] Quoted by John Stott in *Issues Facing Christians Today* (Basingstoke: Marshalls, 1984), p. 19.

## 5. Words and how to control them

[1] Ben Okri, *Birds of Heaven* (London: Phoenix, 1996), pp. 3-5. Quoted in Richard Bauckham, *James* New Testament Readings (London: Routledge, 1999), p. 205.

[2] David Field, *Discovering James*, Crossway Bible Guides (Leicester: Crossway Books, 1998), p. 117.

[3] Especially in Matthew's gospel. E.g., Matthew 8:19; 23:8. On this and the next point see Luke T. Johnson, *The Letter of James* Anchor Bible (New York: Doubleday, 1995), p. 255.

[4] Acts 13:1; Romans 12:7; 1 Corinthians 12:28; Ephesians 4:11 and, of course, the Pastoral Epistles.

[5] 2 Timothy 2:2.

[6] 1 Thessalonians 4:3.

[7] John Chrysostom, *On the Priesthood*, NP-NF (Grand Rapids: Eerdmans, 1889, org. 386), III.7, p. 49.

[8] Luke 12:3.

[9] Johnson, *op. cit.* p. 255.

[10] Proverbs 18:21.

[11] Quoted by Field, *op.cit.,* p. 118.

[12] Quoted in *Ancient Christian Commentary on the Scriptures,* XI, ed. Gerald Bray (Downers Grove: IVP, 2000), p. 39.

[13] Quoted by Douglas Moo, *James*, Tyndale New Testament Commentaries (Leicester: IVP, 1985), p. 125.

[14] Gehenna is mentioned by Jesus in Matthew 5:22.

[15] Thomas Manton, *An Exposition of the Epistle of James* (London: Banner of Truth, 1962, orig. ed., 1693), p. 286.

[16] *The New Testament in Modern English* (London: Geoffrey Bles, 1960).

[17] Psalm 140:1, 3.

[18] Genesis 1:27.

[19] Romans 12:14.

[20] Johnson, *op. cit.,* p. 264.

[21] Motyer, *The Tests of Life* (London: IVP, 1970), p. 68.

[22] Ephesians 4:21.

[23] David W. Gill, *Becoming Good: Building Moral Character* (Downers Grove: IVP, 2000), p. 71.

[24] C. Leslie Mitton *The Epistle of James* (London: Marshall, Morgan and Scott, 1966), p. 164.

[25] James Adamson, *The Epistle of James*, NICNT (Grand Rapids: Eerdmans, 1976), p. 178.

[26] Numbers 14:21; Deuteronomy 7:8; Luke 1:73; Hebrews 6:13.

[27] Exodus 22:10-11.

[28] Matthew 5:33-37.

## 6. Law and how to keep it

[1] Joseph Fletcher, *Situation Ethics: The new morality* (London: SCM, 1966).

[2] Exodus 20:13.

[3] Romans 13:1-7; 1 Timothy 2:1-2; 1 Peter 2:13-17.

[4] E.g., John 1:17.

[5] E.g., Romans 7:7–8:4; Galatians 3:1–4:7.

[6] E.g., John 14:23-24; 15:9-17.

[7] E.g., Galatians 5:13-14, 6:14 and, depending on one's interpretation of the entire chapter, Romans 7.

[8] James 2:1.

[9] For a discussion see Mary Evans, 'The Law in James', *Vox Evangelica* XIII (1983), pp. 29-40.

[10] *Ibid.,* p. 37.

[11] Luke T Johnson, 'The Use of Leviticus 19 in the Letter of James' *Journal of Biblical Literature* 101 (1982), p. 399. The references are Leviticus 19:12 = James 5:12; Leviticus 19:13 = James 5:4; Leviticus 19:15 = James 2:1,9; Leviticus 19:16 = James 4:11; Leviticus 19:17 = James 5:20; Leviticus 19:18 = James 5:9 and Leviticus 19:18 = James 2:8. Only Leviticus 19:14, with its reference to cursing the deaf and tripping up the blind, is not mentioned but is surely embraced by James' demand for impartiality.

[12] Matthew 19:19; 22:39; Mark 12:31, 33.

[13] Luke 10:27.

[14] Matthew 5:21, 27-32; 19:9, 18; Mark 10:11-19; Luke 18:20.

[15] Romans 6:14.

[16] Romans 7:12. Since it is God's revealed will for living how could it be otherwise?

[17] Galatians 5:13-15.

[18] Exodus 20:8-11.

[19] E.g., Mark 2:23-3:6; John 5:1-15; 9:1-34.

[20] Psalm 19:7-9.

[21] Psalm 119:45.

[22] Nick Hornby, *How to be Good* (London: Viking, 2001), p. 48.

[23] Quoted in *Ancient Christian Commentary on the Scriptures,* XI, ed. Gerald Bray (Downers Grove: IVP, 2000), p. 25.

[24] These suggestions are listed by Robert Wall, *Community of the Wise* (Valley Forge: Trinity Press International, 1997), pp. 126-27.

[25] For details see pp. 48-65.

[26] Galatians 5:1.

[27] Galatians 5:13.

[28] Luke T. Johnson, *The Letter of James*, Anchor Bible (New York: Doubleday, 1995), p. 233. Johnson lists: 1:12; 3:1; 4:11-12; 5:5, 9, 12.

[29] 2 Corinthians 5:10.

[30] Matthew 25: 31-46.

[31] Matthew 25:41. Sins of omission are mentioned in James 4:17.

[32] Matthew 25:34.

[33] Bruce Milne, *The Message of Heaven and Hell*, Bible Speaks Today: Bible Themes (Leicester; IVP, 2002), p. 125.

[34] Johnson, *op. cit.,* p. 85. He points to James 4:1-6 as one clear expression of a closed worldview driven by 'the logic of envy'.

[35] For some biblical references see pp. 88-90. Note also Zechariah 7:9-10.

[36] Quoted in Donald E. Messer, *A Conspiracy of Goodness: Contemporary Images of Christian Mission* (Nashville: Abingdon, 1992), p. 75.

[37] Philip Yancey, *What's so Amazing about Grace?* (Grand Rapids: Zondervan, 1997), p. 179.

[38] Matthew 18:21-35.

[39] Matthew 5:7.

[40] Douglas Moo, *James*, Tyndale New Testament Commentaries (Leicester: IVP, 1985), p. 98.

[41] Exodus 34:6.

[42] Luke 6:35.

[43] Luke 6:36.

[44] Bray (ed.), *op. cit.*, p. 25.

## 7. Faith and how to prove it

[1] Ephesians 2:8-9.

[2] Galatians 2:12.

[3] An example of this may be found in James Dunn, *Unity and Diversity in the New Testament* (Philadelphia: Westminster and London: SCM, 1977). The quotation is from page 230. On the specific issue of James and Paul, Dunn (p. 255) speaks of a 'deepening rift between Paul and Jerusalem' and of how 'the sharpness of the rift of the antagonism between Paul and Jerusalem can hardly be over-estimated'.

[4] For a survey of the views of various scholars see Ralph Martin, *James*, Word Biblical Commentary (Waco: Word, 1988), pp. 82-84.

[5] To be more precise some suggest Paul's primary emphasis is on initial faith. But the term 'foundation faith' is preferable for Paul stresses the need for the Christian life both to begin and to continue on the basis of faith. See Galatians 3:3; Colossians 2:6.

[6] Galatians 5:6.

[7] Douglas Moo, *James*, Tyndale New Testament Commentaries (Leicester: IVP, 1985), p. 102. In fairness it should be said that Moo is less convinced about one detail, that of the distinction of others between Paul and James' view of 'works' (p. 101), but the quotation still represents his general position.

[8] Richard Bauckham, *James*, New Testament Readings (London: Routledge, 1999), pp. 113-40.

[9] *Ibid.*, p. 131.

[10] *Ibid.*, p. 119.

[11] *Ibid.*, pp. 120-127.

[12] *Ibid.*, p. 129.

[13] *Ibid.*, pp. 135-140.

[14] James 2:24.

[15] Alec Motyer, *The Tests of Life* (London: IVP, 1970), p. 54.

[16] Luke T. Johnson, *The Letter of James* Anchor Bible (New York: Doubleday, 1995), p. 219. Johnson calls this section 'the formal framework' of what has gone before.

[17] Moo, *op. cit.*, p. 101.

[18] Moo refers to 1:21; 4:12; 5:20 in support of this position.

[19] The thought is that of J. B. Mayor, quoted in Moo, *ibid.*, p. 104

[20] Robert W. Wall, *Community of the Wise* (Valley Forge: Trinity Press Int., 1997), p. 134.

[21] 1 Corinthians 8:4-6; Galatians 3:20; Ephesians 4:4-6; 1 Timothy 2:5.

[22] Mark 5:1-20.

[23] Johnson says it is not clear whether they shudder out of terror or awe (*op. cit.,* p. 241) but most believe it to be out of terror and James Adamson, *The Epistle of James* (Grand Rapids: Eerdmans: 1976), p. 126, states that the idea of demonic terror before the holiness of God was familiar in Jewish apocalyptic literature.

[24] Wall, *op. cit.,* p. 137.

[25] Quoted in *Ancient Christian Commentary on the Scriptures,* XI, ed. Gerald Bray (Downers Grove: IVP, 2000), p. 30.

[26] C. Leslie Mitton, *The Epistle of James* (London: Marshall, Morgan and Scott, 1966), p. 110.

[27] 1 Corinthians 15:14; Galatians 2:2; Philippians 2:16; 1 Thessalonians 3:5. See further *Dictionary of New Testament Theology* ed. Colin Brown (Exeter: Paternoster, 1975), Vol 1, p. 547.

[28] 2 Corinthians 6:1.

[29] Ephesians 4:5-6.

[30] The commentator Oecumenius, a sixth century Bishop, in Bray (ed) *op.cit.,* p. 31.

[31] Wall points out that the choice may not have been so surprising as it appears to us because they were often coupled together in Hellenistic Judaism as example of gentile proselytes, *op. cit.,* p. 143.

[32] *ibid.,* p. 144.

[33] Moo, *op. cit.,* p. 108.

[34] Joyce Baldwin, *The Message of Genesis 12-50*, Bible Speaks Today (Leicester: IVP, 1986), p. 90.

[35] For a full exposition of the chapter see the author's *The Message of the Cross*, Bible Speaks Today (Leicester: IVP, 2000), pp. 36-50.

[36] The same verse is quoted twice by the Apostle Paul to support his argument for the need for faith (Romans 4:3, 22).

[37] Johnson, *op. cit.,* p. 248.

[38] Adamson, *op. cit.,* p. 133.

[39] Joshua 2:11.

[40] Genesis 22:12.

[41] Hebrews 11:31.

[42] Quoted by Moo, *op. cit.,* p. 117.


**8. Relationships and how to handle them**

[1] Jonathan Sacks, *The Politics of Hope* (London: Jonathan Cape, 1997), p. 191. For a similar critique of American society see Robert D. Putnam, *Bowling Alone: The Collapse and Revival of American Community* (New York: Simon and Schuster, 2000).

[2] Galatians 6:2.

[3] Colossians 3:15.

[4] Ralph Martin is the chief recent exponent of a Zealot background to

James. See *James,* Word Biblical Commentary (Waco: Word, 1988), p. 144 and lxii-lxvii. See also Douglas J. Moo, *James*, Tyndale New Testament Commentaries (Leicester: IVP, 1985), p. 141.

[5] See W. J. Heard, 'Revolutionary Movements' in *Dictionary of Jesus and the Gospels* (ed. Joel B. Green, Scott McKnight and I. Howard Marshall, Downers Grove and Leicester: IVP, 1992) pp. 696-97.

[6] 1 Peter 2:11.

[7] R. V. G. Tasker, *The General Epistle of James* (London: Tyndale Press, 1956), p. 85.

[8] Alec Motyer, *The Tests of Faith* (London: IVP, 1970), p. 87.

[9] Jonathan Glover, *Humanity: A Moral History of the Twentieth Century* (London: Jonathan Cape, 1999), p. 89.

[10] The philosopher Friedrich Nietzsche (1844-1900) believed 'the will to power' was the most central characteristic of human beings. The phrase became the title of his posthumously published notebooks. He was admired by the Nazis for providing philosophical support for their policies. For the last year of his life he was judged insane.

[11] Robert W. Wall, *Community of the Wise* (Valley Forge: Trinity Press Int., 1997), p. 198.

[12] John Blanchard, *Not Hearers Only*, Vol. 3 (London: Word, 1973), p. 32.

[13] Luke T. Johnson, 'Friendship with the World/Friendship with God: A study of discipleship in James' in *Discipleship in the New Testament,* ed. F. F. Segovia (Philadelphia: Fortress Press, 1985), pp. 166-83.

[14] Luke T. Johnson, *The Letter of James,* Anchor Bible (New York: Doubleday, 1995), p. 288.

[15] *Ibid.*

[16] James 1:17.

[17] Jeremiah 3:20; Hosea 2:5, 7.

[18] Matthew 12:39; 16:4.

[19] 2 Corinthians 11:2.

[20] James Adamson, *The Epistle of James*, NICNT (Grand Rapids: Eerdmans, 1976), p. 170.

[21] Job 1:6-12; Zechariah 3:1-2; Revelation 12:10.

[22] Isaiah 14:12-15; Luke 10:18.

[23] Genesis 3: 1.

[24] Matthew 4:1-11.

[25] Thomas Manton, *The Epistle of James* (Edinburgh: Banner of Truth, 1992, orig. edn. 1693), pp. 364f.

[26] Matthew 4:1-11

[27] E.g., 2 Corinthians 10:1-13:10 and Ephesians 6:10-20.

[28] Donald Barnhouse, for example, spoke of the ignorance of Satan and said there were things he didn't know and things he couldn't do and that made him vulnerable. 'He is strong but not supreme, he is potent but he is not omnipotent.' Quoted in Blanchard, *op. cit.,* p. 70.

[29] Colossians 2:15.

[30] For an exposition of this position, see Clinton E. Arnold, *Powers of Darkness* (Leicester: IVP, 1992).

[31] Thomas Manton, *op.cit.,* p. 363.

[32] Genesis 5:24.

[33] James 2:23.

[34] Exodus 33:11.

[35] John 15:15.

[36] For example, Exodus 20:5; 34:14; Deuteronomy 4:24; 5:9; 6:15.

[37] A good explanation of the arguments can be found in Moo, *op.cit.,* pp. 144-146.

[38] Philip Yancey, *What's so Amazing about Grace?* (Grand Rapids: Zondervan, 1997), p. 90.

[39] David Wells, *God in the Wasteland* (Grand Rapids: Eerdmans and Leicester: IVP, 1994), p. 114.

[40] *ibid.,* p. 30.

## 9. Tomorrow and how to face it

[1] *The Times,* 13th September, 2001, p. 9.

[2] Alec Motyer, *The Tests of Life* (London: IVP, 1970), p. 94.

[3] Matthew 19:23.

[4] Proverbs 20:4.

[5] James' words closely follow Proverbs 27:1.

[6] Proverbs 19:21. See also Proverbs 16:1, 9.

[7] Leslie Mitton, *The Epistle of James* (Edinburgh: Marshall, Morgan and Scott, 1966), p. 169. Mitton contrasts the pictures the Bible uses to describe the transience of life with the 'everlasting hills' that speak of permanence and durability of God.

[8] Job 7:7; Psalm 39:5.

[9] Job 7:9.

[10] Psalm 102:11.

[11] Psalm 102:11, 103:15

[12] Psalm 139:14.

[13] Acts 17:28.

[14] Calvin referred to in Alec Motyer, *The Message of James*, Bible Speaks Today (Leicester: IVP, 1985), p. 161.

[15] On the role of language in everyday life see Peter Berger and Thomas Luckmann, *The Social Construction of Reality* (Harmondsworth: Penguin, 1967), pp. 49-61.

[16] Exodus 13:3-16.

[17] A random selection of Psalms illustrates the point: 71:18; 78:4, 5; 79:13; 96:10; 102:18; 118:2; 124:1; 129:1; 145:4.

[18] Thomas Manton, *An Exposition of the Epistle of James* (Edinburgh: Banner of Truth, 1962, orig. ed. 1693), p. 392. He cites 1 Corinthians 4:19; 16:7; Romans 1:10 and Philippians 2:19.

[19] To rephrase R. V. G. Tasker, *The General Epistle of James* (London: Tyndale Press, 1956), p. 103.

[20] For a fuller account of this in relation to guidance see, Derek Tidball, *How Does God Guide?* (Fearn: Christian Focus, 2001), pp. 41-59.

[21] Douglas Moo, *James*, Tyndale New Testament Commentaries (Leicester: IVP, 1985), p. 157.

[22] Robert Wall, *Community of the Wise* (Valley Forge: Trinity Press Int., 1997), p. 217.

[23] R. V. G. Tasker, *The General Epistle of James* (London: Tyndale Press, 1956), p. 104.

[24] James 1:22-25.

[25] Joseph Hart (1712-1768).

## 10. Prayer and how to use it

[1] Source unknown.

[2] Ralph Martin writes, 'by common consent the chief emphasis is on prayer.' *James*, Word Biblical Commentary (Waco: Word, 1988), p. 215.

[3] 1 Peter 5:7.

[4] James 1:17.

[5] Deuteronomy 8:1-20.

[6] C. S. Lewis, *Reflections on the Psalms* (London: Fontana Books, 1967), pp. 80-81. I first came across much of this quotation in David Watson, *I Believe in the Church* (London: Hodder and Stoughton, 1978), p. 183.

[7] Alec Motyer, *The Tests of Life* (London: IVP, 1970), p. 112.

[8] For a thorough recent discussion of the significance of his healing ministry by a Pentecostal scholar who questions whether Jesus' ministry was meant to be a paradigm for believers subsequently see Keith Warrington, *Jesus the Healer: Paradigm or Unique Phenomenon?* (Carlisle: Paternoster Press, 2000).

[9] 1 Corinthians 12:9, 28, 30.

[10] For example, Philippians 2:26-27; 2 Timothy 4:20 and his own physical weaknesses which almost certainly included eye trouble, Galatians 4:13-15; 6:11, possibly 2 Corinthians 12:1-10.

[11] John 5:6.

[12] On this discussion see R. A. Campbell, *The Elders: Seniority within Earliest Christianity* (Edinburgh: T & T Clark, 1994).

[13] Mark 8:22-26.

[14] See John 2:18; 4:54; 6:14; 12:18.

[15] Mark 2:1-12, esp. verse 5.

[16] John 4:43-54.

[17] Matthew 17:20; Luke 17:6.

[18] Luke 13:1-2; John 9:1-5.

[19] 1 Corinthians 11:30.

[20] The word for 'well' is *sōzein* which is used several times in the Gospels ambiguously to indicate physical healing and/or eternal salvation. Luke Johnson believes that when, as here, it is connected with faith 'it tends to be used in a religious sense'. But James' vocabulary in the rest of this section

would suggest he has physical healing firmly in view. *The Letter of James,* Anchor Bible (New York: Doubleday, 1995) p. 332.

[21] Motyer, *op.cit.,* p. 117.

[22] James 4:1-3.

[23] Martin, *op.cit.,* p. 215.

[24] Romans 8:28.

[25] Romans 12:10.

[26] Romans 12:16.

[27] Romans 15:7.

[28] Romans 15:14.

[29] Galatians 5:13.

[30] Ephesians 4:32.

[31] Ephesians 4:32; Colossians 3:13.

[32] 1 Thessalonians 5:11.

[33] Hebrews 10:25.

[34] 1 John 3:11, 23; 4:7, 11,12; 2 John 1:5.

[35] Motyer, *op.cit.,* p. 120.

[36] Philippians 4:19.

[37] Mark 6:13.

[38] Thomas Manton, *An Exposition of the Epistle of James* (London: Banner of Truth, 1962, orig. ed. 1693), p. 447.

[39] Matthew 8:8.

[40] Mark 9:24

[41] John 13:10.

[42] E. M. Bounds, *Power through Prayer* (London: Marshall, Morgan and Scott, 1962), p. 30.

[43] Manton, *op. cit.,* p. 469.

[44] Johnson, *op. cit.,* p. 344.

[45] See Michael Fanstone, *The Sheep that Got Away* (Tonbridge Wells: Marc, 1993).

[46] Robert Wall, *Community of the Wise* (Valley Forge, Pa: Trinity Press International, 1997), p. 272.

[47] Quoted in *Ancient Christian Commentary on the Scriptures,* XI, ed. Gerald Bray, (Downers Grove: IVP, 2000), p. 63.

[48] *The Message* (Colorado Springs: NavPress, 1993).

# The Letter of James

*Chapter 1*

[1]James, a servant of God and of the Lord Jesus Christ, To the twelve tribes scattered among the nations: Greetings.

[2]Consider it pure joy, my brothers and sisters, whenever you face trials of many kinds, [3]because you know that the testing of your faith produces perseverance. [4]Let perseverance finish its work so that you may be mature and complete, not lacking anything. [5]If any of you lacks wisdom, you should ask God, who gives generously to all without finding fault, and it will be given to you. [6]But when you ask, you must believe and not doubt, because the one who doubts is like a wave of the sea, blown and tossed by the wind. [7]Those who doubt should not think they will receive anything from the Lord; [8]they are double-minded and unstable in all they do. [9]Believers in humble circumstances ought to take pride in their high position. [10]But the rich should take pride in their humiliation—they will pass away like a wild flower! [11]For the sun rises with scorching heat and withers the plant; its blossom falls and its beauty is destroyed. In the same way, the rich will fade away even while they go about their business. [12]Blessed are those who persevere under trial, because when they have stood the test, they will receive the crown of life that God has promised to those who love him. [13]When tempted, no one should say, 'God is tempting me.' For God cannot be tempted by evil, nor does he tempt anyone; [14]but each of you is tempted when you are dragged away by your own evil desire and enticed. [15]Then, after desire has conceived, it gives birth to sin; and sin, when it is full-grown, gives birth to death. [16]Don't be deceived, my dear brothers and sisters. [17]Every good and perfect gift is from above, coming down from the Father of the heavenly lights, who does not change like shifting shadows. [18]He chose to give us birth through the word of truth, that we might be a kind of firstfruits of all he created.

[19]My dear brothers and sisters, take note of this: Everyone should be quick to listen, slow to speak and slow to become angry,

[20]because our anger does not produce the righteousness that God desires. [21]Therefore, get rid of all moral filth and the evil that is so prevalent and humbly accept the word planted in you, which can save you. [22]Do not merely listen to the word, and so deceive yourselves. Do what it says. [23]Those who listen to the word but do not do what it says are like people who look at their faces in a mirror [24]and, after looking at themselves, go away and immediately forget what they look like. [25]But those who look intently into the perfect law that gives freedom and continue in it—not forgetting what they have heard but doing it—they will be blessed in what they do. [26]Those who consider themselves religious and yet do not keep a tight rein on their tongues deceive themselves, and their religion is worthless. [27]Religion that God our Father accepts as pure and faultless is this: to look after orphans and widows in their distress and to keep oneself from being polluted by the world.

## Chapter 2

[1]My brothers and sisters, believers in our glorious Lord Jesus Christ must not show favoritism. [2]Suppose someone comes into your meeting wearing a gold ring and fine clothes, and a poor person in filthy old clothes also comes in. [3]If you show special attention to the one wearing fine clothes and say, 'Here's a good seat for you,' but say to the one who is poor, 'You stand there' or 'Sit on the floor by my feet,' [4]have you not discriminated among yourselves and become judges with evil thoughts? [5]Listen, my dear brothers and sisters: Has not God chosen those who are poor in the eyes of the world to be rich in faith and to inherit the kingdom he promised those who love him? [6]But you have dishonored the poor. Is it not the rich who are exploiting you? Are they not the ones who are dragging you into court? [7]Are they not the ones who are blaspheming the noble name of him to whom you belong?

[8]If you really keep the royal law found in Scripture, 'Love your neighbor as yourself,' you are doing right. [9]But if you show favoritism, you sin and are convicted by the law as lawbreakers. [10]For whoever keeps the whole law and yet stumbles at just one point is guilty of breaking all of it. [11]For he who said, 'Do not commit adultery,' also

said, 'Do not murder.' If you do not commit adultery but do commit murder, you have become a lawbreaker. [12]Speak and act as those who are going to be judged by the law that gives freedom, [13]because judgment without mercy will be shown to anyone who has not been merciful. Mercy triumphs over judgment.

[14]What good is it, my brothers and sisters, if people claim to have faith but have no deeds? Can such faith save them? [15]Suppose a brother or sister is without clothes and daily food. [16]If one of you says to them, 'Go in peace; keep warm and well fed,' but does nothing about their physical needs, what good is it? [17]In the same way, faith by itself, if it is not accompanied by action, is dead. [18]But someone will say, 'You have faith; I have deeds.' Show me your faith without deeds, and I will show you my faith by what I do. [19]You believe that there is one God. Good! Even the demons believe that—and shudder. [20]You foolish person, do you want evidence that faith without deeds is useless? [21]Was not our father Abraham considered righteous for what he did when he offered his son Isaac on the altar? [22]You see that his faith and his actions were working together, and his faith was made complete by what he did. [23]And the scripture was fulfilled that says, 'Abraham believed God, and it was credited to him as righteousness,' and he was called God's friend. [24]You see that people are justified by what they do and not by faith alone. [25]In the same way, was not even Rahab the prostitute considered righteous for what she did when she gave lodging to the spies and sent them off in a different direction? [26]As the body without the spirit is dead, so faith without deeds is dead.

## Chapter 3

[1]Not many of you should presume to be teachers, my brothers and sisters, because you know that we who teach will be judged more strictly. [2]We all stumble in many ways. Those who are never at fault in what they say are perfect, able to keep their whole body in check. [3]When we put bits into the mouths of horses to make them obey us, we can turn the whole animal. [4]Or take ships as an example. Although they are so large and are driven by strong winds, they are steered by a very small rudder wherever the pilot wants to go. [5]Like-

wise, the tongue is a small part of the body, but it makes great boasts. Consider what a great forest is set on fire by a small spark. [6]The tongue also is a fire, a world of evil among the parts of the body. It corrupts the whole person, sets the whole course of one's life on fire, and is itself set on fire by hell.

[7]All kinds of animals, birds, reptiles and sea creatures are being tamed and have been tamed by human beings, [8]but no one can tame the tongue. It is a restless evil, full of deadly poison. [9]With the tongue we praise our Lord and Father, and with it we curse human beings, who have been made in God's likeness. [10]Out of the same mouth come praise and cursing. My brothers and sisters, this should not be. [11]Can both fresh water and salt water flow from the same spring? [12]My brothers and sisters, can a fig tree bear olives, or a grapevine bear figs? Neither can a salt spring produce fresh water.

[13]Who is wise and understanding among you? Let them show it by their good life, by deeds done in the humility that comes from wisdom. [14]But if you harbor bitter envy and selfish ambition in your hearts, do not boast about it or deny the truth. [15]Such 'wisdom' does not come down from heaven but is earthly, unspiritual, demonic. [16]For where you have envy and selfish ambition, there you find disorder and every evil practice. [17]But the wisdom that comes from heaven is first of all pure; then peace-loving, considerate, submissive, full of mercy and good fruit, impartial and sincere. [18]Peacemakers who sow in peace reap a harvest of righteousness.

## Chapter 4

[1]What causes fights and quarrels among you? Don't they come from your desires that battle within you? [2]You desire but do not have, so you kill. You covet but you cannot get what you want, so you quarrel and fight. You do not have because you do not ask God. [3]When you ask, you do not receive, because you ask with wrong motives, that you may spend what you get on your pleasures.

[4]You adulterous people, don't you know that friendship with the world means enmity against God? Anyone who chooses to be a friend of the world becomes an enemy of God. [5]Or do you think Scripture says without reason that he jealously longs for the spirit he

has caused to dwell in us? [6]But he gives us more grace. That is why Scripture says: 'God opposes the proud but shows favor to the humble and oppressed.' [7]Submit yourselves, then, to God. Resist the devil, and he will flee from you. [8]Come near to God and he will come near to you. Wash your hands, you sinners, and purify your hearts, you double-minded. [9]Grieve, mourn and wail. Change your laughter to mourning and your joy to gloom. [10]Humble yourselves before the Lord, and he will lift you up. [11]Brothers and sisters, do not slander one another. Anyone who speaks against a brother or sister or judges them speaks against the law and judges it. When you judge the law, you are not keeping it, but sitting in judgment on it. [12]There is only one Lawgiver and Judge, the one who is able to save and destroy. But you—who are you to judge your neighbor?

[13]Now listen, you who say, 'Today or tomorrow we will go to this or that city, spend a year there, carry on business and make money.' [14]Why, you do not even know what will happen tomorrow. What is your life? You are a mist that appears for a little while and then vanishes. [15]Instead, you ought to say, 'If it is the Lord's will, we will live and do this or that.' [16]As it is, you boast in your arrogant schemes. All such boasting is evil. [17]So then, if you know the good you ought to do and don't do it, you sin.

## Chapter 5

[1]Now listen, you rich people, weep and wail because of the misery that is coming upon you. [2]Your wealth has rotted, and moths have eaten your clothes. [3]Your gold and silver are corroded. Their corrosion will testify against you and eat your flesh like fire. You have hoarded wealth in the last days. [4]Look! The wages you failed to pay the workers who mowed your fields are crying out against you. The cries of the harvesters have reached the ears of the Lord Almighty. [5]You have lived on earth in luxury and self-indulgence. You have fattened yourselves in the day of slaughter. [6]You have condemned and murdered the innocent one, who was not opposing you.

[7]Be patient, then, brothers and sisters, until the Lord's coming. See how the farmer waits for the land to yield its valuable crop,

patiently waiting for the autumn and spring rains. [8]You too, be patient and stand firm, because the Lord's coming is near. [9]Don't grumble against one another, brothers and sisters, or you will be judged. The Judge is standing at the door! [10]Brothers and sisters, as an example of patience in the face of suffering, take the prophets who spoke in the name of the Lord. [11]As you know, we consider blessed those who have persevered. You have heard of Job's perseverance and have seen what the Lord finally brought about. The Lord is full of compassion and mercy.

[12]Above all, my brothers and sisters, do not swear—not by heaven or by earth or by anything else. All you need to say is a simple 'Yes' or 'No.' Otherwise you will be condemned.

[13]Is any one of you in trouble? You should pray. Is anyone happy? Sing songs of praise. [14]Is any one of you sick? Call the elders of the church to pray over you and anoint you with oil in the name of the Lord. [15]And the prayer offered in faith will make you well; the Lord will raise you up. If you have sinned, you will be forgiven. [16]Therefore confess your sins to each other and pray for each other so that you may be healed. The prayer of a righteous person is powerful and effective.

[17]Elijah was human just as we are. He prayed earnestly that it would not rain, and it did not rain on the land for three and a half years. [18]Again he prayed, and the heavens gave rain, and the earth produced its crops. [19]My brothers and sisters, if one of you should wander from the truth and someone should bring them back, [20]remember this: Whoever turns a sinner from the error of their way will save their soul from death and cover over a multitude of sins.